How Christianity
Made The Modern World

The Legacy of Christian Liberty:
How the Bible Inspired Freedom,
Shaped Western Civilisation, Revolutionised
Human Rights, Transformed Democracy
and Why Free People Owe So Much
to their Christian Heritage

Paul Backholer

'Tell your children about it,
let your children tell their children,
and their children another
generation' (Joel 1:3).

Inscribed on America's Liberty Bell:
'Proclaim liberty throughout the land and
to all the inhabitants thereof' (Leviticus 25:10).

The Founding Verses of The British Empire:
'Those who go down to the sea in ships, who do
business on great waters, they shall see the
works of the Lord and His wonders
in the deep' (Psalm 107:23-24).

How Christianity Made The Modern World

UK ISBN
978-1-907066-02-3

British Library Cataloguing In Publication Data.
A Record of this Publication is available
from the British Library.

First published in 2009 by ByFaith Media.
Second edition © 2014.
Third edition © 2017.
This book is also available as an ebook.

Contents

Preface

'It is the last hour...even now many antichrists have come...they went out from us, but they were not of us...' (1 John 2:18-19).

It has often been indicated by some that the world would be a better place without Christianity, but that conclusion can only be grounded in a cloudy and one-sided view of history. In this book we will examine how Christians were often the pioneers who fought for our liberties and by doing so moulded our values, laws and civilisation. Christians have frequently been at the fore in the development of obtaining our human rights by pioneering healthcare, education, workers' and children's rights etc.; also they helped the evolution of the modern democratic form of government. Throughout this book we shall discover that the modern world owes much to the influence of Bible-believing Christians and that Christianity played a major part in shaping the world as we know it today.

The Forgotten Legacy: 'It is as pernicious to overrate the value of ancient civilisation and to exaggerate the amount of the heritage which the modern world has actually received, as it is foolish to ignore the great achievements of the ancients and to deny that a portion of their assets has leavened progress in later days,' wrote Oxford professor Cyril Bailey (1871-1957) in the 1920s *The Legacy of Rome*.[1]

The legacy of Rome can be found everywhere in the West, from art to architecture, law, language, drama and debate etc. Yet, at the same time Rome lies in the shadow of Greece. The Western world stands in debt to these great civilisations, yet just as we fail to fully appreciate the legacy that these powers have, we also fail to appreciate how Christianity still influences our everyday lives, from the laws that guide and protect us, to the values that shape society.

In the Bible, in Acts chapter seventeen, the Apostle Paul finds in Athens an altar dedicated to an unknown god. The lamentable truth concerning the gods the ancients worshipped is that they did not ameliorate the lives of their devotees; the opposite is often true. The Greek philosopher Apollonius of Tyana (40-120AD) confirms that Athens was, as Paul's observations suggest – 'Where altars are set up in honour even of unknown gods.'[2] Pausanias, the second century Greek writer confirmed that such altars remained in Athens. 'The Temple of...Zeus further off and altars of the unknown gods.'[3] In the West, after Christianity established itself no such altars were required and brutal pagan rituals were abolished. In *The City of God Against the Pagans,* St Augustine (354-430) addresses the moral failure of pagan religions: 'We would ask why their gods took no steps to improve the morals of their worshippers?'[4] In the Christian world, the unknown became known and the non-conformist faith of the early Church became alive, and took on the titans of the world, from slavery to human sacrifice. Christianity brought an end to much oppression, gave human dignity and helped entrench human rights in law. These reforms and the reformers cannot be credited to Rome or Greece, but to non-conformist Christianity and its legacy. English philosopher Bertrand Russell (1872-1970) wrote in *The History of Western Philosophey*: 'When we come to compare Aristotle's ethical tastes with our own, we find...an acceptance of inequality which is repugnant to the modern sentiment.'[5] 'As for the triumph of Christianity,' wrote the historian William Stearns Davis (1877-1930), 'No student of civilisation will ever underestimate its importance. Here, again, conjecture loses itself asking what would have become of arts, laws, and letters if the Germanic invaders had conquered a world knowing no better deities than Jupiter or Isis?'[6]

However, we are reminded of the crimes committed in the name of the Church – exploitation, inquisitions, torture, intolerance and crusader massacres all carried out because of a twisted interpretation of belief. We should never forget these crimes, yet at the same time we should not allow the gross failures of Church history to overshadow the vast contributions which were made in Christ's name towards creating a better age. In addition, the New Testament writers themselves warned that some people would twist and use Scripture with unholy and evil intent. Sadly, history reveals these warnings found fulfilment, as the established Church (at times) became the greatest enemy to the liberty found within the Holy Bible. The failings of the established churches have led people to perceive that the official Church and biblical Christianity are not one and the same. Often Church structures have become the oppressor of true Christianity and the greatest hinderance to its purpose. The freedom fighters in this book are proof of this! Also, the problems of the Church have not been due to Jesus' teaching, but the failure to follow them. How could religious leaders of the past claim to follow and represent Jesus, who told us to love our enemies, whilst they told their followers to kill them?

At times the Roman Empire used Christianity to create a powerful civil religion, which served as a religious focus for citizens, but was devoid of Jesus' message. Now and again the Church leadership was in addition the 'helpless plaything'[7] of the ruler. Later in Europe, Monarchs and their political allies appointed religious leaders whose political and spiritual wings had been clipped. In this way, the state had a veneer of Christianity, but the Christ of Christianity was often ignored. As we ponder this, even the religious wars of Europe begin to find some perspective. It's oversimplified to propose that the wars of Europe were merely about religion; those who suggest such things fail to weigh a host of other political, social, economic and international considerations. However, within the established Churches there has been much corruption, where power was over-exercised, abused and sought for self. At some points there was little or no knowledge of the Bible by many because Church teaching and tradition became the new 'inspired word.' No wonder then that the established Churches became (during some periods) irreconcilable with the teachings of Jesus.

However, in Britain and the United States there has been a long history of non-conformist Christianity. These non-conformists took the Bible far more literally than the establishment and referred to the Bible alone as their sole source of doctrine. In one sense, this book could almost be called *How Non-Conformist Christianity Made The Modern World*. For a thousand years, the most faithful expression of biblical Christianity has often been on the fringe. It has often been a minority that struggle against those who offer lip-service to Christianity, but in practice oppose it. Speaking of William Wilberforce's struggle to end the slave trade, Christianity Today stated: 'Even though Great Britain thought of itself as a Christian nation, political and cultural elites had little tolerance for the kind of religion that called for total immersion in the life of faith, with a deep personal piety, a morally reformed life, and an eagerness to share the faith with the great unwashed, and without regard for existing Church structures.'[8] Wilberforce was so concerned about the loss of genuine faith that he wrote a book about abandoning nominal faith to embrace biblical Christianity.

There will be some who after evaluating the lives of great leaders will attempt to 'dig up the dirt' to overshadow their contributions. Before we start, we should remember that Christian leaders embody all human frailties, they are sinners redeemed, not holy saints revealed. Everyone's experience, understanding, expression and faithfulness to Christianity will be different. Each person's path is full of errors, learning curves and lows, but the central theme for each is faith in Christ. Many represented in this book have had a progressive revelation of God's purpose for the world, whilst being culturally conditioned to accept some things which are now considered wrong; their personal revelation from God helped them pioneer in their work. The believers mentioned here could not battle on every front, nor could they confront every issue at once; but the issues that they did face, were often confronted, overturned and redeemed.

Throughout this book, we are not attempting to dismiss the contributions of any other areas of society, but we are trying to re-engage with the often overlooked influence of Christianity upon the world. This book contains numerous subjects and for each chapter, large volumes have been and could still be written. It is imperative that the reader understands that in each chapter, there could be numerous other contributions, for which space and time does not allow. Also there are many quotes throughout this book from numerous sources and people; it is therefore obvious, just as with any other work that those quoted may not necessarily agree with all of the author's conclusions.

The history of Christianity is not perfect and the crimes of the Church are pitiful, but it is worth putting them in context of the crimes of recent times. The political failings that lead to WWII left seventy-two million dead[9] and vastly eclipsed all religious wars combined. In addition atheist governments in the twentieth century stained the human story with the most grotesque abuse of human rights that dwarf all previous human suffering; it is estimated that one hundred million people died because of them. In addition, now that the West has abandoned much of its Christian moral heritage, many feel that it has become transparently dysfunctional. A nation's ethical health is often tested by how they treat their most vulnerable; yet since legislation in the U.S., forty-seven million abortions have taken place. What does this say about our respect for pregnancy and life itself? When we consider these things, the failings of the established Church find some perspective. The Christian story is not free from failure, but it did give the West an aspiration to drive towards and a dream to fight for. The expert and chief editor of History of the World W.N. Weech posits: 'However hideously debased it may have been in barbarian Europe, Christianity had embedded in it ideals that are probably necessary to the foundation of enduring civilisation, those of sacrifice and restraint. It was capable at its best of inspiring its adherents for the service of their fellows and of bringing the highest motives to bear on mundane affairs.'[10]

William Henry Seward (1801-1872), the American Secretary of State who purchased Alaska from Russia said, "The whole hope of human progress is suspended on the ever growing influence of the Bible."[11] Immanuel Kant (1724-1804), German philosopher and one of the most influential thinkers of his day said, "The existence of the Bible, as a book for the people, is the greatest benefit which the human race has ever experienced."[12] It is true that the King James Bible 'is rightly regarded as the most influential book in the history of English civilisation.'[13]

It was during the Christian age in the West that sadistic pagan religion was brought to nought that universities were founded, mass education was pioneered, healthcare was transformed and the modern concept of human rights and political liberty was fashioned. It was also in the Christian age that dark superstition gave way to scientific inquiry; mass poverty was relieved by charity, and that accepted morality led to social cohesion and economic progress. "The Bible is a book that has not just shaped our country, but shaped the world," said British Prime Minister David Cameron, "and with three Bibles sold or given away every second, a book that is not just important in understanding our past, but which will continue to have a profound impact in shaping our collective future...From human rights and equality, to our constitutional monarchy and parliamentary democracy, from the role of the Church in the first forms of welfare provision, to the many modern day faith-led social action projects the Bible has been a spur to action for people of faith throughout history, and it remains so today."[14]

Chapter One

Christianity and Liberty

'And what great nation is there that has such statutes and righteous judgments as are in all this law?' (Deuteronomy 4:8).

It is a false belief, propagated by too many that Christianity was a great hinderance to the development of liberty, human rights, good government and free Western civilisation. On a consistent basis the mass media and educational institutions unconsciously perpetuate this myth, until public opinion is shaped and even some Christians believe this to be the inerrant truth. Joseph Goebbels said, "If you tell a lie big enough and keep repeating it, people will eventually come to believe it."[1] In fact, the history and development of the West cannot be understood without constant reference to the true expression of the Christian faith. Our modern beliefs in religious freedom, political accountability, good government, charity and community all evolved because of the Christian influence. In 2008, British Prime Minister Gordon Brown said, "People of faith have been at the heart of just about every social movement that has transformed society in this country, from the abolition of slavery through to Make Poverty History."[2] Journalist Simon Heffer wrote, "I appreciate the vital role that Christianity contributes to our way of life. Our history and our culture are utterly inseparable from it."[3] At the fore of the West's development of human rights were often Christians motivated by their faith who helped the creation of accountable democratic institutions, which later honoured workers' rights, provided education and healthcare, abolished slavery and guarded children's rights. At the heart of much of our great art, literature, scientific achievement, architecture and global accomplishments, we often find pioneers who were motivated by their Christian faith. Instead of impeding their progress, the faith of these innovators often propelled their achievements. Only in Christian nations did the modern ideals of political accountability, freedom of speech and religious liberty develop and congeal. Western civilisation, as we know it today, without the influence of Christianity is inconceivable. "Without God," said President Eisenhower, "there could be no American form of government nor an American way of life."[4] Journalist Melanie Phillips said of Great Britain, "The Bible is the moral code that underpins our civilisation...Christianity is still the official religion of this country. All its institutions, its history and its culture are suffused with it."[5] The same is true for Canada, Australia, New Zealand and much of Europe. Professor Stephen McDowell said of the U.S., "The Bible was the most central influence in the beginning, birth, growth and development of the United States – in education, government, law – in every area."[6]

Christianity underpins Western civilisation, its influence is immeasurable, inescapable and profoundly inexhaustible. "I am far within the mark," said the famous preacher James Allan Francis, "when I say that all the armies that ever marched and all the navies that were ever built, and all the parliaments that ever sat and all the kings that ever reigned, put together, have not affected the life of man upon earth as powerfully as has this One solitary life (of Christ)."[7] The foundations of the modern world were laid by Christian nations, who were shaped by the teaching of Jesus Christ. These Christian nations became the dominant powers on the planet and their civilisation has prevailed, creating the free Western world. Since 1500AD, Christian nations have been the world's most powerful economic and military powers[8] and for at least the last two hundred years, the Protestant English speaking nations of the world have prevailed, being responsible for around 1/4 of the global economy; making them the pre-eminent military powers, despite being under 6% of the world's population.[9] Britain has 0.16% of the earth's land area, yet in all her history combined, she has been directly responsible for almost 1/3 of the planet at various times, with 1/4 of the world under her direct rule all at once[10] and the U.S. today has around 320 million of the world's 7 billion population, yet her influence is felt quite literally everywhere.

Today 1/3 of the earth's entire population are Christian and Christianity is still the fastest growing faith on the planet, based upon free-will conversion.[11] In addition, because of the massive religious changes that have taken place globally in the last few centuries, 164 nations are now identified as predominantly Christian.[12] This great sea of religious change is also being witnessed in the world's next great superpower – China, where it is estimated that between 80 to 130 million people are now Christian and if this growth continues, by 2050 Christians could possibly consist of 20% of her population![13]

Chapter Two

The Christian Legacy

'There is neither Jew nor Greek, there is neither slave nor free, there is neither male nor female; for you are all one in Christ Jesus' (Galatians 3:28).

Everything begins with an idea. Dr Francis noted, "No man has ever done a great thing until he has first believed a great thing."[1] Christianity spread with the idea of the fundamental equality of all human beings. The value of a human being in God's sight is so immense, that He sent His only begotten Son to suffer, die and to be raised again so that all could repent, believe and share in His Kingdom. It was the first Kingdom the world had ever heard of, where there was true equality. For this reason, those truly inspired by the Bible felt commissioned to create a world where the doctrine of the fundamental equality of all human beings shaped every area of human experience, from law and politics, to health and wealth. In the English speaking world, this helped the development of a civilisation where no one person should be allowed to be considered 'more equal' than another. 'For you brethren have been called to liberty; only do not use your liberty as an opportunity for the flesh, but through love serve one another' (Galatians 5:13).

'Christians are often reformers,' wrote a British broadcaster, 'in the first part of the nineteenth century, puritanical evangelicals helped abolish slavery and reform the flawed electoral system...examples of philanthropy include the valiant efforts of Lord Shaftesbury to alleviate the harsh economic conditions by campaigning to limit, by law, the number of hours that women and children had to work. Other philanthropists became reformers who tackled public sanitation or the problems of the poor. On a more local level, individual gentlemen and concerned ladies distributed relief to the poor, set up hospitals and schools, or endowed colleges, museums or libraries.'[2] In 2005, the British Prime Minister Tony Blair said, "...Churches are among the most formidable campaigning organisations in history," and, "...faith communities have always played a significant role in social action in Britain – in education, in welfare, in support for so many of the most vulnerable and needy in our society."[3]

In the U.S., the celebrated pastor Rick Warren said, "It was Christians who helped abolish slavery, achieve women's suffrage, led the civil-rights movement and drafted the Bill of Rights."[4] *Time* magazine wrote: 'It's time to remember the spiritual revivals that helped lead to the abolition of slavery in Britain and the United States; the black church's leadership during the American Civil Rights Movement...how Desmond Tutu and the South African churches served to inspire victory over Apartheid...and today, how the growing evangelical and Pentecostal churches of the global South are mobilizing to address the injustices of globalization.'[5]

What is our Christian Heritage? Inspired by their non-conformist faith, Christians became freedom fighters who limited the power of kings, empowered parliament and demanded civil rights for all. Believing all to be created equal in God's image, they made massive contributions to the development of liberty, democracy and human rights. They became pioneers of education, healthcare and fought for rights for children, women and workers. Great Christian reformers helped end the slave trade, slavery, child labour and Apartheid. As Christian soldiers they created modern campaigning, which brought the plight of the oppressed to the masses and forced governments to be accountable and act justly.

Motivated by their Christian faith they became innovators of science and technology, as well as great artists, architects, musicians and authors. Nations embodied the Protestant work ethic, which created unplanned economic expansion that led to wealth and helped gradually end extreme poverty at home. In business they called for shorter working hours, better pay, safer working conditions, humane treatment and a day of rest. For those overlooked, Christianity developed organisations that gave relief to the impoverished, help for the oppressed and rehabilitation for the outcast. They called for prison reform at home to global reform overseas.

Great Christian explorers and adventurers helped end the untouched slave trade abroad, mapped unchartered territories and brought Christianity to those in spiritual darkness. At home believers fought to protect God's creation by saving the countryside, preserving history and guarding nature from exploitation. In the Creator's name they informed the population about cruelty to animals, outlawed many of its crimes and created societies to enforce these laws. In their own nations, spiritual revival often led to social cohesion, uniting people in a common cause with shared values, to cherish the dream of liberty for all. In every area of Western life, the Christian influence is immense and its success widespread; yet the general population often know little of the pioneers who fought for their liberties, nor of the faith that motivated them.

Sir John Mortimer, CBE, QC, (1923-2009), playwright and atheist wrote: 'Our whole history and culture in Europe is based on Christianity, whether you believe in it or not. Our culture is Christian; Shakespeare, Mozart – all that makes life worth living is part of the Christian tradition.'[6] Journalist Jill Parkin said, "Our landscape is peppered with churches that contain our history; our art galleries contain centuries of painting that is either classical or Christian. Some of our greatest literature derives from Christianity and most of our great music...is Christian either in intent or in nature."[7] Journalist Simon Heffer said, "Our society and its values are founded on Christian beliefs. You don't have to be deeply religious – and I certainly am not – to appreciate the part played in the shaping of our country by 1,400 years of British Christianity, and 470 years of the Church of England. For many of us, the Christian rite is present at our births, our marriages and our deaths. Our national flag includes the crosses of our patron saints, and our Head of State is also Supreme Governor of the Church."[8]

In the United States Christianity played a pivotal role at every stage of the development of her history, the same is true for all other English speaking nations and most European states. The broadcaster Joanna Bogle wrote: 'Christianity underpins our laws, has shaped attitudes for generations, and gives our annual calendar its form...and our Christian understanding about education and hospital work comes from the heritage left to us by religious communities.'[9]

Her Majesty Queen Elizabeth II, speaking to the British people on 25 December 2000 said, "Christmas is the traditional, if not the actual, birthday of a Man who was destined to change the course of our history. And today we are celebrating the fact that Jesus Christ was born two thousand years ago; this is the true Millennium anniversary. The simple facts of Jesus' life give us little clue as to the influence He was to have on the world...His death might have been the end of the story, but then came the resurrection and with it the foundation of the Christian faith.

"Even in our very material age, the impact of Christ's life is all around us. If you want to see an expression of Christian faith you have only to look at our awe-inspiring cathedrals and abbeys, listen to their music, or look at their stained glass windows, their books and their pictures. But the true measure of Christ's influence is not only in the lives of the saints but also in the good works quietly done by millions of men and women day in and day out throughout the centuries. Many will have been inspired by Jesus' simple but powerful teaching: love God and love thy neighbour as thyself – in other words, treat others as you would like them to treat you."[10] Two years later in her Christmas speech the Queen said, "Christmas is the anniversary of the birth of Christ over two thousand years ago, but it is much more than that. It is the celebration of the birth of an idea and an ideal. I know just how much I rely on my own faith to guide me through the good times and the bad. Each day is a new beginning, I know that the only way to live my life is to try to do what is right, to take the long view, to give of my best in all that the day brings, and to put my trust in God. Like others of you who draw inspiration from your own faith, I draw strength from the message of hope in the Christian gospel."[11]

In addition, English speaking Christian nations have shaped the world by spreading Christian values and removing vile regimes. These powers were not perfect, but history does reveal that wherever there is a power vacuum, it will be filled. Surely it is better for nations with a Judeo-Christian heritage, a sense of duty towards mankind and a love of justice to fill that vacuum, rather than a dictatorship or team of unelected amoral officials? History also reveals that when a global superpower weakens, the world leans towards anarchy, as others try to fill the power vacuum. Therefore one legacy of these Christian superpowers is that of stable hegemony.[12] British victory in the world led to them presiding over the one hundred years of peace and prosperity beginning in 1815, and the United States has guarded the world since 1945. The Lord 'has determined their preappointed times and the boundaries' (Acts 17:26).

Chapter Three

Great Reformers

'Thus says the Lord God of hosts..."Reform your ways and your actions" ' (Jeremiah 7:3).

"Hail Caesar, we who are about to die salute you." The crowd of tens of thousands in the coliseum of Rome leaned forward, expecting to witness, for sheer pleasure a battle to the death between gladiators. Life and death were all part of the entertainment in Rome. In 403, St Telemachus jumped into the coliseum and cried out for it to end, "In the great name of Him who died for men, Christ Jesus."[1] However, the crowd hooked on the heroin of bloodshed cried out until he was forced aside, but then he intervened again. Now the crowd lusting for blood was angry and in the name of entertainment he was struck down and killed. Silence swept across the coliseum as one by one, they realised that a holy man had died for their entertainment and thus the games were soon finished forever.

One of the great legacies of the Bible is the value that it places on each human life. The intrinsic value of every human life was not respected in the ancient world, but Christianity made the West realise that all life is valuable. When the author visited Rome's coliseum, he could only marvel at the faith of this reformer, who stood in front of an enormous crowd worked up into a frenzy, to challenge them all to a new way of thinking. This reformer brought an end to these games, and taught Rome that to God, all life is valuable and no-one is disposable.

A Powerhouse of Reform: Around fourteen hundred years after the great reform of Telemachus, a team of evangelical Christians known as The Clapham Sect were still going in Christ's name into the world to challenge all assumed abasement in the coliseum of public opinion. Instead of separating themselves from the world and hiding in a holy huddle, they got their hands dirty and became a powerhouse to influence public opinion, and changed the law in Britain to the glory of Christ. Professor Donald M. Lewis wrote: 'While Africans were oppressed abroad, at home in the 1800s England, children were exploited, illiteracy grew, disease ran rampant, and urban slums spread like cancer. So abolition wasn't the only cause that engaged Christian energies.'[2]

The Clapham Sect was led by William Wilberforce and Henry Venn. Together they achieved great reforms – the slave trade was abolished, workers' rights were increased, prisons were redeemed, Christian values became centre ground and parliament was reformed. They also founded several missionary societies, promoted missionary work abroad, and encouraged the creation of tract societies, including the British and Foreign Bible Society and the Church Missionary Society. Considering their achievements at home and abroad, one would expect they would have been highly regarded in their day, but like Christians in every generation, they pioneered against the tide of opinion. They were ridiculed by many and nicknamed 'the saints.'

Professor Irvin Hexham wrote: 'From the start, evangelical reformers and missionaries met dogged resistance from entrenched interests. Initially their opponents, particularly proponents of slavery, argued that Africans had no soul. The publication of Charles Darwin's *Origins of the Species* in 1857 gave them new arguments, as can be seen from debates found in the journals of the London and later Royal Anthropological Institutes. Here one finds travellers and scientists arguing that missionary endeavours impede trade and are doomed to failure because Africans in particular are a subspecies of men, while other races are simply inferior to the more highly evolved Europeans.'[3] At the same time as 'scientific' racism was trying to hinder Christian reform abroad, Lord Shaftesbury and others made a concerted effort to bring reform in the name of Christ to every area of human experience at home. He said, "Our bodies, the temples of the Holy Ghost, ought not to be corrupted by preventable disease, degraded by avoidable filth and disabled for His service by unnecessary suffering."[4]

Christianity is the story of global reform from Rome's coliseum to the industrial heart of England, and from India's villages to America's great cities. On a global scale, the doctrine of the fundamental equality of all human beings has shaped the lives of millions, who have had their rights provided for and protected because of those who took the Christian gospel seriously. Against all odds, they defeated entrenched interests and made Christian values centre ground. In 2005, the British leader of the opposition said, "Wilberforce and Shaftesbury were above all men of deep faith, who found in their religious commitment the inspiration to work tirelessly on behalf of our most deprived people. Through their relentless determination, they changed the political landscape of our nation and indeed the world."[5]

The transforming influence of the Christian faith upon society is still being witnessed around the world today, from the U.S. to the U.K., and from New Zealand, to South Africa. Stephen Timms, a British Member of Parliament pointed to the fact that eighty percent of the activists who joined the Make Poverty History campaign were from churches and said, "The impact (of Christians) on Britain has been immense, and there is today in government and among politicians a new recognition of the value of faith in society."[6] In Australia, Peter Costello, the longest serving treasurer in its history and World Bank adviser said, "Australia's Christian traditions should not be neglected... we need a return to faith and the values which have made our country strong."[7]

In history, Bible-believing Christians have only been a small proportion of the world population, yet they are credited with an overwhelming number of reforms which have shaped the lives of billions of people on the planet! The presumption based upon the teachings of Christ, that every human being is created equal in God's image has led evangelical Christianity to become a transforming force around the world. The recognition and safeguarding of human rights in Western law is a theme which was often birthed out of Christians reading the Holy Bible, and applying it to the world that they lived in.

After hundreds of years of Christians fighting for human rights at home and calling for legal protection, the world recognised the universal application of this pattern and safeguarded human rights in international law. In addition the reforms that Christians led in the West have inspired oppressed citizens around the world to call for similar rights in their own lands. Today, the West can put pressure on developing nations concerning human rights abuses etc., because Christians resolved these very issues at home in previous generations. But without having faith in a God who grants rights, they cannot be guaranteed. Professor John N. Gray wrote: 'Rights are like money and the law – they only exist if enough people accept that they exist. But what if large sections of the population, or those that are the most ruthless in imposing their values, don't accept them?'[8]

Chapter Four

The End of the Slave Trade

"Is this not the fast that I have chosen: to loose the bonds of wickedness, to undo heavy burdens, to let the oppressed go free and that you break every yoke?" (Isaiah 58:6).

It was the early hours of the night when strangers appeared with harsh countenance and haunting eyes. Ambushing the village by brute force and without pity for the human spirit, they rounded the people up and led them, day after day on an interminable journey towards the sea. With little water and no rights, the animals seemed to have a fairer lot than these human beings. Along the way crimes against humanity took place, but only the ground itself would cry out for the spilt blood. There was no way of knowing where one was going or what was happening, because each captive was now deaf and mute. For if one spoke, a cruel beating could follow and the foreign tongue was a mystery. How could their liberty be taken in such ferocity?

The sight of the sea revealed a grave fate, for they would never see home again. Never again would these Africans taste their local food, look into their spouses eyes, or hold their children. Never again would they wake up to the sound of nature, which they had heard every morning for their entire lives. Never again would they be considered human. Now a commodity, the Arab trader bargained for a better deal from the European, until both satisfied with the profit they would make, sealed the deal. An underground, overcrowded cell was the holding bay for these humans who openly suffered during the preparations for their final sight of their homeland. Some would wait here for one day, others for months.

Forcing one to vomit, the smell of death upon entering a slave ship foreshadowed what lay ahead. The stains of blood, odours of malady and the echoes of agony filled these vessels of criminality. The conditions upon a slave ship were paramount to hell; chained together, as if vines around a tree, even those who could sympathise with their plight were escaping to eternity – their bodies thrown overboard and listed as cargo. For those who survived the suffocating unremitting journey to the New

World, a life of hardship, poverty, ill-treatment and slavery was the final insult.

Day by day the guilt of the slave trading nations grew, as Western citizens continued trading with lives without a thought for their fellow man. The slave trade was making many rich and cities were growing from the dust out of its wages. Even the established Church was making profit from the suffering of the slaves and revenues were getting larger.

During those dark days, there was a group of evangelical Christians, who contrary to their culture, believed the Bible taught that each individual possesses inalienable natural rights, granted to them by his or her Creator. To deny these rights was to constitute a complete denial of the Creator's design and of the most basic human right. The historian Professor Niall Ferguson of Harvard and Oxford asked, 'What was going to turn Britain from the world's leading enslaver to the world's leading emancipator?'[1] The answer was Christianity.

William Wilberforce (1759-1833) believed that the teachings of Jesus Christ emphasised the humanity and rights of every person. Inspired by his Christian faith, Wilberforce and his fellow labourers started the campaign of a lifetime to bring a total end to the slave trade within the British Empire and beyond. Granville Sharp (1735-1813) had laid the groundwork for the abolitionists, by using the law to fight slave traders, and he helped set up a free colony in Sierra Leone where freed slaves could prosper. But by the early 1800s, the trade was making fortunes and those who were seeking to bring it to an end were bitterly opposed.

Wilberforce stood against public opinion, and challenged big business who were doing exceptionally well out of cruelty and exploitation. Wilberforce and his friends were often discouraged, beaten back and appeared to fail on many occasions. But as the many years passed, public opinion changed and support grew for the abolition of this vile trade.

On the author's visit to the world's first Methodist Church in Bristol, England, he was able to consider how the revivalist John Wesley (1703-1791) encouraged Wilberforce in his campaign against the slave trade. From the podium in Bristol, Wesley preached against slavery and the last letter he ever wrote was to Wilberforce denouncing the vile practice. As the Christian voice was raised, people in their thousands signed petitions to end the trade and 'this was the birth of a new kind of politics, the politics of pressure groups.'[2] It was no easy campaign though, journalist, author and broadcaster Joanna Bogle in *Celebrating Our Heritage* notes: 'It took Wilberforce over twenty years of campaigning to get the slave trade abolished throughout the British Empire.'[3]

The breakthrough came in 1807, when the British parliament abolished the slave trade and in the following years the British used their influence throughout the world, to negotiate and at times to force other nations to end their trade in slaves. It was a victory for Wilberforce and his friends, but more importantly it was a victory for humanity, accomplished in the name of Christianity.

Christian Powers and Global Values: History teaches us that the world is shaped by superpowers. Every nation on earth today is influenced by the U.S., and as we look back to other Christian superpowers, we realise that they too set the moral and legal tone of the modern world. The British superpower led the way to make a complete end of the slave trade and as other chapters of this book reveal, what happened hundreds of years ago in Britain or the U.S. still has a profound influence upon the rights and privileges that we all take for granted today. Christian nations have created the most influential civilisation in all history; never before have citizens had so many rights and liberties as they do in the Christian West, yet when we evaluate history, we realise that human effort alone cannot claim the glory. When we consider how this civilisation developed, we realise that before Christianity arrived, Northern Europe[4] had nothing compared to other civilisations like ancient Egypt or Persia. But after biblical Christianity had time to influence its peoples, they went on to lead the world towards a new age of liberty. The power of religion is often overlooked in its ability to evolve nations, but we can understand its efficacy when we compare the Christian West with other parts of the world which follow other religions. One could watch the news today and ask which religion led to liberty and which to tyranny?

Chapter Five

The End of Slavery

"The Spirit of the Lord God is upon Me, because the Lord has anointed Me...to proclaim liberty to the captives and the opening of the prison to those who are bound" (Isaiah 61:1).

The quality of life around the world in the nineteenth century was very poor. Injustice was normal and avoidable suffering was a part of life. In 1807, the slave trade had been abolished, but slavery itself still continued. Sir Thomas Foxwell Buxton (1786-1845), was an evangelical reformer and an anti-slavery campaigner. At home and abroad he was prepared to give his time and money to help those who suffered with injustice and cruelty. The factories of Great Britain had made the nation the Workshop of the World, but the conditions came close to slavery themselves – but one could not complain because there was always another worker ready to labour for lower wages, in harsher conditions. In 1818, he was elected as a Member of Parliament; he used his influence to call for the abolition of slavery itself and to call for reform in criminal law, and within prisons. When people questioned why he cared for the prisoners, his ideals were reflected by his thoughts, "One of the ill effects of cruelty is that it makes the bystanders cruel." As a man of faith, he was committed to his relationship with God saying, "You know the value of prayer; it is precious beyond all price. Never, never neglect it."

He was a co-founder of the Society for the Mitigation and Gradual Abolition of Slavery and the mantle of William Wilberforce came upon him, as he emerged as the leader of the abolition movement in the British House of Commons. His victory came when slavery itself was formally abrogated in 1833. An estimated 700,000 slaves were freed because Christianity stepped in and demanded that the law should respect the doctrine of the fundamental equality of all human beings. In the 1920s, the prolific author Ernest Protheroe celebrated how Christianity had brought liberty to the British people and how the faith haemorrhaged it to the world. Commenting on the British flag he wrote: 'It is the world's emblem of freedom; if a slave can only set his foot upon soil over which the flag flies, his shackles fall off and henceforth he can defy those who would again enthral him.'[1] Sir Thomas Foxwell Buxton is one of many great Christian reformers who are largely forgotten today, but the British establishment has marked his achievements. He was featured on an English five pound note, and in Westminster Abbey there is a monument dedicated to him and another in Victoria Tower Gardens which marks the emancipation of the slaves.

American Slavery: Slavery began in North America in 1509, when a Roman Catholic bishop encouraged Spanish settlers to bring a certain number of African slaves to the New World. The bishop who encouraged the importing of African slaves knew that slavery existed in Africa, but not on the American continent. He encouraged the shipping of slaves from Africa to America, as a concession to stop indigenous Americans being taken as slaves, but he soon regretted his actions as he realised that he had unleashed a tidal wave of human suffering. Over time, laws were created to deny any claim to rights for slaves, including restricting their movements, banning them from owning property and in some cases, even declaring them slaves for life.

In 1775, the first formal anti-slavery society was founded by a Christian group called the Society of Friends. By 1807 the British parliament set a precedent by abolishing the slave trade and it was sure to have an impact across the Atlantic. One year later, the U.S. Act to Prohibit the Importation of Slaves came into effect for the entire U.S. and its territories. However, there was a great difference between having a law and implementing that law; for an estimated quarter million slaves arrived up until the American Civil War of 1861-1865.

William Wilberforce believed the U.S. would live up to the aspiration of liberty for all. Speaking in parliament in 1811 he said, "America and Britain are two nations who are children of the same family, and brothers in the same inheritance of common liberty."[2] In the next generation President Abraham Lincoln spoke of William Wilberforce and the influence he had upon changing the opinions of the American people, especially the youth – "Every school boy knows the name of William Wilberforce," said Lincoln.

By 1820, an American census revealed that thirty percent of the population were still slaves. In the midst of the tribulations of the slaves, there were many Christians whose voices were raised calling for justice. Sojourner Truth (1797-1883) was a Christian evangelist and reformer, who was once a slave. In Massachusetts she took a stand for justice and later her achievements were marked by President Lincoln, who in 1864 received her at the White House. Charles Finney (1792-1875) is known as a revivalist, but he was in addition a leader in the abolition movement. He denounced slavery from the pulpit and refused communion to slaveholders who came to his church. He later became president of Oberlin College, which under his leadership became a centre for the abolition movement and was one hundred years before its time, being among the first colleges in the U.S. to educate women, men and African Americans together.

America's Independence from Britain gave citizens of the U.S. a new found self-confidence, but in the short-term it was a tragedy for African Americans. For in 1834 the British Empire freed all slaves held in its territories, but the U.S. was no longer a British territory. For this reason over 2,009,043[3] African Americans continued as slaves who would have been freed, if the U.S. had remained part of the British Empire. By 1860, there were over 3,953,760[4] slaves in the United States and it was America's most costly war – the Civil War, which consumed over 600,000 lives, which finally settled the fate of the North American slaves. The U.S. National Archives noted: 'President Abraham Lincoln issued the Emancipation Proclamation on January 1, 1863, declaring, "all persons held as slaves" within the rebellious areas "are and henceforward shall be free." '[5]

Abraham Lincoln called 'the Civil War God's punishment for the sin of slavery, and the presidency an office that drove him to his knees "by the overwhelming conviction that I had nowhere else to go." '[6] The Emancipation Proclamation and the Thirteenth Amendment to the Constitution sealed the fate of slavery in the U.S., but we should never forget the Christian reformers of all races who set the scene for this advancement of human rights.

Chapter Six

The Birth of Modern Campaigning

"For if you remain completely silent at this time, relief and deliverance will arise for the Jews from another place...yet who knows whether you have come to the kingdom for such a time as this?" (Esther 4:14).

'If you have ever signed a petition, worn a charity wristband or taken part in a demonstration you owe something to Thomas Clarkson,' wrote the journalist Brian Wheeler. Clarkson was a leading figure fighting for the overthrow of the trade in slaves and later the institution of slavery itself. He was a fellow Christian labourer with Wilberforce and is considered one of the leading planners of the abolition campaign. Wilberforce was in the spotlight, but it was Clarkson that kept him there. Thomas Clarkson was the first to lead a membership organisation to campaign for political change and he helped set a precedent for all others because of his successful lobbying of MPs.[1]

'What is even less well known is the extent to which Clarkson and his fellow abolitionists set the template for all future protest movements,' wrote Brian Wheeler. 'Every modern campaigning technique – from celebrity endorsement to political lobbying and consumer boycotts – was pioneered by the abolitionists more than 200 years ago...the growth of their movement went hand in hand with the birth of parliamentary democracy and the idea that if enough people band together around a common cause they can change the law...everything that followed – from the Suffragettes to the U.S. Civil Rights Movement in the 1960s to Live Aid and Make Poverty History owes a debt to the abolitionists.'[2]

There were many who tried to make slavery and the slave trade appear legitimate, and even theologians came forward to offer a doctrinal basis to continue slavery. But Clarkson cut through the nonsense, and confronted the prejudices and lies that were being promoted by the pro-slavery lobby. He started a campaign to raise public awareness – he encouraged the boycott of sugar harvested by slaves and after winning the backing of celebrities, over 300,000 people supported the boycott.

Pioneering investigative journalism he travelled 35,000 miles over a seven year period collecting irrefutable evidence of gross abuse which could be presented to parliament and to the general public. In 1787, the forerunner of today's campaign logo was designed by Josiah Wedgwood. On the logo was an image of an African praying which said, 'Am I not a man and a brother?' Clarkson understood the 'turn-off' dilemma of dedicated Christians trying to motivate sceptics with Scriptural quotes and faith based values; so instead he chose to present the evidence in a way that would appeal to all. Forsaking condemnation from the pulpit, he sought to move the emotions by holding meetings where former slaves told their stories of abuse. At the same time he used statistics to prove that British sailors were dying in significant numbers on the slave ships and therefore the whole idea was flawed. Clarkson understood the power of a single image and one picture of the interior of a slave ship, packed with hundreds of slaves has become an enduring shocking representation to the inhumanity of slavery. It is an image that the reader can probably still visualise in his or her own mind.

Clarkson is often forgotten because he encouraged Wilberforce to be the central figure in the campaign, yet in 1996 his ministry was honoured. The Bishop of Ely, speaking in Westminster Abby at the unveiling of a memorial to Clarkson said, "...Then there was his Christian faith, which was totally integrated with his passion. He argued that slavery was incompatible with Christianity, a proposition advanced by numerous others before him, among them Gregory of Nyssa, in the fourth century, Pope Leo X, in the sixteenth century and by the extraordinary Anglican Bishop Warburton in the eighteenth."[3]

The campaigners of today still follow the precedent that was set by Clarkson and his team – "We totally copy those methods," said Sarah Green, of Amnesty International (itself founded in a church), who says the abolition movement continues to be an "inspiration."[4] Today, we are familiar with campaigning from Hollywood celebrities to charities; but do we realise that it was the inspirational leadership of these Christian innovators who set the template for all other campaigns?

Chapter Seven

Workers' Rights

'The wages of the labourers who mowed your fields, which you kept back by fraud, cry out and the cries of the reapers have reached the ears of the Lord of Sabaoth' (James 5:4).

In the small hours of the morning, the family awoke in their squalid home; before the sun rose the wife had to make her way to the factory, the father to the mine and the children all under the age of thirteen, not to school, but to work. The entire neighbourhood was foul and run-down. Poor sanitation, infestation and low wages made life repulsive. The industrial cities of England were overrun with the poor; choking like rats in decrepit streets, asphyxiating in smog and fostering disease. Home felt like a shantytown and work was hell on earth. A generation of peasants lived and died in hot smutty factories, for industrialisation was coming at the price of the human spirit.

There were no choices and no-one to stand up for the rights of the worker. Only a day before a young lady had been sacked because she went for water without permission; but the owner was not concerned about her leaving, for she was only a number and another was waiting in line outside. The factory had developed a style of natural selection which crushed the weak and systematically diminished the strong. The repetitive job of the employee cleansed the mind of worth, turning the day into a wearisome fight for survival. It was a Friday morning when the accident happened. The job of keeping bread on the table and a roof over her family's head meant that even her children had to work down the mine. The entire family had gone for weeks without seeing the sun or breathing clean air. Exhausted by constant labour and in ill-health because of the conditions, this woman's concentration was lost for a second and her arm was caught in the machine. The excruciating pain caught the attention of all – the arm was lost and so was the job. There was no compensation or help from others. Without her wage, the family's income was too small to keep a home; by the end of the week they were homeless.

This type of story, told many times over, was a regular occurrence in Christian England, and the faith was crying out for people to take the message of Christ out of the Church and into the public square. Who would stand up for the rights of these poor workers and their colleagues? Addressing these concerns in 1891, the author of *What Are Churches For?* wrote: 'The presence of...ever-increasing poverty in the midst of abounding wealth, is the true sphinx enigma which this civilisation must solve, or else be devoured by the monster itself has generated.'[1]

Battling For Better Conditions: John Wesley (1703-1791) is better known as a revivalist and founder of Methodism, but he also cared about the every day lives of people; for he fought for better working conditions at home and for an end to slavery worldwide. He wrote *Work and Slavery* in 1773, in which he called for an end to many of the social evils of the day and many other Christians of all denominations would follow in Wesley's footsteps.

Charlotte Elizabeth Tonna (1790-1846) was a Bible-believing Christian and an industrious exponent for labour reform. She carefully researched and exposed the distressing working conditions in English factories. She specifically focused on the plight of women and children by making her findings known in fictional and non-fictional works. Her fictional accounts of families destroyed by the abuses of industrialisation brought the facts to the fore of the conscience of many who were unaware of the problem. Her novel of 1841, *Helen Fleetwood: A Tale of the Factories* is perhaps her most famous work. Despite being fiction, people knew the story was based upon the terrible working conditions of many of her age. She helped reveal to the public the hardships endured by working people, which she hoped would encourage others to help alleviate this suffering, whilst motivating legislation to protect them. Her fiction moved the emotion and her non-fiction exposed the facts. Her work of 1843, *The Perils of the Nation: An Appeal to the Legislature, the Clergy, and the Higher and Middle Classes* was commissioned by the Christian Influence Society in an effort to advance godly legislation. As the editor of *The Christian Lady's* magazine she also produced many Christian tracts and works, especially for children. 'Tonna's most important contribution to the history of English literature was her representation of working-class women to the middle and upper classes. She was able, according to Deborah Kaplan, to translate the dry facts of parliamentary reports – a largely male discourse – into fictional accounts that were far more accessible to her female readers. As a result "her industrial fictions show these readers that women whom they assumed to be different, unfamiliar, 'other' are, in fact, like themselves." [2]

Battling For Workers' Rights: The Industrial Revolution that began in Britain would change the world forever. However, as Britain became the Workshop of the World the rights of the workers were largely ignored. For Christians in Britain, they knew that whatever they allowed at the heart of the Industrial Revolution would set the tone for all other nations that followed. For this reason it was very important that the Christian voice would be heard now, otherwise misery could spread. So, Christian leaders used their voice to call for better working conditions and rights to protect employees from abuse. In addition calls came from Christians and later from others to end child labour. During this era there were many great evils being inflicted upon children and the working classes; some mills never stopped working day or night and children were labouring up to eighteen hours a day! Even those under five were working down the mines in appalling conditions. The author frequented an old mine site in South Wales, U.K., which reveals to visitors the appalling conditions in which children and adults worked. On one hand there is a startling exhibition showing how the Industrial Revolution created machines that still look spectacular, but on the other hand we realise that progress came at a time when workers had little or no rights.

Anthony Ashley Cooper (1801-1885), later to be known as Lord Shaftesbury was raised into a life of privilege and was expected to reach the greatest heights of power in Britain. However as a devout Christian he chose to seek the good of the people in the name of Christ, rather than seek glory for his own name. Challenging big business, the wealthy and the most powerful never made Lord Shaftesbury's life an easy one, but by firsthand experience he explored the terrible conditions of the working classes and managed to get public opinion changed and passed laws to protect children, women and the rights of all to a better working life. His work led to The Factory Act of 1847, which restricted the working day for women and children between the ages of 13-18 and a year later, the first Public Health Act was established. Many other Acts led to greater human rights and the protection of children. For Shaftesbury, this was the first of many steps which would need to be taken to protect the rights of workers and it was his Christian faith which was the inspiration.

Battling For Fair Pay: In the village of Tolpuddle, Dorset, England, lived many Bible-believing Christians who trusted that all humans were fundamentally equal in the sight of God. However, England did not represent this view in its distribution of land and wealth. Instead, the poorest were oppressed by the wealthy and in Tolpuddle these Christians would lead the battle for equality, as their own liberty was at threat. The Tolpuddle Martyrs Museum states: 'Between 1770 and 1830, enclosures changed the English rural landscape forever. Landowners annexed vast acreages, producing even greater wealth from the now familiar pattern of small hedged fields. Peasants no longer had plots to grow vegetables nor open commons for grazing their single cow or sheep and pigs. Wages of 9 or 10 shillings a week reduced families to starvation level unless they could be supplemented by working wives and children. Low wages, appalling conditions and unemployment, bad winters and poor harvests in 1829 and 1830 fuelled a great explosion of anger, resulting in riots.'[3]

The author has visited Tolpuddle on several occasions and saw at another location the fabricated village which was built for the filming of the movie about these events. Whilst surveying the area, one can begin to understand the real sense of isolation and injustice that must have been felt by these workers. Their suffering was grave, but they were far beyond the hearts and minds of people in the great cities of England, yet they raised their Christian voices and made the nation stand up to attention. To protect their rights, The Friendly Society of Agricultural Labourers was set up by six men from Tolpuddle, with the preacher George Loveless as their leader. They worked out that they needed a wage of at least thirteen shillings a week to be able to purchase their basic needs, but they were prepared to work for ten. However, the landowners did not want to pay this minimal wage and had them arrested, convicted under trumped-up charges and transported to Australia. Throughout England there was uproar at this injustice as sympathy for the workers grew. This led to a quarter of a million people signing a petition and 30,000 people marching in London to support the labourers. The government could not ignore the passionate demands of the masses, and they were freed and given passage back from Australia. When the first four arrived home in England, they came ashore at Plymouth, next to the point where the Mayflower Pilgrims left for the New World many generations before. The Tolpuddle Martyrs helped give the defenceless worker a voice in England, for after them workers knew that if they banded together their common voice could demand justice. They started the first Trade Union with the Christian principles of fairness and justice; not to be confused with the development of Marxist Unions of later eras, which were in conflict with Christianity.

A Battle Worth Fighting: Christians from all backgrounds have won great victories for the worker in the name of Jesus Christ. From the Christian labourers who worked the fields, to godly politicians who graced parliament, they all fought for equality in the work place. They won the right to fair pay and better conditions for each individual, and they set a modern precedent which by law employers had to follow. They won the right for workers to join together in one common cause, to be represented before their employers and they helped publicise the plight of the working classes. This was Christian justice in action and every citizen of the English speaking world felt the reverberations of the actions of these faithful warriors, from Australia, where the Tolpuddle Martyrs are still considered heroes, to Canada, where laws were changed for the better. Today the rights of millions of workers are still protected by law because Christians took their faith into the public square and called for action. For these Christians who fought for the rights of all, their motivation was not rights as and end unto themselves, but their underlining belief in God's gift of equality to all. On 21 May 1988, Prime Minister Margaret Thatcher told the General Assembly of the Church of Scotland, "We must not profess the Christian faith and go to church simply because we want social reforms and benefits, or a better standard of behaviour, but because we accept the sanctity of life, the responsibility that comes with freedom and the supreme sacrifice of Christ...we are a nation whose ideals are founded on the Bible."

Chapter Eight

Children's Rights

"Let the little children be filled first" (Mark 7:27).

The clouds menacing in the dark evolved into a tapestry of horror; it was as if the demons themselves were finding their expressions through them. But it was not these that ravished her with fear – it was the slow footsteps that echoed down the streets that were the real threat. In the silence of the night every drip of water, every fox howling and all noises were magnified until dread took hold. As the human shadow began to fall over the entrance of the back-street where she lived, her body would withdraw into itself. Hiding, shaking, freezing – there would be no sleep tonight, nor any other. She knew the stories of the adults who walked the streets at night and of the missing children whose lives were cut short. She had learnt not to make friends, because one of them still haunts her dreams, and she can never forget the screams of this child as she disappeared off the streets into oblivion.

The night was the enemy and the sun rising marked the end of one terror, unto another. In the night she was afraid, in the day she was worthless. Every eye would watch her walk the streets and she would overhear adults telling their children not to talk to her. With no family, no hope and no money, she only had one choice. She would hang around the market, looking at the bread and wait for her chance. When the time was right, she would run, grab something and escape, hoping that the police were not following. As the clock struck nine at night, the worries of the day came to an end as the terror of the night began once again. She once again found her way to the backstreet and attempted to hide amongst the rubbish. She was only seven years old.

A Father to the Fatherless: George Müller (1805-1898) was a Prussian born minister who made England his home. He felt the burden of the lost children on England's streets and founded orphanages in Bristol with three key principles: faith, care and evangelism. He made the choice never to ask for people to support his work or to make appeals asking for money. His ambition in providing for masses of children was to prove that God could be fully trusted to supply all of one's needs. With this in mind, he would pray to God asking for the needs of the orphanages and trust in Him alone to provide. During his lifetime he cared for 100,000 children who were saved from a life on the street. He provided for a basic education, as well as their practical needs and helped these young people to get a job before they left. His pioneering work was so successful that some of the upper class began to be disturbed that poor street children were being raised "above their natural station in life!"

His ministry as a philanthropist gained a worldwide reputation and the Bristol orphanage was a model for others to follow. In his later years Müller did not settle down into retirement, but spent twenty years travelling the globe, preaching the word and sharing personal experience of answered prayer. There were days of terrible trials and limited income for the work, but it has been estimated that in today's money Müller received over one hundred million British pounds in his lifetime through prayer alone. Julian Marsh, the Chief Executive of the George Müller foundation said, "He says therefore in his diaries later in his life that he had documentary evidence that he had received 50,000 answers to prayer and went on to say something even more remarkable – that 30,000 of those prayers had been answered in 24 hours or less."[1] Julian Marsh continued, "It is amazing that the story of a life that was lived trusting only in God, a life in love with Jesus Christ and a lasting testimony of a God who cares for us and who is totally trustworthy is still fresh and challenging today, even though this man was born 200 years ago."[2]

Müller began his life saving work, when the state did little or nothing to help homeless children. He truly was a Christian pioneer in a day when very few other people cared for the most vulnerable within society. The old Müller children's homes are no longer needed today, but they still dominate a large area of Bristol. When the author visited the city, he was able to see the tombstone of Müller which is set in a huge forty-three acre forest-type graveyard. The cemetery workers explained that people from all over the world come to pay respect.

Child Life and Labour in England: The U.K. National Archives revealed that 'in 1821, approximately 49% of the workforce was under twenty. In rural areas, children as young as five or six joined women in 'agricultural gangs' that worked in fields often a long way from their homes.'[3] Previously, we have considered

Lord Shaftesbury, who fought to protect the rights of many workers and his battles included fighting for the rights of young people, women and children. Prolific author Ernest Hayes wrote of Shaftesbury, the great Christian innovator, revealing how very difficult life was for children in those days: 'The gravest social evils that followed in the wake of the Industrial Revolution in England were borne by the children of the poor. The introduction of machinery brought pauperism to large masses of people and the parish authorities often claimed the right to dispose of the children of any person accepting relief. These children were consigned to employers at the age of seven upwards till they were twenty-one. Next door to the mills, apprentice-houses were built and in these two buildings young lives were spent at the best in monotonous toil, at worst in the hell of inhuman cruelty. The majority of mills worked fifteen hours a day, while some of them never stopped day or night. The children who attended the machines by day crept into beds just left vacant by the children who were to attend them by night. In the mines children were employed as trappers for opening and shutting the doors that regulated the ventilation of the workings. Others were employed to draw trucks along the mine corridors, often on their hands and knees.'[4]

Shaftesbury devoted himself to helping all workers, including children and in his lifetime he managed to get laws passed which prevented children under the age of nine from working in factories, and made it illegal for children aged nine to thirteen, to work more than eight hours a day. This was major progress for his day. Women and teenagers were also protected from being forced to work every hour under the sun; chimney sweeps and young miners also found protection. Shaftesbury, amongst many others, awoke the conscience of his nation and called the people to apply the principles of the Christian faith into every area of national life.

A Home and Education: Thomas John Barnardo (1845-1905) in his lifetime rescued nearly 60,000 children and rehabilitated them to help them find their place in society. The Barnardo's charity says of him: 'At the age of 16, after converting to Protestant evangelicalism he decided to become a medical missionary in China and so set out for London to train as a doctor.'[5] But whilst in London, his attention was drawn to the great numbers of homeless children. With the support of Christian leaders, he gave up his vision of China, to help the destitute children of England.

In 1870, the first Dr Barnardo's home was opened, in which he would provide for the basic needs of children – food, clothing, housing, education and care. The BBC's Songs of Praise featured a programme recognising this Christian hero in which they reported: 'Dr Barnardo's belief that the most vulnerable and disadvantaged children deserve a better start in life and the chance of a better future remains the philosophy of Barnardo's today.'[6]

Child Abuse – An Invisible Social Evil: "My father and mother are both dead. I don't know how old I am. I have no recollection of a time when I did not live with the Connolly's. Mamma has been in the habit of whipping and beating me almost every day," said American child Mary Ellen. "I have now the black and blue marks on my head which were made by mamma, and also a cut on the left side of my forehead which was made by a pair of scissors. She struck me with the scissors and cut me; I have no recollection of ever having been kissed by anyone...never dared to speak to anybody, because if I did I would get whipped."[7]

In 1874, Etta Wheeler, a Christian missionary was carrying out door to door work in the U.S., offering help to impoverished residents. During these visits she became aware of the plight of Mary Ellen Wilson, who was being tormented by her cruel abuser, Mary Connolly. Under the pretext of offering the family help she visited the home to determine the state of the child. She found a malnourished nine year old girl, who looked as if she was five; she was bruised, battered and barely dressed despite being winter. Across the table lay a brutal whip of twisted leather strands, and the child's meagre arms and legs bore many marks of its use," said Etta. "But the saddest part of her story was written on her face in its look of suppression and misery, the face of a child unloved, of a child that had seen only the fearsome side of life. These things I saw while seeming not to see and I left without speaking to, or of, the child. I never saw her again until the day of her rescue, three months later, but I went away determined, with the help of a kind Providence, to rescue her from her miserable life."[8]

Etta knew that she needed legal help to formally rescue this child, so she sought Henry Bergh. The story of Mary's abuse made the press and this invisible social evil of child abuse was exposed. During the case, Judge Lawrence called upon section 65 of the American version of the ancient English Habeas Corpus Act, to rescue Mary. At the happy conclusion, the thoughts of Etta Wheeler went towards all the other children who were secretly being abused. She realised from experience that even though she found abuse, she had no legal right or provision to help victims. There needed to be an organisation which had power and legal standing to help others. With this in mind she saw Henry Bergh and asked, "If there could not now be a society for the prevention of cruelty to children which should do for abused children what was being so well done for animals?"[9] "There shall be one," was the reply. It was this event which became the catalyst for the creation in 1875 of the New York Society for the Prevention of Cruelty to Children (NYSPCC) – the first child protection agency in the world.

In England, the Rev. Benjamin Waugh (1839-1908) had witnessed first hand the deprivation and child cruelty which had gone unnoticed by many. His experience as a writer for the *Christian Sunday* magazine gave him the skills to write in 1873, *The Gaol Cradle, Who Rocks It?* in which he addressed the evil of child abuse and neglect. The movement took ground and the NYSPCC provided the inspiration to start a similar work in England. In July 1884, three Christian leaders, Lord Shaftesbury, Rev. Benjamin Waugh and Rev. Edward Rudolf founded what would become the National Society for the Prevention of Cruelty to Children (NSPCC) with Queen Victoria as patron. They helped raise funds to employ inspectors, who investigated reports of child abuse and took action to end it.

The NSPCC became an integral part in developing child protection policy and practice in Britain, and from that point on, children had some hope that they did not have to suffer in silence. The NSPCC reported that our society 'has helped more than 10 million children since our inspectors first began their work within the London community in the 1880s. But although our society is now radically different in many ways, the emergence of new and different social pressures means that today's children need the help of the NSPCC as desperately as children did in late Victorian England.'[10]

Protecting The Most Vulnerable: Before modern nation states began to take responsibility for caring for the most vulnerable in society, it was Christian leaders who saw the evil, challenged it and changed it. Hundreds of thousands of children were rescued from poverty because of the works of Müller, Barnardo and others like them. Today there are numerous descendants of these children who were rescued from the dark streets, who may have no idea that Christianity rescued their families in their darkest hour. At the same time, Shaftesbury was able to get the law changed in Christ's name, to save the smallest child from working, and as time went on others stood in his footsteps and called for a total end of child labour.

Christian concern also made the world notice not only the work place, but what happened behind closed doors. Looking back, child protection agencies have helped bring an end to the abuse of millions of children worldwide. The events retold here have made an impact globally – there were the direct changes; where English speaking colonies had laws changed following the mother country and societies were created in various nations. In addition, there were the indirect changes, where other nations gained the momentum to require the same protection for children in their homelands.

When the author visited Brazil, he toured a large hostel run by Christians who were rescuing children from the streets. There are places like that hostel all over the world, because Christians have always been the greatest volunteer force on the planet! Where else is there such a large body of people, who are willing to forsake pay, career advancement and comfort, to help the poor, vulnerable and forgotten? British MP Alun Michael explained that people of faith were the 'bedrock' of the voluntary sector saying, "That chain from faith to values, from values to social action has been absolutely essential to the health of the nation over many, many years; and I would go further in saying that from social action to politics is also a very necessary step as well."[11] Christian actions have spoken louder than words all over the world. In the Sudan, the author visited a Christian orphanage and school in the traditional Islamic centre of Khartoum. The founder was an English missionary whose exceptional work has been allowed to flourish because the fruit of changed lives speaks for itself. In India, every Christian ministry that the author worked with had a programme to help orphans and the impoverished. Also, in India, there is a growing recognition of the influence of the small but growing Christian Church. Indian Prime Minister Dr Manmohan Singh said, "Christianity is part of our national heritage," and he made reference to the fact that Christianity arrived in India before it came to many Western nations.[12]

The broadcaster Jeremy Paxman explained how missionaries, following the example of David Livingstone helped improve the rights of many children worldwide and continue to do so. "They often brought with them education and modern medicine," he said, "more than one hundred years after Livingstone, much of the missionary legacy is alive and well...Today, the work started by Church of Scotland missionaries has, as all over Africa, become a local African activity. The Nkolokoti Primary School was founded in 1935 in what was then the British colony of Nyasaland. The school now has almost 8,000 pupils. Missionaries have come in for a lot of stick for providing an excuse for flag-planting and land-grabbing, but the fact of the matter is, that without missionaries, this school wouldn't exist, and so 8,000 children would get no education and, come to that, no breakfast either."[13]

In the modern age, Christian agencies are working all over the developing world attempting to help and rescue children from poverty and abuse; as we consider this, we would do well to remember that Christians were the ones who addressed these very issues at home, and helped end the silent neglect of children. Visitors to churches in the West today will realise that there are several major campaigns which Christians are now involved with. One is to end worldwide poverty and injustice, which has caused endless suffering for millions, especially for children and another, is to end the modern slave trade – which usually presents itself through people trafficking and prostitution. Making poverty history caught the world's attention and it is the aim of many Christians to make other causes as well known.

Chapter Nine

Women's Rights

'Strength and honour are her clothing...she opens her mouth with wisdom' (Proverbs 31:25-26).

The Bible and Christian history are full of examples of women who have been used by God and have added valuable contributions to every area of society. The Bible divulges women playing roles in all areas of society including leadership, national defence, humanitarian exploits and spiritual exhortation. In addition, we discover that the Bible offered rights to women which were not available to many women a few hundred years ago, and are still not available to women in other nations, where other faiths have shaped their society.

The book of Job is a unique book from the Bible and at the end of his story which questions suffering and injustice, we discover that Job gave his daughters a legal right to become heirs; these were days when sons could get everything. Throughout the Law of Moses, we find the provision of many rights for women, including some inheritance rights and protection from crime. In the Old Testament we find that the prophetic gifts of Deborah were used to lead and provide a defence strategy for an entire nation. Ushering in the era of the prophets, the faith of Hannah was the cornerstone upon which Samuel would enter the world as a prophet to his nation and Esther can rightly be judged as the saviour of all Jewish people throughout the Herculean empire of her day.

In Scripture, we also discover that godly women played a role in reforming men, for the tenderness of the Shulamite woman revealed the poet of love in the womaniser Solomon. In Proverbs 31 we discover the dilemma of many twenty-first century women being witnessed thousands of years earlier than anticipated; she is a business woman, a mother, a wife, a homemaker, a humanitarian, a person of wisdom and integrity, and one who fears the Lord. She is up early, working all day and is still busy after dark! In the New Testament, the first revelation of the Saviour's birth came to Mary and the aged prophetess at the temple knew before many men, that she had seen the salvation of God. The gospel also records in Luke 8:1-3 that it was often women who provided for the material necessities of

Jesus. It was to two women that Jesus' resurrection was first heralded and whilst the disciples did not believe them, their faith was strong in the Lord. Australian journalist and broadcaster Clive James wrote that Jesus was, 'The first great man to be a champion of women.'[1] In addition, during the birth of the Church, the Holy Spirit descended and empowered all who were present for service, including women. Throughout the letters in the New Testament, we also find a husband and wife team who led a church and the specific mention of some women's ministry.

In history and in almost every culture, it was considered normal to grant lower status to women than to men. Christianity arose in a culture where the widespread oppression of women was as regular as the sunrise, yet Jesus rejected cultural oppression and showed respect for women, by honouring them with the greatest news the world had ever heard of – He is risen!

Professor Kate Cooper, a leading authority on the role of women in the early Church said, "In the early Christian communities," women "were seen as equal sharers in the job of preaching and teaching."[2] In Romans 16 Paul mentions many women whose contributions to early Christianity were important, including Phoebe who gets a special commendation. The historian Bettany Hughes said, "In the first two centuries of Christianity, at least fifty percent of the churches in Rome were founded by women." Inside the Catacombs of St Priscilla in Rome, which date between the second and forth centuries AD, the historian Bettany Hughes noted, "All over this subterranean world there are images of not just men leading worship, but women."[3] However, when Christianity was adopted as the official religion of the Roman Empire, the Church reverted to reflecting culture.

In the modern age, many people of various outlooks contributed to women gaining the right to vote, to receive an education, obtain a career and hold public office etc., but it is worth remembering that many Christian women who were motivated by their faith, led by example to gain their rights and others followed in their footsteps. In addition, Christian women played a primary role in creating a faith based education system across the world which helped men and women understand that before God, they have equal rights.

Yet, in regions of the world with a different religious heritage, things are still grim. Former British politician Edwina Currie wrote: 'There is precious little equality in countries like Iran...there is none whatsoever in countries like Afghanistan,' where a new law 'denies Afghan Shi'a women the right to leave their homes except for 'legitimate' purposes; forbids women from working or receiving education without their husbands' express permission; explicitly permits marital rape; diminishes the right of mothers to be their children's guardians after divorce; and makes it impossible for wives to inherit property from their husbands.'[4] In addition, in Saudi Arabia women are not considered capable to drive a car. Things are changing, but we must ask ourselves why in the Christian West did women gain rights, while in other cultures they are still often denied?

Best-Selling Author and School Founder: Hannah More (1745-1833) was an Esther of her day; for truly she was chosen for such a time as hers. Having fought against the prejudices of her age, she became a best-selling author, founded many parish schools, helped eradicate slavery and became a Christian forerunner in the struggle for women's rights. At the first parliamentary debate on the slave trade, she used her literacy skills to promote abolition; she wrote *Slavery,* a poem which was dedicated to the anti-slavery movement and her support gave more weight to the cause of abolition. She obtained a large fortune because of the success of her writings and was very generous towards charity. Her own life was an example to all of what a woman of God could achieve in the cause of Christ.

One of Hannah's most famous works was *Strictures on the Modern System of Female Education* (1799). In the book she reveals how women were given a second class education which short-changed them of their true abilities. Her personal example revealed that Christ could lead women to succeed in every area of society. People standing on all sides of the feminist movement, from the extreme to the faith-based, have acknowledged her contribution as a pivotal player in the battle for equality. For Christians, they honour her courage for fighting for the rights of women to play a fuller role in society, without the desire to destabilise the family or degrade womanhood by encouraging promiscuous behaviour, excessive drinking or the copying of other male dominated failings. Hannah was one of many Christian women who helped free women, yet at the same time, respected the dignity and grace of womanhood. The Victorian Web states, 'She was one of the most successful writers and perhaps the most influential woman of her day.'[5]

Better Working Conditions for Women and Children: Charlotte Elizabeth Tonna (1790-1846) was a writer and campaigner for better working conditions, especially for women and children. In 1844, she published *The Wrongs of Woman*, designed to confront the garment industry with the abuses of women and children in their factories. Originally part-published in *The Christian Lady's* magazine her thoughts were designed to make a wider audience aware of the human cost of high production, high profits and low pay.

Famous Reformer: Elizabeth Fry (1780-1845) was raised in a generation when a woman's role was severely restricted. She was expected to get married, stay at home and keep a respectable household. Instead of succumbing to the pressure of her day, she became a famous reformer who even found a friend in the Monarch. Using the text of Matthew 25 as her commission, she helped reform the prison system and gave strength to the poor and lowly. In days when it was unusual for a woman to have a voice outside of the home, she became a friend to the outcasts and took the story of their plight to the highest places of power. Her Christian example encouraged other women to play a fuller role in society.

Abolitionist and Advocate of Women's Rights: Sojourner Truth (1797-1883) was a former U.S. slave who was given her freedom by her last master in 1827. Truth became a Christian evangelist, and a leading advocate of the abolition of slavery and for the rights of women.

Contributions to Literature and the Women's Movement: Florence Nightingale (1820-1910) played an important role in the growth of women's rights, even though she is best known for her staggering contributions in the medical and mathematical fields. Florence's mother and sister were well educated, but instead of fully employing themselves, they accepted the quiet lifestyle that society demanded of women. A life of thoughtless ease was rejected by Nightingale whose story includes her personal battle to follow God's call into a career when society, family and the establishment were all against her. She was the author of *Suggestions for Thought to Searchers after Religious Truth* which contained in one part, the history of the women's movement. Her life was a personal example of what godly women could do, instead of allowing culture to dictate they had to become ineffective and incapacitated outside of the home.

A College Education and an Army of Labourers: Charles Kingsley (1819-1875) was concerned about all aspects of the life of the nation. When London's Queen's College dared to go against public opinion and offer a college education to women, he supported the plan and even became a lecturer. Nonconformist Christians not only helped to pioneer equal opportunities for women in education, but they were also on the faith based front line. Whilst women were encouraged to stay at home and follow etiquette, the Salvation Army was pioneering a brilliant work in the tragic streets of London. From the early days, the Army has accorded women equal opportunities with every rank being open to them.

Christian Medical Pioneers: 'There was a strong Christian element in the motivation of the pioneers of medical education for women,' wrote Dr Rosie Beal-Preston. 'Elizabeth Blackwell, the first woman doctor was a Quaker, while Elizabeth Garrett came from a very devout family. Ann Clark, another Quaker, was the first woman surgeon and worked at the Women's Hospital and the Children's Hospital in Birmingham. Sophia Jex-Blake, another devout Christian founded the London School of Medicine for Women while Clara Swain was the first woman doctor to go overseas (to Asia) as a medical missionary.'[6]

Elsie Inglis (1864-1917) started training for her profession when women were greatly frowned upon for attempting to enter any career path, but to become a doctor was especially discouraged. She was one of many who began to open the doors of professions that were traditionally closed to women and by doing so, reshaped the world. Her passion was for women, to play a full role in society and with this in mind, she fought for women's right to vote as well. When she offered her services to her nation during the First World War the doors of power closed to her. Instead of giving up, her Christian faith motivated her and she formed independent hospital and transport units which served in Belgium, France, Sicily, Serbia and Russia. Her biography states: 'By her knowledge she cured the physical wounds of the Serb soldiers. By her shining face she cured their souls. Silent, busy, smiling, that was her method. She strengthened the faith of her patients in knowledge and in Christianity. Scotland hardly could send to Serbia a better missionary.'[7]

Protecting Women's Rights Abroad: Mary Slessor (1848-1915) was a sacrificial missionary who went to Africa and confronted customs which treated human life as expendable. She ended tribal wars, saved the lives of slaves, and she was especially worried about the way African women were treated. 'Women were treated as lower than cattle, and Mary was so successful in raising their standing in society that she may be considered as one of the pioneers of women's rights in Africa,' explained a representative of Dundee City Council, Scotland.[8]

'One of the most notable features of Christian missionary work in what we would now call the Third World was that the first to become converted to Christianity were always the women,' wrote the journalist Mary Kenny. 'It was obvious that Christianity brought women higher status and more respect. The British Empire was, simultaneously, working to halt some of the cruelties visited upon women in some native cultures – stopping, for example, the Indian practice of forcing a widow to throw herself on the funeral pyre of her dead husband. In China, missionaries tried to stop the cruel foot-binding of females. I have read some grisly accounts by late Victorian British missionaries who tried to stop little girls being sold into prostitution on the Indian subcontinent. There was a superstitious belief...that a man could get rid of venereal disease by having intercourse with a young virgin. And thus poor little girls of nine and ten were being subjected to penetration by diseased older men. The missionaries crusaded repeatedly against this.'[9] The article then tells how a female missionary fought to protect girls from forcible circumcision, but was hacked to death by locals for 'interfering.' We must never forget that brave missionaries across the globe often gave their all to protect the rights of women abroad and to give all they served, dignity in Christ.

Rights At Home: The contribution of female missionaries to women's rights at home in the West is often forgotten. These pioneers were prepared to go to the most dangerous parts of the world, risking all for the sake of the Christian gospel. When they came home (not that many did), men often slumped back into their chairs, humbled by the passion and backbone that these female missionaries had shown. After all, if a woman can civilise a tribe of lawless cannibals, they can surely do any other job at home. As one preacher said, "If we can send our women to the ends of the earth to preach, we can surely open all of our institutions at home to them too."

The first mass organisation of women committed to social reform, founded in 1874, was the effectual Christian Women's Temperance Union, who campaigned on a large number of issues facing women, from equal pay, protection at home and voting rights. This organisation is the oldest continuing women's organisation worldwide and it was key to fighting for universal suffrage. In the U.S. there is an obvious link between Christian women's movements and the struggle for rights, and they have inspired women all over the world. In fact, it could be argued that these Christian women made the largest single contribution to the advancement in women's rights in the modern age, because they mobilised many hearts with concise objectives.

Christianity and Women: In the context of women's rights, it may be true that the established Church often reflected culture, instead of transforming it. Yet the Christian women here (and many others not cited), led by example to revolutionise the place of women in society. During the late twentieth century, many of the contributions of these great Christian women were sidelined because they did not cry for sexual promiscuity or the demise of marriage. In the twenty-first century, perhaps some are now beginning to understand that these Christian women got the balance right. There are few today who would want to argue that the women (or men), who fall out of clubs drunk in the early hours of the morning, and who subsequently wake up in a strangers bed have a better standard of living, or more self respect, than these Christian women who championed female dignity and grace. Christianity demands respect for women, it honours their bodies and requires men to show their love in the lifetime commitment of marriage, as they take full responsibility for the results of their actions.

Chapter Ten

Education: Schools and Universities

'He spoke three thousand proverbs and his songs were one thousand and five. Also he spoke of trees, from the cedar tree of Lebanon even to the hyssop that springs out of the wall; he spoke also of animals, of birds, of creeping things and of fish' (1 Kings 4:32-33).

Throughout history, education was mostly for a select few. The rich and powerful used their knowledge to rule over the majority, but things started to change when Christian centres began to grow in influence around Europe. The Bible revealed a God who valued knowledge and the Church often represented this ideal. During the poorly named 'Dark Ages' and throughout the times when secular government collapsed, it was the Christian Church which kept learning alive, and helped forever seal our link with much ancient wisdom and learning; in many cases, it was monks who saved ancient texts for posterity. During the long development of the modern state all education was frequently in the hands of the Church and for that reason, Christianity became the cornerstone upon which Western education was built. The Western belief in education for the masses is rooted in the Christian faith, for it was Christians who were the first to attempt universal education and it was missionaries who promoted literacy on a worldwide basis.

The Beginnings: Alexandria in Egypt was a fascinating place to walk around for the author; the imagination comes alive at the quest to know what was lost from the famous library, which was sadly destroyed. The modern library is wonderful to visit, but it feels like an empty promise. Alexander the Great may be the first person who comes to mind upon the mention of this city, but this was also a Christian beacon before the Islamic invasion. It was home to the Catechetical School of Alexandria, which was founded in 190AD. Pantaenus, Clement, Origen and Athanasius were scholars, teaching not only the Bible and Christian doctrine, but a host of other subjects including mathematics and medicine. As time went on Christian education for the few was growing and the subjects studied were expanding too, from basic astronomy to geometry.

The first major change that Christianity brought to education was that of making no distinction of gender. Before the time of Christianity, the standard for education amongst the Greeks or Romans was that of teaching the male offspring of wealthy people. Girls were in general, not given a formal education, but Christianity challenged this. The second great change that Christianity offered was that of opening the doors of education to some of the poor – for the call of God was now more important than one's social or financial status.

Northern Europe: Before Christianity penetrated Northern Europe, the region was a very dark place, lost in pessimistic pagan superstitions, with people estranged and entrapped by a foreboding sense of helplessness. Christianity was the power which changed this and opened the door for personal hope and national awakening. The first step of changing these backward lands into the leading powers on the planet was to educate the masses in Judeo-Christian ethics and biblical culture. One commentator wrote: 'Turning the bloodthirsty savages of North Western Europe into mild Swedes, Norwegians, Danes and Englishmen is a revolution of the spirit not to be sneezed at!'

Monasteries: Monastic centres in Europe became the primary centres of learning and it was from these Christian sources that universities would develop. Within these Christian faith based communities, monks would lead a hard life, but much time would be taken to collect books and the laborious task of copying them by hand continued. Reading and copying manuscripts were two of the most important parts of the lives of these monks and because of their scholarly backgrounds, they also became the lecturers in the newly founded universities.

Oxford University: 'Oxford is the oldest university in the English-speaking world and lays claim to nine centuries of continuous existence.'[1] The motto of Oxford is 'Dominus Illuminatio Mea' – 'The Lord is my Light,' from Psalm 27. Christianity has played a central role in the development of Oxford from its beginning in 1249: members of several Christian orders shaped its infancy, later the Bishop of Rochester and Walter De Merton developed college life. William Grocyn, a biblical scholar during the Renaissance period helped revive the Greek language and the Archbishop of Canterbury codified Oxford's status. It became a powerhouse of Christianity and biblical reform, from John Wycliffe to John Wesley, to the writings of C.S. Lewis.

Cambridge University: The story of the University of Cambridge, in England, is similar to Oxford. It is the second oldest university in the English speaking world and was shaped by Christianity – a decree by Pope Gregory IX confirmed its status. The first college was founded by Hugh Balsham, the Bishop of Ely. During medieval times, many colleges were established with the religious concerns of the founders in mind and when Britain turned Protestant, the curriculum turned from Canon Law, towards the Bible, mathematics and the classics.

Encouraging Learning: William Wykeham (1324-1404) was a senior clergyman, bishop and statesman who used his wealth and influence for the greater good of the people. As he progressed in his walk of faith, he felt guilty that he had been given so much in a world where there was great lack. He served as the Chancellor of England and used his political power as well as his ecclesiastical influence, to encourage learning and founded schools and colleges. The school at Winchester remains the oldest scholarly foundation in England. The Society For Promoting Christian Knowledge in 1898 expressed how Christian donors funded many universities: 'The monasteries had for a long time been the chief seat of learning, but there were now a number of other schools besides...by the middle of the fourteenth century Merton, Baliol, Exeter, Oriel University and Queen's College at Oxford were flourishing; most of which had been promoted by people who believed that such benevolence would obtain for them pardon and grace in the world to come.'[2]

Aberdeen University: Bishop William Elphinstone (1431-1514) helped introduce printing into Scotland, but is best known as the founder of the University of Aberdeen in 1494. Leslie Macfarlane wrote of him: 'For despite his formidable administrative gifts, he remained at heart a devout Christian, as we may see for ourselves – in the commentaries he made in the margins of his legal text books, and in the comments he silently made in the margins of the homilies and sermons to be found in his devotionals, not meant for others to see.'[3]

Luther and Calvin: In Europe, we find that the idea of universal education was grounded in non-conformist Christianity. In Germany Martin Luther (1483-1546) taught that parents had a duty before God to teach their children, and that education should be wide and varied. In Geneva, Switzerland, John Calvin (1509-1564) promoted 'a system of elementary education in the vernacular for all, including reading, writing, arithmetic, grammar and religion, and the establishment of secondary schools for the purpose of training citizens for civil and ecclesiastical leadership.' In Germany, the Christian Johann Sturm (1507-1589) introduced a system of grading students hoping this would encourage them to learn by reaching for the next grade.

The Bible: One of the greatest leaps forward towards universal education was the translation of the Bible into the vernacular in many European nations. For the first time, every citizen had a special reason to learn how to read, for now they could read the very words of God in the vernacular.

Revival, Education and Sunday Schools: As Europe developed, it was still the social elites that had access to education. Wells Cathedral School in England is one of the oldest boarding schools in Europe and was founded in 909. After 1547, grammar schools began appearing in every city of England with biblical studies, Latin and Greek all in the curriculum. But as these were fee paying schools, the masses were still disenfranchised. Consequently, it was during the great Evangelical Revival (1739-1791) that Christianity brought another fundamental change to education – it began to take action by providing education for the masses. In England, John Wesley (1703-1791) not only cared about the eternal salvation of the people who came under his preaching, but he proved by example that the gospel cared about the whole person. He wrote many practical books to help people, including *Grammar* in 1751, to help people read and write.

During the eighteenth century newspaperman Robert Raikes (1736-1811) realised that something had to be done about the impoverished and uneducated children of England. His response was to prove by personal experience that the poorest children can be helped and educated in Sunday schools. He wrote: 'Vice is preventable. Idleness is the parent of vice.

Ignorance is the cause of idleness,' and finally, 'Vice is preventable – begin with a child.'

He believed that children could get a better start in life with a Christian education and therefore they would avoid crime, laziness and all the associated sins of that era. It was a hard start, but after success he published his reports in his newspaper and others followed his example. Sunday schools had existed before, but Raikes popularised the successful model. In November 1783, he proved to his readers that his scheme had helped end the riotous behaviour of the youth on Sundays in his area of England, and encouraged all to help the youth of their day. The work grew and became a vital international movement, bringing children by their masses into God's house for instruction. King George III (1738-1820) saw the positive outcome of this Christian fervour, which led to greater education and said, "It is my wish that every poor child in my dominion shall be taught to read the Bible." In 1784, the Society for the Support and Encouragement of Sunday Schools Through-out British Dominions was founded and before fifty years had passed, one quarter of the English population were already registered in a Sunday school.[4] By 1903, six million children across the country regularly attended Sunday school.

Hannah More: Hannah (1745-1833) was one of the greatest social reformers of the eighteenth and nineteenth centuries. It was her devotion to the Christian faith, and her desire to follow the Master which led her to establish a network of parish schools to educate the children of the poor, and Raikes was one of her inspirations. This evangelical philanthropist was a citizen of high class and was well connected in polite society. But she did not lose her purpose in the grandeur of her position. She became friends with John Newton, the evangelical hymn writer and abolitionist William Wilberforce. As a best-selling author and poet she used her influence to forward the cause of Christ. In the film *Amazing Grace* by Walden Media, Hannah More is often featured and is one of the people who 'humbly suggests' that Wilberforce can better serve God in politics.

In Germany, Frederick Froebel (1782-1852) the son of a Christian minister became the founder of preschools. As a boy he learnt much from his Christian father, but realised that not everyone had this kind of expertise available to them. He developed the idea of kindergartens based upon his experience of playing and learning as a child in the family garden, as he was taught by his wise father.

American Christian Education: In British America, the first law which passed concerning public education was founded by the concern that all should have a thorough knowledge of the Holy Bible. In 1647, The Old Deluder Satan Act was passed to make sure that all were taught the Holy Scriptures. In 1690, America had its first textbook, *The New England Primer;* with the Bible as its foundation, it contains numerous references to Holy Scripture and an underlining Judeo-Christian ethic. *The New England Primer* was used up until the beginning of the twentieth century and contained a statement of faith in Christ, prayers that finished in the name of Jesus and a song of praise in the Christian theme. Also, Harvard, Yale and Princeton all had solid Christian foundations. Broadcaster Wendy Griffith noted: 'Harvard was established primarily to train ministers to evangelise the Atlantic seaboard. A statue of John Harvard – a young minister when he came over from England, still stands in Harvard yard. Chartered in 1636, Harvard remained dedicated to Christian education for more than 200 years.' Historian Peter Marshall said, "The rules of Harvard said if any student does not believe that the Scriptures are the inspired word of God – he is subject to immediate dismissal. So you're going to get thrown out of the college if you reject the infallible role of Holy Scripture."[5] Benjamin Silliaman (1779-1864) was a Yale faculty member who wrote: 'Yale College is a little temple; prayer and praise seem to be the delight of the greater part of the students.'[6]

In 1749, Benjamin Franklin (1706-1790) presented his plan for public education in Pennsylvania, which contained his passion that students should be taught, 'The excellency of the Christian religion above all others.' Benjamin Rush (1745-1813) a signatory of the Declaration of Independence wrote: 'Let the children who are sent to those schools be taught to read and write and above all, let both sexes be carefully instructed in the principles and obligations of the Christian religion. This is the most essential part of education.'[7] In 1782, the Continental Congress published an English language Bible calling it an 'edition of the Holy Scriptures for the use of our schools,' and when Benjamin Franklin University was founded in 1787, it was dedicated as 'a nursery of religion and learning, built on Christ, the Cornerstone.' Francis Scott Key (1779-1843), the author of the poem that became America's national anthem – *The Star-Spangled Banner* was in addition the president of the American Sunday School Union. In 1828, following Britain's Sunday school movement he called for a rapid expansion of the cause, asking for Sunday schools to be established all over the Midwest. Fifty years later over two and a half million students attended in over sixty thousand schools.

Special Needs: In the ancient world, people with special needs were often treated appallingly, many were murdered as babies and others survived to live a life of poverty or abuse. The Christian Church was the first institution to truly commit to helping those who were often excluded from society. When Christianity became a tolerated religion within the Roman Empire, it was able to help those in need, starting by opening shelters for the blind. In the modern age, Louis Braille (1809-1852) was the man whose invention would give millions of blind people the chance to read. He developed an alphabet system of raised dots which could be read by fingers. He was a committed Christian, who believed God had a destiny and purpose for him in life. Some of his last words were, "I am convinced that my mission is finished on earth; I tasted yesterday the supreme delight; God condescended to brighten my eyes for the splendour of eternal hope."

Church and the State: 'From medieval times, the Church provided education to all classes of society, in monasteries, at public schools, orphanages, charity schools, grammar schools, Church foundations, or by the chaplains to private households. Until as late as the nineteenth century, all university fellows and many schoolmasters were expected or required to be in holy orders.'[8] From 1833 onward in Britain, the state began to follow the Church's example and invest in education. 'Twenty years before state education began in 1870, a government commission found that about two and half million children in England attended day school. Almost all of these were run by churches, chapels and Christian charities.'[9] Journalist Cristina Odone wrote: 'Until the 19th century, churches and religious charities were the only providers of education in this country. Those schools, with their endowments, scholarships and sense of mission, were the sole promoters of social mobility. The 7,000 church schools in Britain still offer an escalator to better opportunities.'[10]

Queen Elizabeth II addressed how the legacy of the national endowment of the King James Bible and the work of the Church played a significant role in establishing the right to education in England. "The Authorised Version has remained one of the defining elements of our heritage. Similarly the Church of England's initiative to build new schools at the beginning of the nineteenth century created a momentum which led eventually to Parliament establishing a universal right to education."[11] Lord Ian Blair, the former Met chief of Scotland Yard said, "The greatest achievements and ambitions of human social history, such as the abolition of slavery and the provision of universal education or free health care for all have had their origins in religious impulse."[12]

Heritage: The first schools opened during the English colonial era in North America and churches established most universities as a training ground for new ministers. In the 1840s, American schools were largely private, run by Christians, and steps were made to create a public education system for all. The state took more control and more recently, the agenda of the separation of Church and state has had a major impact upon the teaching of the Christian heritage in U.S. schools. In twenty-first century England, one in three publicly funded schools are still run by religious faiths, the overwhelming majority being Christian. Religious education is important and by law, schools in the public education system are required to perform a daily act of worship which must be 'wholly or mainly broadly Christian.' In Canada, the Christian heritage in education is evident in the mottos of the Universities: in Dalhousie, Nova Scotia - 'Pray and work;' in the University of Alberta – 'Whatsoever things are true;' and the University of Ottawa – 'God is the Lord of the sciences.'

Around the world, it was Christian missionaries who started tens of thousands of schools throughout Africa, Asia and beyond, providing for the very first time a modern education for the masses and in many places, a written language. In Korea, Christianity was the dynamic force that helped change an illiterate nation into an Asian 'tiger economy.' Author Douglas Porter wrote: 'Missionaries required illiterate Korean adult converts to learn and read Korean...before they could be admitted into membership...the result was one hundred percent literacy rate in a largely illiterate nation. Their ability to read made Christians the nation's natural leaders of Korean society.'[13] UNESCO also proved in a report which they sent to the U.N. that Christian action in educating the masses was essential to the development of Africa. The 1960s report showed that 85% of all school children in Africa were in Christian schools; even the former head of the U.N. Kofi Annan, was educated in a Christian school. Around the world in many places today, the story is still the same.

Christian Legacy: Education throughout history has been the key to the liberation of people from oppression and it was Christianity that celebrated education, expanded and provided it freely to millions when the state was still sleeping. Looking back at two thousand years of Christian history in education, we realise that our Christian heritage has played the most significant role in laying the foundations for our modern educational system, which benefits millions today, and helps our nations to continue to be world leaders. At the same time, missionary leaders like David Livingstone supplied the impetus for Christians to provide a Western education to the masses of the world, by showing that Christianity was making that possible at home. In 1852, David Livingstone (1813-1873) wrote: 'The English universities were founded and endowed chiefly by clergy, and the first thought of the first Bishop the English Church sent to Africa, was to found a college. The missionaries too, have always laboured to the benefit of their means to establish such institutions for the benefits of their converts. New England, with a population of about three million, has thirteen incorporated colleges. The United States generally have upwards of one hundred and twenty. Nearly all the universities of the Christian world have been founded by the clergy, and most of them have been conducted as schools of the Church.'[14]

St Augustine (354-430) told us in his *Confessions* that seeing the Scriptures he heard a voice saying, "Take up and read, take up and read." Over 1500 years later, the Church was saying the same thing to entire nations, because Christianity made it possible.

Chapter Eleven
The Right To Healthcare

"Your faith has made you well, go in peace" (Mark 5:34).

The Greek philosopher Herophilos (334-279BC) analysed that 'science and art have equally nothing to show, that strength is incapable of effort, wealth useless and eloquence powerless if health be wanting.'[1] The Christian Medical Fellowship revealed the Christian response: 'Over two millennia, Christian doctors and nurses, inspired by the example and teaching of Jesus of Nazareth, have been at the forefront of efforts to alleviate human suffering, cure disease, and advance knowledge and understanding.'[2] Christianity first began to have an impact upon healthcare, when it became the state religion of the Roman Empire. There had been care before, but under the Christian influence it rapidly expanded. By 323, the Church began an official policy of encouraging care for the poor, widows, strangers and the sick. The first Council of Nicea of 325 encouraged this action and Christian leaders were asked to create a hospital in every town. This act by the Church should never be underestimated, for it set in motion the creation of a healthcare system which became the forerunner of all healthcare in the Christian world. Without this official policy of the Church, the story of the development of healthcare or the lack thereof, would have been very different. By the medieval period, monks and nuns were the primary care givers because they created centres for care within their Christian communities.

A Founding Father: In 1123, Raherus founded Saint Bartholomew's Hospital – the oldest surviving hospital in England. He felt a distinct call from God to give up personal wealth to live the life of a servant. After falling sick in Rome, he was taken to a Christian hospital where, 'he made a bargain with God; he vowed that if health were given him, he would return home and set up a similar hospital to relieve the sufferings of the poor.'[3] Raherus is one of the founding fathers of healthcare in the English speaking world, and set an example which helped create a faith based healthcare system, which for centuries was almost the only provider of care for the sick.

The Founder of Modern Nursing: The treatment of the poor and sick at home and of the soldiers on the front during the

Crimean War (1853-1856) was appalling. With no money or training, the sick, the infirm, the aged and mentally unstable were all thrown together into wretched dirty institutions, full of untrained despairing nurses with poor reputations. Florence Nightingale (1820-1910) is famous as the founder of the modern nursing profession, which centred upon sacrificial commitment to compassionate patient care. Her modern approach focused orderly cleanliness and intelligent hospital administration, based upon statistical research. Florence felt that God was calling her to serve mankind when she was only sixteen years old.

Today, nursing is a respected profession but this was not the case in the early 1800s, and for an upper class wealthy family from which she descended, nursing was unacceptable and considered similar to being a maid. Therefore, Florence was expected to accept her status as a woman, to marry and to become an obedient wife. For many reasons, her parents forbade her to practice nursing, however, Florence could not shake-off her calling and rejected the cultural pressure that she was experiencing, and would not disobey God to satisfy her parents. She spent many years waiting for the right opportunity to follow God's call, until she was given the chance to travel around Europe, where she viewed several hospitals and found inspiration. By the age of thirty-three she finally got the opportunity to become a nurse and worked for an ill governess in Upper Harley Street in London.

Against all the odds, she found her way to the frontline during the Crimean War and led a nursing team to pioneer new methods. In 1854, in modern day Istanbul, Turkey, she discovered the wounded in terrible conditions and reported back to Britain her findings. The medical staff was overworked, under trained and short of all that was needed. Infections were common and often fatal, sewers were broken and ventilation was poor. More soldiers died from illness than from battle wounds, and so Nightingale and her fellow nurses thoroughly organised patient care, cleansed the hospital and all the equipment. She returned to England as a hero, but physically broken; her health would fail her for the rest of her life. She reformed nursing and in so doing saved many lives and found fame, which she used to raise money to help train other nurses. Her primary desire as a nurse was to serve others, as if they were Christ and when training people she consistently made mention of Holy Scripture. Writing to a fellow nurse of the conditions of the sick, the wretched, the forsaken and sinful people, she wrote: 'It was to these Christ came.'

Florence believed that Christians were not supposed to shut themselves away behind church doors, only praying for a mighty deliverance, when God has given them the ability to change the world for the better. She once marvelled that people would pray for deliverance from the plague and sickness, when at the same time the common sewers ran into London's River Thames! Why would people pray such a thing when it was in their power to deal with these unsanitary practises? Nightingale believed that a noble expression of womanhood was a life of service and sacrifice – following the example of her Lord. She published her *Notes on Nursing* in 1860, which was primary reading for nurses of her day. She also worked hard to improve conditions for the poor at home and took an active role in reforming the Poor Laws. In 1883, Queen Victoria presented her with the Royal Red Cross. She was an example to all nurses; she had played the central role in the establishment of the Royal Commission on the Health of the Army and was also called upon for advice during the American Civil War. On the author's visit to the Nightingale family grave at East Wellow, he found the four sided family monument, with the humble letters F.N., born 1820, Died 1910. Inside the church dating to 1215, is a replica of the Scutari Cross, made of bullets from the Crimea.

Christianity In Action: Early medical care was primitive, but as scientific knowledge grew, Christians were at the fore. John Wesley (1703-1791) followed his great revivals with practical help and advice for the people. His book *Primitive Physic* of 1747 gave simple medical advice which was relevant for his day. William Wilberforce and the Clapham Sect called for the widespread vaccination of the people of London against smallpox. One of the first female doctors, Annie McCall, was concerned about the number of women who died in childbirth, and in 1889 she began an ante-natal and post-natal clinic, and founded the Clapham Maternity Hospital. Elizabeth Fry started an Institute for Nursing Sisters and the hospice movement began largely through the influence of Christians. William Tuke, Lord Kinnaird and others helped to improve the care of children with special needs, and children received special homes, which Andrew Reed began. Also, the Royal National Institute For The Blind was opened by a Christian doctor. Christians not only provided care, but they pioneered new scientific advances in care. 'For example, Joseph Lister introduced antiseptic procedure into his surgery at a time when half of all patients died from infections; Sir James Simpson discovered chloroform as the first effective anesthetic and Professor Arthur Rendle Short pioneered the use of blood transfusions.'[4]

Healthcare: In the U.S., Pennsylvania Hospital was the first hospital to come into being in the British colonies. William Penn was the Christian founder of the Province of Pennsylvania, who also created another pioneering hospital. The link between Christianity and healthcare is an obvious one: 'In the U.S. the traditional hospital is a non-profit hospital, usually sponsored by a religious denomination.'[5] In the U.S., healthcare systems evolved relying primarily on private health insurance. In Britain in 1948, the National Health Service (NHS) was formed to provide free healthcare for all, to continue the work begun by Christian pioneers. According to the Archbishop of York, the foundations of the NHS can be sourced back to William Beveridge's experience at Oxford University, where he was challenge by Christians to see what poverty is and how it can be alleviated.[6]

Christianity for over a thousand years was pretty much the only provider of healthcare for the average person in the West. Without the healthcare that the Christian faith made available, there would be no hope or assistance for the majority. Around the world today, Christianity is still the major contributor to healthcare in many developing nations and Christians could well remember that this was once the case in the West. With the development of science many Christians were innovators and gave sacrificially of themselves. Nightingale was one who helped change the lives, not only of her patients but of every patient who would later benefit from the new systems that she helped develop. When people asked what was the motivation of these Christian pioneers? The words of Jesus often find reference in their diaries and biographies. 'Lord when did we see You sick and come to You? "Inasmuch as you did it to one of the least of these My brethren, you did it to Me" ' (Matthew 25:35-40).

Chapter Twelve

The Impoverished Masses

'Pure and undefiled religion before God and the Father is this; to visit orphans and widows in their trouble...' (James 1:27). 'If there is among you a poor man...you shall not harden your heart nor shut your hand from your poor brother' (Deuteronomy 15:7).

Christian revival and social justice often went hand in hand. John Wesley encouraged prison reform, desired the end of slavery, set up the means to distribute food and clothes to the poor, and helped people to get on their feet. *A Lion Handbook: The History of Christianity* reveals more: 'A lending bank was opened by Christians in 1746. Legal advice and aid was made available. Widows and orphans were housed...(in other words) the evangelical revival made England aware of its social obligation.'[1]

In the nineteenth century, social commentator and Christian Frank Ballard helped record the terrible conditions people in Britain were still living in, whilst it was enjoying prosperity which no other nation had known. 'In London alone, 44,000 little children daily attending boarding schools are in want of food. In the same city, there are 100,000 paupers, 80,000 fallen women, 60,000 married people living in single rooms...the average lifetime of the well-to-do is 55 years, that of the working-classes is 25! And 82 percent of their children die before the age of five!'[2] In the midst of this great poverty, many had no idea where to start to improve the lives of the average citizen – some even suggested that poverty was the lot of the masses. In these very dark days, it was William Booth (1829-1912) and many others like him who took their Christian faith into the public sphere to challenge and changed the status quo.

William Booth proclaimed, "While women weep, as they do now, I'll fight; while children go hungry, as they do now I'll fight; while men go to prison, in and out, in and out, as they do now, I'll fight; while there is a drunkard left, while there is a poor lost girl upon the streets, while there remains one dark soul without the light of God, I'll fight, I'll fight to the very end!" Booth founded the Salvation Army which took the gospel to slums and removed the slums from the hearts of people. The Army spread from

London, England, to every corner of the world and today is one of the largest distributors of humanitarian aid, and has been called the world's third largest army.

Booth started work at age thirteen and knew how poverty wrecked the human spirit and humiliated the soul. He spent several years as a minister, until he left to follow God's new call upon his heart. In London, he felt the burden of the poor and founded an organisation to help them. The work was outrageously hard, his wife wrote that he would, 'stumble home night after night haggard with fatigue, often his clothes were torn and bloody bandages swathed his head where a stone had struck.'[3] Booth knew that his mission was a direct work of God and despite his methods being questioned by many, he kept battling against the current and said, "We must wake ourselves up! Or somebody else will take our place and bear our cross, and thereby rob us of our crown." In 1878, the work was renamed The Salvation Army, and the image of an army defeating sin and restoring hope captured many hearts.

Booth led by example and spoke of the secret of their success, "The greatness of a man's power is the measure of his surrender." 'In 1890, Booth's controversial book, *In Darkest England And The Way Out* was published. In it he presented his plans for a programme which helped the poor and needy. His ideas were summarised in what he termed The Cab-Horse Charter which read: 'When a horse is down he is helped up, and while he lives he has food, shelter and work.' Booth realised that this meagre standard was absolutely unattainable by millions of people in Britain, yet the fact remained that cab horses were treated to a better standard of living than many people.'[4]

Booth set up hostels for the homeless, a poor man's bank, a missing persons bureau, training facilities to teach a trade and a job centre for people to find work. In addition he started a match factory that did not use sulphur which harmed people. Many of these ideas became commonplace in the future, but it was Booth who pioneered these self-help steps, so people could work out of poverty into providence. By 1899, the Army had lodged 11 million homeless people, served 27 million meals, found work for 9,000 people and even traced 18,000 missing people. The International Heritage Centre states: 'Booth's book was used as a blueprint for the present day welfare state when it was set up by the government in 1948. Many of Booth's ideas were incorporated into the welfare state system.'[5]

Booth's passion to help people practically never overshadowed the gospel message. He said, "To get a man soundly saved it is not enough to put on him a pair of new breeches, to give him regular work, or even to give him a university education. These things are all outside a man and if the inside remains unchanged you have wasted your labour. You must in some way or other graft upon the man's nature a new nature, which has in it the element of the Divine." By 1912, the Army had spread to 58 nations, by 2008 it operated in more than 100 nations and it is a significant player in the U.S., always ready to help when disaster strikes and when daily tragedy goes unnoticed.

Cleaning Up All England: Charles Kingsley (1819-1875) was the rector at Eversley Parish Church and his concern for others overwhelmed him. He found it hard to believe that in every town or small village, English people were living in appalling poverty. The very basics of life were expensive, work was hard and wages low. He was sceptical of large political rallies, especially as churchmen feared encouraging campaigning which could lead to a French style bloodbath of a revolution. Instead, he favoured direct action, in which Christians could become knights in a modern chivalry, fighting for justice and the rights of all. He began his work in his own parish; when he arrived the church was in a poor state, but soon it had become the centre of the community, giving life and hope to all in need. The work grew and even adults would attend evening classes to be educated as the first step to a better life. Ernest Hayes wrote: 'Kingsley took no notice of such false distinctions between sacred and secular. He believed God wanted all men to have the chance of living good, all-round, healthy, intelligent lives and he determined that he would do all he could to bring that about...he went into the worst slums of London and other cities, finding out the horrors of sweated labour, bad housing and overcrowding. Then he denounced these evils in his articles.'[6] His concern was not only for the salvation of men, but for their practical needs as well. As a pioneer 'green campaigner' (by placing people first, he urged for cleaning up the environment), he called for rubbish to be cleared, polluted wells to be cleaned and drains to be made hygienic. In his parish church he had learnt how to help the sick, but he demanded more direct action – if the water was pure and proper sanitation was available, the epidemics that had plagued generations would be thwarted. Kingsley preached the need for Christianity to find its way outside of the Church into every day life – calling for justice, freedom, fairness and liberty for all. His lifetimes work was acknowledged by many and he became Queen Victoria's chaplain in 1859, the Canon of Chester in 1869 and the Canon of Westminster in 1873.

Care For All: In 2005, England's Archbishop of York said, "In our time, this socialising and transforming power of corporate-discipleship is illustrated further by three Christian men at the University of Oxford: Richard Tawney, William Beveridge and William Temple, who were challenged to go to the East End of London to 'find friends among the poor, as well as finding out what poverty is and what can be done about it.' In the East End their consciences were pricked by poverty: visible, audible, smellable. After university, Tawney worked at Toynbee Hall, creating a fraternal community; William Beveridge paved the way for the welfare state in his report which for the first time set out to embody the whole spirit of the Christian ethic in an Act of parliament. William Temple, as Archbishop of York and then Canterbury, mobilised the church support for a more just, equal and fraternal Britain. His book *Christianity and Social Order* is one of the foundation pillars of the welfare state as we know it today."[7] The modern welfare state can of course be abused, but Christians in Britain had to ask themselves one difficult question – "What would Jesus do?" How would Jesus want the poor, the vulnerable and hard working families to be treated in one of the wealthiest countries in the world? Should everything they worked for during their entire lives be lost and help denied, because of a tragic event (like the credit crunch / recession) which was beyond their control?

Ending Extreme Poverty: In the history of the world, there had never been an enduring civilisation which was not plagued by large numbers of impoverished citizens, but these Christians believed in the biblical teaching of the fundamental equality of all. Thus, if we are all created in God's image, then we all deserve the right to live our lives without being plagued by extreme poverty. William Booth helped the world to understand that they already had the money to take people out of extreme poverty, if only they would stop talking and start moving with direct action. Charles Kingsley and others, not only looked at the fruit, but tackled the root. He realised that if there was clean healthy living conditions with good food and clean water, many of the problems that wrecked lives would be dealt with. These Christian pioneers and many others like them gave the world a new vision to achieve. They began the work that ended extreme poverty at home and set a basic standard of living of which millions of Western citizens have benefited from. Previously extreme poverty was a part of life, after them it was avoidable.

"The Bible provides a defining influence on the formation of the first welfare state," said British Prime Minister David Cameron. "In Matthew's Gospel, Jesus says that whatever people have done 'unto one of the least of these My brethren' they have done unto Him. Just as in the past it was the influence of the church that enabled hospitals to be built, charities created, the hungry fed, the sick nursed and the poor given shelter so today faith based groups are at the heart of modern social action...The Bible has helped to give Britain a set of values and morals which make Britain what it is today. Values and morals we should actively stand up and defend. The alternative of moral neutrality should not be an option. You can't fight something with nothing. Because if we don't stand for something, we can't stand against anything."[8]

National Justice: One of the greatest differences between Western Europe and the U.S. is the ideological approach to helping the impoverished. In Western Europe, Christians who despise Communism and embrace ethical capitalism and democracy, still believe that the state has a responsibility to help the poor based upon the teachings about national justice by the Old Testament prophets. In the U.S., as the country was the primary power which challenged the Soviet Union, the culture developed with a highly sensitive defiance of socialism. Therefore, the welfare state is often associated with puritanical socialism, rather than a national expression of Christian justice. America has often preferred personal charity to state help. In Europe, Christians made their values a concern of the state (as ancient Israel did), believing it fulfilled on a national level the Lord's command of, "Love your neighbour as yourself." See Deuteronomy 15, Isaiah 58, Amos 5, Acts 4:32-35.

Chapter Thirteen

The Preservation of Nature, History and Places of Natural Beauty

"Woe to those who join house to house; they add field to field, till there is no place where they may dwell alone in the midst of the land!" (Isaiah 5:8).

History is often the story of mankind struggling to survive against the forces of nature; however during the Agricultural and Industrial Revolutions, people began to realise that humans could do endless damage to the environment. A Christian leader was the first in modern history to suggest that the world could not be incessantly exploited, in other words, its resources are limited and valuable. Former director of Denmark's National Environmental Assessment Institute and best selling author Bjørn Lomborg, was named one of the world's 100 most influential people by *Time* magazine.[1] Considering big ideas that changed the world, he pointed out that it was the Rev. Thomas Robert Malthus who first addressed the challenge of earth's limited resources.[2]

The Rev. Thomas R. Malthus (1766-1834) was a man of strong faith who created a stir with his *Essay on the Principle of Population* (1798). His concern about the population out growing its food supply was reinvigorated during the global food crisis of 2008. The author was in Ethiopia when this crisis began to hit. Reports began with 50,000 people being in immediate danger; within a few months the number was multiplied. Back in the eighteenth century, the question this preacher posed concerned the sustainability of the rapid increase in the world's population. People are still asking the same question that his essay presented in the modern context – can our mismanaged earth really sustain a future population of nine billion? He may not have foresaw the future advance in farming techniques, colonisation of barren lands and scientific progress, but he was the first who helped create a paradigm shift, where people began to realise that we could not endlessly exploit the planet.

Protecting Nature From Industrialisation: With the rapid industrialisation and development of Britain, the nation was in grave danger of losing some of its great treasures of natural beauty. Social commentator J.B. Priestly in *Our Nation's*

Heritage noted: 'The private enterprise of the nineteenth century has turned a fair land into hell.'[3] During the same season, some of the most important buildings in the long story of Britain were in danger of being ruined; in this grave situation Canon Hardwick stepped in to save British heritage for posterity.

Canon Hardwick Rawnsley (1851-1920) realised that Britain could have turned into one big factory, if people were not prepared to stand up and fight for God's gift to the people of the British nation. Millions were in danger of never being able to walk in the hills or sit by the still waters to enjoy God's creation. In response, Canon Hardwick founded the Lake District Defence Society, which would help protect the splendour of the Lake District, as it included England's largest lake and highest mountain. Visit Cumbria wrote of the Canon's work: 'No-one has achieved more for the Lake District in the last 200 years than Canon Rawnsley.'[4]

Industrial revolutions worldwide led to most of the population leaving the countryside to reside in towns and cities; this happened first in Britain and spread; today it is still happening in China and India. 'The turning point is 1851, when for the first time in history anywhere in the world more people in Britain lived in towns than in the countryside. By 1901, only one fifth of the British population remained rural.'[5] In the U.K., practically this meant that some people could live much of their lives without ever feeling the beauty of nature.

One poor person who realised the Canon's mission sent a donation to help the work and said, "All my life I have longed to see the lakes," and added, "I shall never see them now, but I should like to help keep them for others."[6] Following Canon Hardwick's success at preservation, he joined with two other philanthropists who set their sights on saving the treasures of the nation. Together they formed the National Trust to buy and preserve places of historic interest and natural beauty. Rupert Potter was the first life member of the National Trust, who was a family friend of the Canon. During their friendship, Hardwick learnt that Rupert's daughter had been working on her first book, and he was instrumental in encouraging young Beatrix Potter (1866-1943) to get her book published and *The Tales of Peter Rabbit* became one of the most successful children's books of all time. Beatrix Potter was inspired by Canon Rawnsley and after finding financial success with her books, she used much of her wealth to purchase land to protect it from developers, so that future generations could benefit from it. This was correctly portrayed in the 2006 film *Miss Potter*, but there was no mention of her inspiration, Canon Rawnsley.

The National Trust testifies of their three founders, 'Concerned about the impact of uncontrolled development and industrialisation, they set up the Trust to act as a guardian for the nation in the acquisition and protection of threatened coastline, countryside and buildings. More than a century later, we now care for over 248,000 hectares (612,000 acres) of beautiful countryside in England, Wales and Northern Ireland, plus more than 700 miles of coastline and more than 200 buildings and gardens of outstanding interest and importance.'[7]

Protecting America: John Muir (1838-1914) was born in Britain and emigrated to the U.S. He 'was raised in a home heavy with the theology of Reformed Scottish Presbyterianism, and he inherited and maintained a fundamental set of orthodox Christian values about people, nature, and the relations between them.'[8] He had a wonderful love for nature which was informed by his faith and he saw the need for conservation. In one of his books he wrote: 'The universe would be incomplete without man; but it would also be incomplete without the smallest transmicroscopic creature that dwells beyond our conceitful eyes and knowledge. From the dust of the earth, from the common elementary fund, the Creator has made Homo Sapiens.'[9]

John Muir became one of the first modern preservationists whose writings helped inspire many others to enjoy nature and to protect it for future generations. He helped save many areas of special interest and is known today as the Father of American National Parks. He founded the Sierra Club in 1892, 'America's oldest, largest and most influential grassroots environmental organization.'[10]

Muir had a balanced view about conservation; his writings suggest that man could continue to trade and prosper, as long as they were careful to protect the environment. We can only guess what he may have thought of the constant barrage of warnings declaring 'imminent environmental catastrophe' and the sensationalism which accompanies such reports for ratings sake or to gain further funding. The U.S. owes much to Muir, even though it was inevitable that some would add to and misuse his ideas. Muir said, "Everybody needs beauty as well as bread, places to play in and pray in, where nature may heal and give strength to body and soul alike."[11]

Confronting Pollution: Titus Salt (1803-1876) was an incredibly wealthy man who became the largest employer in Bradford, England. The city was in a terrible state; pollution was just one threat that led to life expectancy of just eighteen years! Deeply concerned about the situation he found that pollution could be reduced by the use of a new smoke burner and in 1842 he converted his factories. As the mayor he tried to pass 'green laws' which would force all the other factories to follow suit, but he was opposed. Eventually he decided to build his own village based upon his Christian values. In the centre was Europe's largest and most modern textile mill, which was designed to remove dust and reduce noise pollution. It included 850 homes, a park, a school, hospital, library, shops and public baths.

A Healthy World with Healthy People: Charles Kingsley was a preacher with a social conscience. In the cities and villages he called for polluted water sources to be cleaned, he required rubbish to be cleared properly, and desired a proper drainage and sanitation system which would benefit all. He left an amazing legacy which saved lives, and raised living standards in the towns and cities.

Titus Salt helped pioneer the idea that prosperous companies could also be environmentally friendly, if the effort was put in and it was his faith that motivated his actions to encourage others to follow suit. Also, Canon Hardwick and Muir worked to protect the beautiful countryside which was in danger of being turned into cities. Without the legacy of these Christian people, the quality of life in our nations would be significantly lower, and without them, vast parts of our beautiful lands and heritage would have been lost forever.

The Future: Critics of the Christian response to the environment today need to evaluate the reason for some scepticism towards the latest bright idea. At the heart of Christian care for the environment is the concern for fellow human beings – we need to protect the planet because it is where humans live. For some believers, it appears that in some places environmentalism has become a religion of sort, where its needs are put before the welfare of people. One example is bioenergy; for a long time it was hailed as the perfect green fuel, but now the heavily subsided biofuel industry is criticised as being too energy dependant itself. For some Christians, the recent approach to biofuels is highly questionable. In one view, by redirecting land for biofuels we have lowered global food stocks which increased prices; therefore we have chosen to take food out of the mouths of the poorest in the world to feed our vehicles. One year before the global food crisis of 2008, the International Food Policy Research Institute found that the 30% price increase in the cereals price index was due to biofuels.[12] In addition, the increase in food prices led to riots around the world, from South America to North Africa, as the hardships of the poor grew greater still, due to these price gains. It must be understood that Christians are often sceptical of knee-jerk reactions based upon the ideas of 'experts', who years later may be proved wrong – just consider the 1970s predictions of a new ice age! *Newsweek* of April 1975 concluded the results of the cooling world: 'The resulting famines could be catastrophic.'[13]

For many Christians it is self-evident that the needs of the poorest of the world today must come before the desires of the rich in the West. Yet, at the same time, addressing the immediate and long-term concerns of the environment is something that will affect every generation and Christian leaders are already tackling them. The Rev. Richard Cizik, of the Office of Government Affairs for the National Association of Evangelicals was named by *Time* magazine as among the top 100 most influential people in the world for 2008, because of his work for the environment.

Chapter Fourteen
Animal Welfare

'A righteous man regards the life of his animal' (Proverbs 12:10).

The book of Proverbs encourages owners to treat their animals righteously and throughout the Bible there are numerous references to the care of animals. Over the years, inspired by their belief in the Bible, many Christians challenged the acceptance of cruelty to animals and fought to protect them against brutal treatment.

Public Awareness: Charlotte Elizabeth Tonna (1790-1846) is famous for her humanitarian work, but she also laboured to protect the rights of animals and to cause a change in public opinion. In her book about the subject she says, 'It is a creature of God not of ours and if we do anything that He does not approve of, He will surely reckon with us for it. When I call this to mind, I am alarmed – though I do not think I have often been cruel to animals, or any such thing - and I am ready to pray, "Lord, if I have hurt any of Thy creatures, pardon my past sin, for Jesus Christ's sake, I beseech thee; and give me grace to be merciful for the future." '[1]

The Puritans: The campaigns of evangelicals like Tonna's were not the start of Christian concern for animals. The Puritans made important steps forward, but not everyone was impressed with the evangelical zeal to protect animal rights; 'The Puritans banned bear-baiting not because it harmed the bear, but because it gave pleasure to people,' wrote the historian Lord Thomas Macaulay (1800-1859). In addition the great Christian revivals in the West led to the decline in cock-fighting and other forms of entertainment which showed great cruelty to animals. The conscience of the West was awakened by the message of Christianity.

The RSPCA: William Wilberforce is best remembered as the evangelical Christian who led the charge to end the slave trade, but it is worth remembering that believers of his time were engaged in numerous campaigns on many levels, including protecting the rights of mankind, animals and creation alike. Wilberforce was able to ban cock-fighting and as public opinion was changed, bull and bear-baiting ended. In 1824, what became the Royal Society for the Prevention of Cruelty to Animals (RSPCA) was founded by twenty-two reformers. Two years previous, the MP Richard Martin navigated the first anti-cruelty bill, which helped protect by law a number of animals. To make sure this legislation would actually be enforced, Richard Martin, William Wilberforce and the Rev. Arthur Broome, led the group of twenty-two to form a society which would turn law into action. The SPCA was the first animal welfare society in the world, and in 1840 Queen Victoria recognised its pioneering work and granted it royal status and it became the RSPCA. Since the founder's generation, the Society has worked indefatigably to advance kindness to animals and to prevent cruelty. In 2008, the British charity declared: 'There are now 323 uniformed RSPCA inspectors and 146 Animal Collection Officers in England and Wales working tirelessly for animals in distress.' In 2007, 'inspectors investigated 110,841 animal cruelty complaints which resulted in 2,071 convictions.'[2]

From Concern to Action: Evangelical Christians were at the fore of ending cruelty to animals, whilst the populace had little interest. Cromwell and the Puritans made the first modern advances and later, it was writers like Tonna who helped change public opinion. As public concern grew, it was Wilberforce and his friends who created the world's first animal welfare society. Very soon the U.S. would have their own society and other English speaking nations would have their own versions of the RSPCA. Christians changed the law, then they created organisations to enforce these laws, and the suffering and cruelty which had been inflicted upon animals with little or no respite, was finally checked and challenged.

Visitors to foreign countries will quickly notice how very different the attitude is towards the treatment of animals, from that which in common in the West. In the Middle East the author has witnessed donkeys overloaded with goods, which are beaten without mercy to force them on and horses carry scars because of whippings. In the Christian West this type of behaviour was made completely unacceptable because Christians took action and changed the culture. Recently, theologian Andrew Linzey wrote *Christianity and the Rights of Animals*, arguing that all animals are created by God, therefore they are of 'inherent value to God.'

Chapter Fifteen

Time

'In hope of eternal life which God, who cannot lie, promised before time began' (Titus 1:2).

Great people are sometimes honoured by having holidays named after them, but greater still is to have time itself paying homage to one's birth – this is the case with Jesus. Time itself, as we choose to define and count it, is subject to Christ's life.[1]

In 325, the first ecumenical council met at Nicea (Turkey) and tried to calculate a standardised date for all the churches to celebrate Easter. They accepted the Julian calendar which was later updated creating the Gregorian calendar of 1582. The system became standard in the Western world after being adopted by the English historian Bede (672-735), who was the first to use the equivalent of Before Christ (BC). In Rome in 525, a monk called Dionysius Exiguus first devised the Anno Domini system and for hundreds of years in Europe, all types of religious and secular documents were dated 'in the year of our Lord' Anno Domini (AD); thus for some, this tiny statement became a proclamation of faith in Christ's Lordship over all things. European Christian nations later became the pre-eminent powers on the planet, and they colonised the nations and laid foundations for new ones too. The original thirteen States that ratified the U.S. Constitution all pledged in "the year of our Lord, one thousand seven hundred and eighty seven."[2]

As Europe dominated the progress of the world, European standards in the fields of science and administration were exported globally, along with the Christian dating system. Today, the Anno Domini system is the most widespread numbering system in the world, recognised by the United Nations as a global standard. This means that the dates of the greatest discoveries, the longevity of Monarchs, the seasons of war and peace, the rise and fall of great empires, dictators and diplomats are all in subjection to the birth of Christ. Today, billions of people number their days, births, marriages, successes and most enduring memories within the timeline that Christ's life began. In the twentieth century, we may note that 'nineteen hundred and sixty nine years after Christ's birth, man took their first steps on the moon.'[3] In the twentieth century, the most populous nation on earth accepted this calendar – consequently, the times of the Communist government of China and her population are all subject, albeit in ritual rather than religious belief, to Christ's birth. However, it now seems that the terms Before Christ (BC) and Anno Domini (AD) are no longer politically correct, our abbreviations may change, but the calendar will always be fundamentally Christian.

The Seven-Day Week: Over the past few decades there has been great debate over the interpretation of Genesis chapters one and two; perhaps in the controversy we have forgotten one of the greatest legacies of these passages. The legacy of the seven-day week in Europe can be traced back to Genesis. In the history of other civilisations there is reference to the seven-day week. Two thousand and five hundred years ago, India followed this pattern and in fourth century China, there is a reference to a seven-day week and looking further back, ancient Babylon, Persia and others knew this concept too. However, these powers did not make the modern world. The Western world looks back to Rome which often used the nundinal cycle or 'market week' of eight days. As Christianity spread in the Roman Empire, the tradition of the eight-day week grew weaker, as Christianity brought the seven-day design to the fore. It was the Christian Church in Europe which continued this legacy, and later Europeans made it the standard for the world.

Today millions of people look forward to their 'day of rest,' so to speak and dread Monday, the first working day of the week. In the Jewish and Islamic world the Sabbath and first day of the week reside on other days. One of the interesting legacies of empire, the author discovered on his travels, is that there is great incertitude in the Islamic world on the weekends. Businesses, transport hubs and normal life comes to a stop on Friday because of Islamic tradition, on Saturday the system is still in flux, then on Sunday, because of the legacy of European empires, things are still semi-paralysed.

Greenwich Mean Time: 'Greenwich, England, defines both time and place for the whole world. All time is measured relative to Greenwich Mean Time (GMT) and all places have a latitude (their distance North or South of the Equator) and a longitude (their distance East or West of the Greenwich Meridian). So whether you are flying an aircraft, sailing a ship or just planning to meet up using your GPS remember that it's measured from Greenwich, England: Longitude 0° 0' 0", Latitude 51° 28' 38" N (North of the Equator).'[4]

A visit to Greenwich is the most quotidian, yet exceptional of experiences, where you can find tourists with GPS devices looking for zero degrees longitude, hoping to stand with one foot in the Western hemisphere and one in the Eastern. Those who visit will learn of the Rev. John Flamsteed (1646-1719), who was a preacher first, then the first Astronomer Royal and founder of the Greenwich Observatory. In his forty year career he took over 50,000 observations which led to Greenwich becoming home of the prime meridian. His work saw 'astronomy emerge from the mysteries and myths of the Middle Ages to become a modern, mathematical and scientific discipline.'[5] He balanced his poorly paid work with a deep seated faith. He died before his work was published, but his observations 'contained the most accurate information on the position of the stars and planets available for many years to come.'[6] GMT was most important to aid the British in their worldwide oceanic navigation, as mariners calculated their longitude from the Greenwich Meridian. Today GMT is often used to refer to Coordinated Universal Time (UTC), its technical replacement.

Celebrations: Our months are a debt we pay to ancient Rome; August was named after Augustus Caesar, Julius Caesar gave us July and so forth. Our week days are a part of pagan history – Sunday from the sun, Monday after the moon etc. Our Christian tradition attempted to redeem these former pagan ways, which included transforming pagan celebrations to mark Christian history. Today, the celebration of Easter and to greater extent Christmas marks a rest and turning point in our expression of each year. Also, for many people in the West, our births, marriages and deaths are all intertwined into customary observance of Christian tradition.

Chapter Sixteen

Music

'Praise Him with loud cymbals, praise Him with clashing cymbals!' (Psalm 150:5).

Two thousand years after Christ's birth, the sun rose on a small island somewhere in the Pacific. The world's media was present and in a live broadcast the local chief and his people raised their voices singing the Hallelujah chorus – 'And He shall reign forever and ever...Hallelujah,' as they were the first on earth to welcome in the twenty-first century.

When one studies the influence of Christianity upon music, the names of some of the most famous songs and the greatest composers...Handel, Bach, Mendelssohn and Spohr come to the fore. Then we must consider the numerous great hymn writers – Paul Gerhardt, Isaac Watts, John Newton, Charles Wesley and Sankey etc. How many number one hits of today will be remembered in one hundred years, and how many Christian hymns will be loved and sung time and again by the multitudes of Africa, Asia, America and Europe?

Christian music has become so embedded into Western culture, that it is loved by the secular and saved. How many times have Amazing Grace or other classic hymns moved a crowd? We might well ask ourselves, what would Christmas be without hearing Christian hymns? Famously these hymns led to the 1914 WWI Christmas truce, as soldiers saw their common humanity in the cruelty of war. Traditional Christian music has survived the test of time and will surely continue to live on. Still in Europe and America, the majority of the population will hear a hymn during Christmas, Easter, at a wedding or other special event. In Britain during peak-time TV viewing, millions tune in weekly to Songs of Praise on BBC1, to join in a nationwide celebration of Christian hymns and modern choruses. There are also several programmes from other broadcasters which have interviewed celebrities and MPs to find what their favourite hymns are and how they influenced their lives. In addition British Broadcasters have produced other great musical events which interweave Christian themes and music – such as the Manchester Passion and Liverpool's Nativity. This is true of other nations, in South Africa gospel artist Rebecca Malope has a primetime gospel show on the number one TV channel.

Anointing: The Christian tradition in music is also of the utmost importance during the coronation of the Head of State in Britain. In 1 Kings 1:38-40, Zadok the priest and Nathan the prophet anoint Solomon King of Israel. The people sang, 'God save the king, long live the king, may the king live for ever! Amen, Hallelujah!' Almost 3000 years later, this scene is still repeated during the British coronation. 'Zadok the Priest' composed by George Frideric Handel (1685-1759) is sung at every British coronation service, beginning in 1727 with King George II (1683-1760), and in accordance with the prophet Nathan's role, the British sovereign is anointed by the most prominent religious leader in the nation. Those close to Queen Elizabeth II, have expressed that during her coronation in 1953, the anointing was considered as the pre-eminent and most moving part of her enthronement – as it was felt that her promise to serve the nation was made to God, as well as to the people. Also, the British National Anthem itself is a repetition of events which took place in Israel thousands of years ago when the people cried out, 'God save the king' in 1 Samuel 10:24.

A Call to Justice: Christian music has in addition been a source of comfort to millions including those suffering as slaves. The musician Larry Norman (1947-2008) wrote: 'American slaves, beginning in the mid-1600s, without the benefit of a formal education or writing instruments, began creating songs of praise and lamentation as they worked and sweated side by side in the fields and estates of Southern slaveholders. Once slavery was abolished, jobless itinerant field hands and blues singers would spread the black hymns into the white man's cities.'[1] President G.W. Bush said, "The gospel music tradition was born from great pain. Slaves sang spirituals to communicate with one another in the fields, and songs of faith helped black Americans endure the injustice of segregation. Today, gospel is more than an anchor for black culture and history – it's a source of inspiration for the whole nation. Gospel has influenced some of the legends of other forms of American music. Louis Armstrong once said that when he sang in church his heart went into every song. Aretha Franklin wowed crowds in her dad's church in Detroit. Elvis Presley listened to gospel music after rock concerts to calm his mind, and Bob Dylan won a Grammy for a song for his album of gospel hymns."[2]

A New Dawn In Music: The Elvis Presley Memorial Foundation (EPMF) which is overseen by Lisa Marie Presley stated: 'Church and especially the music of the church, was the motivation for Elvis to become a performer. After the Presleys moved to Memphis in 1948, Elvis regularly went to the all night gospel sings at Ellis Auditorium, near his home in Lauderdale Courts. His burning ambition was to become a member of a gospel quartet. He never realised his dream of becoming a member of the Statesmen or the Blackwood Brothers. He had other worlds to conquer. Throughout the rest of his life, Elvis recorded many of the beloved songs of his youth, the emotional and uplifting music of the church.' Executive Director of EPMF Dick Guyton said, "The First Assembly of God Church in East Tupelo was at the centre of the Presley family's life and provided the social structure as well as entertainment on which the family thrived. Young Elvis regularly sang in church, as did many of the members, but according to his minister, Brother Frank Smith, Elvis was fascinated with music and the prospect of learning to play the guitar. Brother Frank taught Elvis how to make a D chord, an A chord and an E chord…all he needed to play 'Ole Shep'…The church has now been acquired…for the Elvis Presley Birthplace and Park.'[3]

The restless and sputtering faith of Elvis Presley is one of the enduring characteristics of the man who had the greatest influence upon music in his generation. It is no surprise then that Elvis ended up publishing some of the greatest interpretations of gospel music that has ever been recorded. Johnny Cash is another great artist who grew up in a gospel tradition and recorded his own versions. U2 front man Bono, has made it no secret that the teachings of Jesus Christ has personally inspired him in the fight for global justice, and the music of U2, the most successful rock group ever, also testifies of Christ – "One man betrayed with a kiss."[4] In fact, when we examine the chart toppers of the past few decades we often find that large numbers of these successful artists began their singing careers in the modern church choir. Fans of Disney productions will also know that many of their most successful performers of the last few years have come from a Christian background. In addition, the 2008 U.K. Christmas number one and two were different versions of 'Hallelujah,' meaning 'praise the Lord.' In 2010, Florence and the Machine re-released, 'You've Got The Love' with the lyrics: '...I know My Saviour's love is real...sometimes I feel like saying Lord I just don't care, but You've got the love...'

CCM: In recent decades Contemporary Christian Music (CCM) has grown and at times moved into the mainstream charts. Krystal Meyer's song 'Make Some Noise' was chosen to feature on the official 2008 Olympics album, which was approved by the International Olympics Committee. Disney also commissioned Christian bands and artists to create albums like, 'Music Inspired by the Chronicles of Narnia,' and it is now common to find CCM in other Disney movies. Rebecca St James is only the eighth Australian artist (or group) to win a Grammy Award; when her album 'God' went gold, Australian Prime Minister John Howard was among those who sent congratulatory letters.[5] *Time* magazine said of worship author Chris Tomlin that he is 'the most often sung artist anywhere!'[6] To his credit are seven number one radio singles, one platinum and one gold album, two Grammy nominations and fourteen Dove Awards. Then of course, there is the legacy of Delirious, the BBC wrote: 'Delirious are one of Britain's best-kept rock secrets.'[7]

By 2008, there were four major global record companies, one of them Britain's EMI, decided to invest in what was called not too long ago 'the fastest growing genre of music.' EMI, through its subsidiary EMI Christian Music Group, is one of the forces behind a lot of the CCM released today and the sales have been healthy. Overall music sales of Christian/Gospel music between 2002-2007 reveals that nearly one quarter of a billion units were sold![8] Today, the future of the entire music industry is in flux, as CD sales continue to decline and illegal downloading and sharing continues. Christian music, with all other genres is entering these troubled waters, but there are still signs of strength. Grammy Award-winning band Casting Crowns made a historic number two debut with 'The Altar and The Door' on America's billboard, which ranks the highest-selling units in the U.S. In 2008, despite having no mainstream TV or radio exposure, the album was only just passed at the finish line, by the explosive inexorable force of the (gospel influenced) High

School Musical franchise. In addition, the Bible has inspired many musicals, including Joseph and others.

Divine Inspiration: James MacMillan, regarded as the pre-eminent Scottish composer of his generation and one of the conductors of the BBC Philharmonic Orchestra, believes that embracing spiritual truth is now one of the most radical and counter-cultural moves a musician can make. "I believe it is God's divine spark which kindles the musical imagination now, as it has always done, and reminds us, in an increasingly dehumanised world, of what it means to be human." MacMillan, a Christian, argues that faith has played an important role in the creative arts, but he is saddened by the secular hostility to faith in the modern media. In his message he quoted from surveys which have shown that only one in five people who work in TV consider themselves as religious, compared with seven out of ten among the general public. "If this is the case with the TV industry," he said, "you can be sure it is the same for the metropolitan arts, cultural and media elites."[9]

Christianity and the Arts: The Rt. Rev. Michael Nazir-Ali has also explained that Britons are suffering from 'cultural amnesia' about the Christian origins of the country's music, art and language. Dr Nazir-Ali explained that great paintings and pieces of music were inspired by Christianity. "What amazes me is how people in this country don't take account of the brute fact that the Bible and the Prayer Book have shaped so much of its literary and cultural achievements. Without the translation of the Bible into English and the creation of the Prayer Book it would have been impossible to have a Donne or a Shakespeare or a Milton. Certainly with art, poetry and music, people aren't exposed to the biblical root of what has inspired people to create these themes."[10] British Prime Minister David Cameron addressed this culture amnesia by explaining the impact of the Bible upon music, "The Bible runs through our music too. From the great oratorios like J S Bach's Matthew and John Passions and Handel's Messiah to the wealth of music written across the ages for mass and evensong in great cathedrals like this one. The Biblical settings of composers from Tallis to Taverner are regularly celebrated here in this great cathedral and will sustain our great British tradition of choral music for generations to come."[11]

Chapter Seventeen

Art and Architecture

'He has filled him with the Spirit of God...to design artistic works' (Exodus 35:31-32).

"By art, more is meant than at first may be thought," said Campbell Morgan (1863-1945) of Westminster Chapel, London, "for it includes architecture, sculpture, symbolism, painting, mosaics, monograms, frescoes, stained glass windows and decorated manuscripts, and on all these Christianity has left its imprint. In architecture, from the basilicas of the time of Constantine to the magnificent cathedrals of our own time and country – the Christian idea and ideal have stood in marked contrast to the pagan temples of the ancient Greeks. Christian architecture, as Forsyth has said, 'Is stone made spiritual and musical – a symphony in stone.' "[1]

The catacombs of Rome are a startling reminder of the times of early Christianity. Walking around them is a clandestine experience where early Christian art, Roman in style, rekindles the imagination to meditate upon the symbols of the faith, or to ponder the simplicity of the image of a fish and its deeper meaning to the persecuted. In 313, the Edict of Toleration allowed Christians and their art to come out of the shadows; the creativity which followed began in simplicity and led to masterpieces.

The story of Christian art is vast and unequalled, from the mosaics of Turkey, to the basilica of Santa Pudenziana in Rome. In Coptic Cairo and St Catherine's in Sinai, the author witnessed the treasures of old, and the new interpretations springing from the same source. In Ethiopia, a priest opened one of their oldest Christian books which was full of illustrations. The same tradition can be found in Western Christianity; one of the most famous is the sixth century Vienna Genesis. A visit to Iona in Britain makes one wonder how St Columba (521-591) survived in such a wind-swept place, yet this was the base for the evangelisation of North England and Scotland. It was also a leading centre of Christian scholarship and the home of many great art treasures, including the one thousand adorned stone crosses and most probably the treasure of the *Book of Kells*.

In Canterbury Cathedral there are in addition early Saxon wall paintings which can still be seen. Turkey holds perhaps one of the greatest inadvertently forgotten examples of Christian art, from the churches carved out of a volcanic landscape, to the newly recovered depictions that were covered over in Aya Sofya (the Church of Holy Wisdom), after the Islamic conquest.

In Christian Europe, many of the greatest artists of all time expressed devotion by creating masterpieces which illuminated the experience of faith. Leonardo da Vinci (1452-1519) is the artist of The Virgin and Child amongst many other Christian classics. He is credited with taking the dry and hard manner of the Early Renaissance, and transforming it to the complex style of the High Renaissance. Raphael (1483-1520), creator of The Procession to Calvary is considered the supreme High Renaissance painter. The National Gallery in London states: 'From 1508 to 1512 Michelangelo (1475-1564) painted the vault of the Sistine Chapel with scenes from the Old Testament. Immediately celebrated, the Sistine Chapel ceiling, with its innumerable figures in complex, twisting poses and its exuberant use of colour, is the chief source of the Mannerist style.'[2] Walking around the Sistine Chapel, it becomes clear that visitors often express an overwhelming feeling of wonder, at the magnitude of the undertaking. In an article titled *God is Behind some of our Greatest Art,* journalist Mark Ravenhill wrote: 'This idea that all artists are essentially humanists is a comforting myth for an agnostic age. There is little evidence to support it. It is, if you like, the agnostic's delusion – because the very opposite is true. The greatest artists, from Matthias Grünewald in the 15th century to Benjamin Britten in the 20th, had a genuine Christian faith...we should celebrate the Christian legacy in Western art and society.'[3]

On the following page with the exception of the last three pieces of art, there is reference to a tiny selection of the collection of the National Gallery in London, England. It should be considered that we have not even began to count the collections which reside in France, Russia, Holland, Italy, the Netherlands, Germany, Austria, Spain, Portugal and Poland etc. They are all part of the great Christian tradition.

Work of Art		Artist
Pentecost	14th century	Giotto
The Transfiguration		Duccio
The Annunciation		Duccio
The Baptism of Christ		Lorenzo Monaco
The Dead Christ and the Virgin		Italian Florentine
The Betrayal of Christ		Ugolino di Nerio
Moses		Ugolino di Nerio
The Crucifixion		Jacopo di Cione
The Madonna of Humility		Lippo di Dalmasio
The Virgin and Child	15th century	Michelangelo
The Entombment		Michelangelo
Christ Crowned with Thorns		Matteo di Giovanni
Christ Nailed to the Cross		Gerard David
The Israelites Gathering Manna		Ercole de' Roberti
Saint Michael Triumphs over the Devil		Bermejo
Mary, Apostles and other Saints		Angelico
The Agony in the Garden		Bellini
A Bishop Saint		Zoppo
The Immaculate Conception		Crivelli
The Virgin of the Rocks	16th century	Leonardo da Vinci
An Angel in Green with a Veil		Leonardo da Vinci
The Mond Crucifixion		Raphael
St John the Baptist Preaching		Raphael
The Purification of the Temple		Vemisti
Mystic Nativity		Botticelli
Adoration of the (three) Kings		Botticelli
The Tribute Money (Widow's Mite)		Titian
The Virgin and Child with Saints		Titian
The Assassination of St Peter		Giovanni Bellini
The Lamentation over Christ	17th century	Rembrandt
An Elderly Man as St Paul		Rembrandt
Christ in the House of Martha / Mary		Diego Velázquez
St John on the Island of Patmos		Diego Velázquez
The Adoration of the Shepherds		Poussin
Christ Cleansing the Temple		El Greco
The Massacre of the Innocents		Rubens
Christ Teaching from St Peter's Boat		Saftleven
Mourning Over the Dead Christ	18th century	Stanzione
The Lamentation at the Cross		Tiepolo
The Rest on the Flight into Egypt		Werff
The Risen Christ Noli Me Tangere		Mengs
Saint Martin Sharing his Cloak		Solimena
St Anthony with the Infant Christ		Bazzani
Rome: The Interior of St Peter's		Panini
Christ on the Cross	19th century	Delacroix
St Paul's from Surrey Side		Daubigny
The Head of Christ		Nikolai Koshelev
Pietà Mary and Christ		Vincent van Gogh
The Raising of Lazarus		Vincent van Gogh

The Galleries of Europe: Could you imagine walking around London, Paris or Rome with all the Christian influence in art or architecture gone? "One need only mention The Madonna of Rubens, Raphael, Michelangelo and of others," said Campbell Morgan..."Rembrandt's great works on The Supper at Emmaus, Christ Before Pilate, The Descent from the Cross and many more...Raphael's Transfiguration; Botticelli's Adoration of the Magi; Tintoretto's The Marriage Feast; Leonardo da Vinci's The Last Supper and Mary Magdalene by Titian; Correggio's Assumption of the Virgin and The Crucifixion by Van Dyck, Velasquez and Fra Angelico; and the more modern religious studies by Millais, Hole, Holman Hunt, Millet, G.F. Watts, Burne-Jones, Gabriel Rossetti...but for the Bible these works would never have existed and art galleries in London, Dresden, Florence, Venice, Paris, Antwerp and Milan would never have housed these great creations of Christian art."[4] Modern artists have also produced works of art for the Christian community, including Graham Sutherland, Eric Gill, Henri Matisse, Elizabeth Frink and Jacob Epstein.[5]

Architecture: For the first few centuries of Christian witness, places of worship were by necessity inconspicuous; believers met in homes or in secret hiding places. As liberty flowed, pagan temples were converted into churches and in time purpose built churches were created. Hellenistic and Roman styles were adopted, and by the fourth century the first Christian basilica in Rome was built. In Southern Macedonia the ruins of a fifth century Christian basilica can be found in Ohrid, with beautiful mosaics. Near by is the thirteenth century lakeside Church of Sveti Jovan Bogoslov Kaneo, which embraces Armenian and Byzantine elements. In Europe, during the ninth to thirteenth centuries, the Romanesque style came to the fore, bearing thick walls to hold the load, buttresses and conforming to the cruciform plan. In Prague, the Basilica of St George is perhaps the Czechs finest Romanesque church, characterised by round arches and vaults. During the twelfth to sixteenth centuries, the Gothic style replaced the heavy fort-like churches, with new pointed arches and an overall look of nimbleness. These great cathedrals appear to point to heaven in angelic poise and are counted as one of the great achievements of Christian civilisation. In France, the Cathedral of Notre Dame in Paris is a magnificent expression of Gothic architecture.

St Paul's in London is one of the greatest cathedrals in Europe; it stands as a testament to the genius of Sir Christopher Wren (1632-1723), blending the Baroque styles of the fifteenth to eighteenth centuries, into a uniquely British design. In Frankfurt, Germany, the Cathedral marks the site where the Holy Roman Emperors of 1562-1792 were crowned. Sadly the author found that most of the Cathedral was destroyed during WWII, but the fifteenth century Gothic style tower did survive as a focus for rebuilding. In Budapest, Hungry, Matthias Church was rebuilt in 1896, with a Neo-Gothic tower of the eighteenth and nineteenth century style. Visitors to Salisbury in England will also find a fine example of a Gothic style Cathedral; they may also notice the similarities between it and Britain's Houses of Parliament. If one stops at parliament to ponder all that is before them, it's not hard to witness the Christian style, pointing upwards towards God – rather than modern parliaments that glorify the moment and may find themselves confined as a testament to short-term thinking. This Neo-Gothic style commands authority, yet still shows humility, as if the building itself is looking up to heaven for help. Britain's Houses of Parliament are a classic example of Christian architecture entering into the secular domain. The design appeals to the sentiment that these houses are timeless and this is one of the reasons why so few can judge their age.

Heritage of Beauty: The legacy of Christian art and architecture is a longstanding two thousand year story beginning with persecuted believers hiding and painting, to Europeans creating the largest buildings that their nations had ever known up until that point. As Campbell Morgan concluded, "It is not too much to say that some of the finest work that has ever been done by pen, brush, chisel and trowel have been done in the presentation of themes and scenes which only the Bible can supply."[6] Bishop Nazir-Ali said, "The Judaeo-Christian tradition provides the connecting link to 'our island story.' Without that tradition it is impossible to understand the language, the literature, the art or even the science of our civilisation. It provides the grand themes in art and literature – of virtue and vice, atonement and repentance, resurrection and immortality. It has inspired the best, most accessible architecture. It undergirds and safeguards our constitutional and legal tradition."[7]

Chapter Eighteen

Language

'I looked and behold, a great multitude...of all nations, tribes, peoples and tongues standing before the throne' (Rev. 7:9).

European Language: The impact of the Christian gospel upon the development of language is staggering. In England, Bible translators had to invent words, establish spelling, order grammar and create new styles of writing to truly express the word of God in the written form. Beginning with Bede (672-735), many had translated parts of the Bible into the vernacular, but it was John Wycliffe who began to translate the entire Bible from the Latin. 'The influence of Wycliffe's Bible upon our language... is not to be ignored,' wrote the author C.A. Lane.[1] The Bible defined the English language and helped secure freedom of thought and speech for the English speaking peoples of the world. 'In 1370 John Wycliffe, a scholar at Oxford University, challenged the central role of the Catholic Mass,' said the journalist and broadcaster Rod Liddle. 'He said that the Bible was the sole source of Christian authority, not the Pope. The Church declared him a heretic...by translating the Bible into English, Wycliffe and those who followed him not only opened that door to the Scriptures, they also started to rescue and define the English language which had become overlaid by French and Latin since the Norman Conquest.'[2]

Later, William Tyndale (1494-1536) wanted to translate the Bible into the English tongue from the original languages; it is his work that has become the foundation of all English Bibles and his translation became the river into which all English would flow. Only William Shakespeare (1564-1616) can claim this status with Tyndale and his great works are also laced with biblical influence. In fact, Shakespeare drew so heavily upon the Bible, that it is no exaggeration to suggest that many passages of his great works cannot be fully understood by those who have no acquaintance with the Bible. So versed in the Bible was Shakespeare that he made 1,300 direct quotes or allusions towards Scripture, using forty-two of its books! Later the King James Bible added to the English language and the historian Lord Macaulay (1800-1859) said of the English Bible, 'If everything else in our language should perish, it would alone suffice to show the whole extent of its beauty and power.' The historian J.R. Green in his *History of the English People* wrote: 'As a mere literary monument, the English version of the Bible remains the noblest example of the English tongue, while its perpetual use made it, from the instant of its appearance, the standard of our language.' Dr Samuel Johnson (1709-1784), the Christian compiler of the great dictionary, also helped set a standard for spelling. Journalist Clive James wrote: 'Much of the beauty of the English language has the Bible as its fountain,' and he noted that 'an education without a Bible education is no education.'[3] In Germany, the story is similar to that of England. There is no other who can claim to have contributed more to the development of the German language than Martin Luther (1484-1546), with his translation of the Bible. Russia can also trace its language back to the influence of Christianity. Around 860, two missionary brothers were sent to Moravia to teach the message of Jesus and translate the Scriptures; before they left they prepared an alphabet for the unwritten language of their mission field. Professor Paul D. Steeves wrote: 'This script, known as Glagolitic, was the forerunner of the form or writing now used in South-Eastern Europe and Russia.'[4] Throughout Europe, the story of language, the story of Christianity and the translation of the Bible into the mother tongue are instinctively interlinked.

Going back further in time we can still find a sixth century copy of Ulfilas' Bible translation. 'Ulfilas took very great care of the Goths...he reduced their language to writing and translated the books of the Bible[5] into their everyday speech.'[6]

The influence of Christianity upon linguistics can also be attested by the phrases that people use: 'The patience of Job', 'It's not gospel truth,' and, 'The blind leading the blind' etc. Christianity has also been the inspiration for the names of millions of people. In the West, the first name is often called the 'Christian name,' even today when people from non-Christian nations convert, they often search the Bible for a new 'Christian name.' In the West, Paul, Peter and John etc., became popular, whilst Judas and Ichabod were blacklisted! Also our towns, roads, hospitals and schools etc., often have Christian names.

British Prime Minister David Cameron, noting the influence of the King James Bible said, "Phrases like strength to strength, how the mighty are fallen, the skin of my teeth, the salt of the earth and nothing new under the sun. According to one recent study there are 257 of these phrases and idioms that come from the Bible. These phrases are all around us from court cases to TV sitcoms and from recipe books to pop music lyrics."[7]

Global Languages: In the modern era, as the world got smaller, anthropologists began to worry that historic languages were being lost; it seemed possible that thousands of years of language history could actually be lost forever. How could these languages be saved? If an attempt could be made to record every language, it would turn out to be too costly and too sacrificial to even consider. Why would anyone leave a well paid job in the first world, to live in a developing world without pay to save a language? Many attempts have been made to lay claims that missionaries have destroyed indigenous culture and erased history, but it was these very missionaries who were and are saving language, and preserving history for posterity. Forsaking pay and the comfort of home, missionaries have gone around the world, analysed the local language, written it down, taught it to the locals and thus preserved a language in written form, which may have otherwise been lost. The Bible is available today in whole or in part to some 98% of the world's population, in a language in which they are fluent. Practically this means that nearly 2,500 languages[8] have God's word in written form; we shall never know how many of these languages would have become extinct, but we can be sure that Christianity played the major role in preserving and recording many of these languages for posterity. There are still thousands of other languages that missionaries intend to learn and the first book to be published in these languages, like many others, will be the Bible. Prolific author Louise Creighton wrote: 'Missionaries...all over the world have been the first to reduce illiterate language to writing, to make grammars for them, to provide them with translation of the Bible and other books.'[9] Many have accused missionaries of bequeathing a legacy of indignation, but William Carey, the famous Protestant missionary was cordially honoured by the Indian Government in 1993, who printed a stamp in his honour. 'The Department of Posts is privileged to issue a stamp on Dr William Carey, who adopted India as his country and strived to serve her people. The stamp design depicts Dr William Carey's portrait at his writing desk, against the backdrop of Serampore College.'[10] Carey not only brought the gospel and opened the first Christian college in Asia, but he also introduced the first printing press to India and worked hard to print works in local languages. He translated much besides the Bible. 'Carey was instrumental in translating the Bible into Marathi, Hindi, Oriya, Panjabi, Assamese and Gujarati. While others did help, Carey was also totally involved in all these translations. In a rough estimate we may say that Carey either worked or influenced heavily the translation of the Bible into as many as forty languages. William Carey was breaking new ground and laying the path for the development of these languages as vehicles of education. It is no wonder then that Rabindranath Tagore, a master of Bengali wrote: 'I must acknowledge that whatever has been done towards the revival of the Bengali language and its improvement must be attributed to Dr Carey and his colleagues. Carey was the pioneer of the revived interest in the vernaculars.' '[11] The author visited India and was given a tour of this college by the principal. They still have the original dictionaries that Carey made, as he translated words from one language to another. It was staggering just to see them, let alone consider writing and translating them all! Carey, as the Father of Modern Missions, set an example in the translation of languages that many would follow. Learning from him, many missionaries have had to devise alphabets and writing styles, transmitting the spoken language into the written word, which not only helped save languages but created new literary traditions.

Historical Language: In European history, it was the desire to read the Bible in the mother tongue which helped to gather a resurgence in Greek, Hebrew and Aramaic. Knowledge of classical Greek was essential to the translation of the Rosetta Stone[12] which was a major key to understanding ancient Egyptian hieroglyphics. In 1802, when the Greek text of the Rosetta Stone was translated, it was the Rev. S. Weston who explained it before the Society of Antiquaries. In addition it is less commonly known that linguistic experts visited Egyptian Christian monasteries to hear them read the Scriptures and learn about their language.[13] As part of their lingual tradition, Christians would read the Bible in their traditional language, which was the closest link to the original Egyptian tongue and by studying them, experts gained some understanding on how to read and pronounce hieroglyphics.

Chapter Nineteen

Law and Order

'Teach them the statutes and the laws' (Exodus 18:20).

'Our legal system was formed and developed over centuries under the dominating influence of the Christian religion,' wrote the author Stephen C. Perks. 'Our very concepts of justice, due process and the rule of law are Christian ideals that we should never have known had the Christian faith not taken root in this land and transformed the nation from a pagan into a civilised society.'[1] U.S. President Barack Obama in *The Audacity of Hope* wrote: 'Our law is by definition a codification of morality, much of it grounded in the Judeo-Christian tradition.'

In Western civilisation, the Judaic and Christian roots which influenced our nations led to the creation of social, political and legal institutions that still dominate our lives today. The rights and laws which protect us today often found their genesis in people who took their Bible seriously and called for legislation which guarded our God-given liberties. From the highest court in the U.K., to the U.S. Supreme Court, these historic landmarks recognise and celebrate the influence of Christianity upon law, from plaques of the Ten Commandments, to paintings of Jesus; even their very architecture echoes our Christian heritage. At the U.S. Supreme Court there are at least six major representations of Christian influence – mostly concerning Moses and the Ten Commandments. In the United States House Chambers there is a relief of Moses, in the Congressional Library there is a large statue of Moses holding the Ten Commandments, and in the Department of Justice there is a statue including the Ten Commandments.

'Towards the close of the sixth century the Christian Church had become an important factor in the government of the world,' wrote the author C.A. Lane in *English Church History*. 'The city of Rome, once the centre of civilisation and refinement rapidly declined in influence after the government was transferred to Constantinople, no more important person than the bishop remaining in residence, who, by reason of this prominence became its virtual ruler.'[2] When Rome declined, Christianity was the chief guardian in the West of much of history, and the process of bringing pagan law under the Christian influence that began with Emperor Justinian (527-565) continued. When Roman rule in Britain and later in Europe collapsed, Christianity eventually filled the vacuum.

'For more than a thousand years Christianity has shaped our laws. The earliest document written in the English language is the law code of the Anglo-Saxon King Ethelbert (560-616).'[3] This English king's Christian faith is the foundation of all law in England, from protecting the day of rest, to the rights of people and property. Later King Alfred the Great (849-899), perhaps the first true King of England defended the nation from the Vikings. British MP Ann Widdecombe said, "Alfred didn't just save his Kingdom, he founded the English nation. But to secure his rule he needed to establish law and order. So where did the first King of the English look for his inspiration? To the Bible of course! He used Moses as his role model, to found one of the first and certainly the most influential codes of English law."[4] Ann Widdecombe continued, "As a Christian and a law maker, it's exciting to discover that English law began with the Ten Commandments." Over the next one thousand years the Bible and the Ten Commandments remained centre stage. "When Elizabeth I came to the throne in 1558," said Ann Widdecombe, "The laws of the Bible took on even more significance."[5] Elizabeth I ordered every parish church should have the Ten Commandments displayed prominently, as Christianity was to remain at the heart of English law. "Both Edward the Confessor and the saintly Alfred made sure that English Common Law was founded on Judaeo-Christian principles," said Bishop Nazir-Ali.[5a]

Over time, British Christians expected rulers to respect their God-given rights; it was their unwillingness to do this which helped shape the creation of modern democracy. Creation Ministries International wrote: 'In declaring the equality of all human souls in the sight of God, Christianity compelled the kings of England to recognise the supremacy of the divine law over their arbitrary will....the Christian faith provided to the people of England a status libertatis (state of liberty), which rested on the Christian presumption that God's law always works for the good of society. With their conversion to Christianity, the kings of England would no longer possess an arbitrary power over the life and property of individuals...'[6] Winston Churchill recorded his history of the English speaking peoples of the world and showed how Christianity prevailed in their culture and law. He wrote: 'England became finally and for all time one coherent Kingdom based on Christianity.'[7] History later records how Christian leaders continued to influence the law over time by campaigning for individual rights, demanding the limitation of the Monarchs power and calling for tolerance – all of which shaped legal theory, nation states and empires.

The story of reform and Christianity go hand in hand from Tertullian who argued in *Apology* that Christianity should be tolerated by Rome, to Shaftesbury who informed politics. From workers' rights, child protection, healthcare to liberty, Christian leaders called for change and they shaped the law. There are too many to mention, but consider the influence of Eusebius, Augustine, Gelasius, Gregrory, Raherus, Thomas Aquinas, Ball, Hogarth, Milton, Tyndale, Calvin, Luther, Tonna, Shaftesbury, More, Nightingale, Wilberforce, Clarkson, Foxwell and Buxton.

In North America, the English speaking colonies were founded on English law, with Christianity as their foundation. By 1787, James Madison (1751-1836) who became the fourth president of the U.S., was reading Isaiah 33:22, 'For the Lord is our judge, the Lord is our lawgiver, the Lord is our king.' He took this Scripture as a confirmation for the plan to divide the central government into three branches – Judicial, Legislative and Executive. The sixth president of the United States, John Quincy Adams (1767-1848) believed that religious faith played a central role in shaping law in the United States. Concerning the Ten Commandments he wrote: 'The law given from Sinai was a civil and municipal as well as a moral and religious code.'[8] Also, the founding documents of the U.S. divulge that a belief in the Creator is essential to American liberty and law. They convey transparently that all men 'are endowed by their Creator with certain inalienable rights,' and that governments must protect them – 'to secure these rights, governments are instituted among men.' These God given rights are those of life, liberty, religious freedom, property, due process, as well as all others within the Declaration of Independence and the Bill of Rights.

The influence of Christianity upon common law is foundational. Joseph Story (1779-1845) served on the Supreme Court of the United States from 1811-1845. He said, "I verily believe Christianity necessary to the support of civil society. One of the beautiful boasts of our municipal jurisprudence is that Christianity is a part of the common law. There never has been a period in which the common law did not recognise Christianity as laying its foundations."[9] Common law places the jury at the heart of justice, as judges base their rulings on previous cases, following precedents. In these courts, the laws of parliament should be implemented in a consistent, coherent and just way.

Lord Denning, often described as Britain's most influential judge of the twentieth century wrote: 'Without Christianity, there can be no morality – there can be no law.'[9a] George Polson, QC, agreed saying, "The true basis of English common law is Christianity."[10] Director of the Kuyper Foundation Stephen C. Perks in *Christianity and Law* reveals: 'The ideals and standards of justice that informed our law were derived largely either from the Bible directly or from ancient pre-Christian institutions that have been so completely transformed under the influence of the Church, that the original pre-Christian practices from which they originate are no longer discernible in the Christianised forms in which we know them.'[11] Ginsberg on justice in society wrote: 'The ultimate justice of law is that it serves moral ends. On this conviction, endorsed by Christians, our legal system and indeed the whole of Western civilisation has been built.'[12]

Britain as a nation with no definable genesis has no written constitution because British liberty was won over time, as non-conformist Christianity and the people triumphed over injustice. On every page of British history, the influence of Christianity can be found. For younger nations, such as Australia, New Zealand, Canada and the U.S., they can trace not only their recent foundations, but the laws from which they were drawn. These nations have in many ways become the legal and political continuity of English Christian heritage. Knowing this, adds credence to the fact that the U.S. and other English speaking nations were founded upon Christian principles; not only in direct action, but also by indirect implementation of English law which was shaped by Christianity. Winston Churchill was right when he surveyed our heritage, calling it, 'Christian civilisation.'

In Britain, the Christian legal legacy is ever present, not only in the heritage of law but in the unwritten constitution. The Church of England is established into England's constitutional arrangement, with the Monarch as the head. The House of

Lords is the upper house of parliament which checks the government and currently the Church of England has twenty-six places for automatic representation secured. In education, one third of all publicly funded schools are run by religious faiths, mostly Christian. The state still supports the civil and legal purposes of the Church within the context of conducting marriages. In addition the state still funds and supports Christian chaplains in the armed forces, prisons and hospitals. The British army itself is shaped by Christian thinking. Michael Portillo, the former Secretary of State for Defence (1995-1997), noted that Augustine's 'Just War Theory' has always shaped British foreign policy.[13] Still today, when a new Monarch is crowned in Britain they are required to place one hand on an open Bible, to take a solemn oath before Almighty God, "To uphold to the utmost of my power, the laws of God within this realm and the true profession of the Christian faith." In addition, prayers are said everyday in parliament and when MPs swear the Oath of Allegiance on taking up their seats, they do so with a hand on the Bible. The general public still back Britain as a Christian nation; a BBC poll revealed that 'most Britons describe themselves as Christian,' and '75% of respondents said the U.K. should retain Christian values.'[14] Speaking in the House of Lords, the Archbishop of York, Dr John Sentamu said, "The place of Christianity in the constitutional framework of our country, governed as it is by the Queen, in parliament, under God, is not in question...the Christian faith has weaved the very fabric of our society just as the oceans around this island have shaped the contours of our geographical identity."[15] British Prime Minister David Cameron said in 2011, "We are a Christian country and we should not be afraid to say so."[15a]

In the U.S., the Christian legal heritage is ever present; Christian values can be sourced from the original colonial charters, to the foundational English laws, all the way into the Declaration of Independence, to the Bill of Rights and beyond. "The fundamental basis of this nation's laws was given to Moses on the Mount," said President Harry Truman. "The fundamental basis of our Bill of Rights comes from the teachings we get from Exodus and Saint Matthew, from Isaiah and Saint Paul. I don't think we emphasize that enough these days."[16] Sam Casey, executive director of the Christian Legal Society said, "Fundamentally, law in the West is a Judeo-Christian tradition."

In the U.S. many federal buildings and monuments bear the image of this Christian tradition. The House and Senate chamber are inscribed with 'In God We Trust' as is all U.S. legal tender, and in a poll, 86% voted in favour of keeping these phrases.[17] On the floor of the National Archives is a Ten Commandments medallion and the Washington Monument is inscribed in Latin with 'Praise be to God.' Also, on the third panel of the Jefferson Memorial is inscribed: 'God who gave us life gave us liberty – Can the liberties of a nation be secure when we have removed a conviction that these liberties are the gift of God?'

Around the world there are a host of other former British colonies whose legal systems are based upon Christian foundations, even if their religions are different. H.M. Queen Elizabeth II is Head of the Commonwealth, which is a voluntary association of 53 nations with a combined population of nearly 1/3 of the planet. Together they promote democracy, the rule of law, good governance and individual liberty etc. Many of these nations have based their legal system on English law and have British models of the civil services, police and military etc. In addition many have an English style parliamentary democracy and as most are former British colonies, they carry on other traditions, including using English as a main language. Britain may well have left a legal footprint upon much of the world, but first it was Christianity that left the lasting legal legacy upon her.

A Future and a Hope: Christian nations have a legal heritage of hope because their institutions were shaped by the belief in the universal equality of all human beings. In the Christian world, a legal system developed in which there was a healthy respect for human dignity; in nations with other foundations, sometimes the opposite was true. Journalist Jill Parkin wrote: 'Our legal system is inherently Christian, that's why we don't cut off people's hands for theft or stone women for adultery.'[18] In countries with a Christian heritage, millions of people benefit from a legal system in which the individuals rights are respected and official power is limited. Though our systems are not perfect, they are the envy of the world. For in the twenty-first century, there are still millions of people who do not have their individual rights protected by law.

Human Rights: In 1948, the non-binding Universal Declaration of Human Rights (UDHR) was adopted by the U.N. Since that time, many other declarations have been presented which update these ideals. These documents cover the right to life, freedom from slavery, liberty of thought, freedom of religious belief, the right to education, fair working conditions and medical assistance etc., as well as the concept of innocence until proven guilt, impartial courts, and the supremacy of a just and fair rule of law. All of these rights and others have been fought for by Christians and the law has changed because of these battles. In fact, the concept of universal human rights is one of the pre-eminent legacies of the Bible. To mark the 60th anniversary of the UDHR the Community of Protestant Churches in Europe said that human rights should not be curtailed on the grounds of religion or culture – which still happens worldwide.

When Said Rajaie-Khorassani of Iran spoke at the United Nations he explained the position of his country that the Universal Declaration of Human Rights is essentially a Christian based document;[19] saying it was a "secular understanding of the Judeo-Christian tradition." He also explained that many rights (especially freedom of religious belief, the right to convert and women's rights) cannot be given to Muslims without a clear breach of Islamic law. In response, the Islamic world created a gravely criticised declaration which is overshadowed by Sharia, imposing 'restrictions on nearly every human right based on Islamic Sharia law.'[20] There are 50 nations which are majority Muslim, and in 2008, they had around 25% of the world's population and controlled 8.7% of the world's GDP.[21] Sadly many of these nations, along with Communist countries, have often held the premier positions in the world for having the worst human rights record. Studies from human rights organisations reveal severe limitations of human rights in these countries. In Turkey in 1998, the Constitutional Court banned and dissolved the Refah Party on the grounds that the 'rules of Sharia', which Refah sought to introduce, 'were incompatible with the democratic regime,' stating that 'democracy is the antithesis of Sharia.' In the appeal by the Refah Party, the European Court of Human Rights found that 'Sharia is incompatible with the fundamental principles of democracy.'[22]

Chapter Twenty

Family and Community

'A man shall leave his father and mother and be joined to his wife and they shall become one flesh' (Genesis 2:24).

For two thousand years, following Jesus' definition of marriage as being the union of one male and one female for life (Matthew 19:4-9), Christianity solidified into Western civilisation that the family should be a stabilising institution at the centre of society. One may ask, is this truly a legacy of Christianity in the West or is this just the natural prospect of all mankind? During the author's travels around the world, it was revealed that our Western ideals about the family and the community though popular, are not completely universal, nor are they the absolute expected outcome of the human experience. Outside of the Christian West there are many social traditions that have accepted polygamous marriage; Islam and traditional religions in Africa have contributed to the continent having the highest rate of polygamy in the world. In Senegal, with a 92 percent Muslim population, nearly 47 percent of marriages are multiple.[1] In a few cases around the world, anthropologists found communities where women had several husbands. In parts of South-Western China, men become responsible for supporting their sister's children, because fathers do not live with their children or the child's mother.[2] China, earth's most populist nation, only finally accepted the superiority of the one man, one woman model in the 1953 Marriage Act which encouraged abandoning polygamy.

If we consider the modern West, we learn that the Christian ideal is not a blueprint written in the conscience of man. Today many secular people are exploring what the alternatives could be to the one man, one woman model. There are many alternative lifestyles which have been and are being experienced by those who choose not to own the Christian tradition, and objective statistics have proved that they lead to disastrous consequences for individuals and society as a whole.

One Man, One Woman: In history, 'Roman Law permitted prostitution, concubinage and sexual access to slaves. The Christian West formally banned these practices with laws against adultery, fornication, and other relationships outside a monogamous, lifelong covenant.'[3] The Bible assigned the fundamentals, which led to the modern marriage covenant and holy blessing of the monogamous institution. In Genesis chapter two, the founding of the monogamous lifelong relationship began, but it only really established itself in the Christian era. Perhaps one of the reasons for this is that Abraham came from Ur of the Chaldeans (Iraq), where it was common for men to have several wives and Moses was raised in Egypt, and continued the tradition in Jewish thought. However, the stories in the Bible provide ample evidence of the distinct problems with polygamy.

In the Christian era, the monogamous marriage model became the absolute standard for the creation of family. In this setting there should be provided companionship, commitment and protected sexual union, where children could be raised in a stable environment. The Christian tradition favours marriage until death because God hates divorce and all it does to the family, especially to children. Remember the Bible says that God hates divorce, not the divorcee. The Bible is also honest about man's failings, and there are provisions for divorce in cases of adultery and the debated Pauline principle of abandonment etc.

Christianity led to a monogamous culture in the West and this helped create rights and responsibilities for the couple, including financial, sexual and legal security. In recent years, a significant amount of this status has been lost by couples who live together, especially when considering financial settlements after separation, inheritance rights, or even hospital visitation rights. After a generation of cohabitation the facts show that the Christian ideal is far superior. A study for a major U.K. political party revealed that 'unmarried parents are up to five times more likely to experience family breakdown,' and that 'by tacitly promoting cohabitation and undermining marriage, policy-makers are exposing more children to the perils of family breakdown, reflected in higher levels of crime, anti-social behaviour, education failure, mental and emotional disturbance.'[4] A report from the Centre for Social Justice states: 'A child not growing up in a two-parent family is 75 percent more likely to fail at school, 70 percent more likely to be a drug addict, 50 percent more likely to have an alcohol problem, 40 percent more likely to have serious debt and 35 percent more likely to be without work.'[5] Marriage has taken a terrible beating in modern days, yet in our history it is the most common and most successful foundation for the family. Even in the post-Christian West, the concept of making her 'an honest woman' is still stated amongst men. Secular people may have to their peril abandoned the ceremony and covenant of a lifetime marriage, but most still hold to the one man one woman commitment and many still hope it will be for life.

'Over the thousands of years since the books of Deuteronomy and Leviticus set out the code of ethics on which Christianity was founded,' wrote Lord Tebbit, 'our Western society has been built on the basic, but vital, institution of family. Not just any old group of people shacked up together for a while, but the exclusive partnership of one man and one woman bearing and bringing up children. That way, the traditions, rules and customs of society have been passed from one generation to the next and children have been cared for in a safe, nurturing and responsible environment. The Christian West is not alone in following this format. Every lasting civilisation has done so....it is, in short, a formula that works. So why meddle with it? In recent years, the family formula has begun to disintegrate and with disastrous results. The downgrading of marriage and the shattering of the family unit that has inevitably followed the granting of equivalent status to other forms of partnership are already having an effect on the levels of crime, unhappiness and deprivation among children – the damage they suffer will be passed on to the next generation.'[6]

Studies have shown that the Christian ideal of marriage has valuable contributions for the individual and society. In most European states, this has been recognised by offering tax breaks to married couples, especially as marriage is a healthy environment for child development. Chancellor of the Exchequer George Osborne, speaking for the British Conservative party in an interview praised marriage and said, "The statistics are clear: children with married parents perform better in school, are happier and less likely to commit crime."[7] 'New research also shows that not only does having a good marriage keep you healthy, it can also prolong life. It's long been reported that those in a good relationship have a lower risk of high blood pressure, but now studies are finding that couples enjoying wedded bliss seem to experience lower levels of heart disease, cancers, flu, Alzheimer's, depression and stress.'[8]

Accepted Sexual Behaviour: Christianity was born into a loose age, and it had to confront the amoral legacy of Greece and Rome. When Plato (424-348BC) referred to a prostitute, he used the expression 'Corinthian girl.' Hundreds of years later, Paul writes to the Corinthians to teach them about acceptable sexual behaviour and the Christian virtue of faithfulness. The Bible has also helped the West develop acceptable expressions of sexual behaviour. Leviticus eighteen is just one chapter that deals with this subject – we discover that sexual relations are forbidden with close relatives: mother, father or their in-laws, brothers and sisters. The extended family is also protected by forbidding sexual relationships with step-brothers, sisters, uncles and aunts. Same sex and bestiality is forbidden. Before we knew anything about genetic mutations in the babies of very close relatives, Christianity made this marriage concept abhorrent to us. In the Christian world, sexuality found its virtuous demeanour in the lifetime commitment of two people of the opposite sex both secured by a holy covenant.

A Moral Foundation: Christianity also provided a moral foundation upon which the West could develop. Thomas Jefferson (1743-1826), America's third president said, "I have always said and will always say that the studious perusal of the Sacred Volume (the Bible) will make better homes, better citizens, better fathers and better husbands." U.S. Secretary of State Daniel Webster (1782-1817) agreed saying, "The Bible fits man for life and prepares him for death." If we consider just the Ten Commandments, we discover that the first few laws encourage civilisation to abandon the tomfoolery of worshipping man-made images, and stresses the importance of submitting ourselves to God and to His moral authority. This created a moral 'ring of steel,' in which the West could over time affirm certain rights before God. The Sabbath law promoted the idea that mankind cannot work 24/7, and needs a day of rest in every week from which no-one should be excluded. The honour law, helped to create a culture of respect, beginning with parents. By banning murder and adultery, the sanctity of life and marriage was safeguarded. Also, the requirement not to steal protects the individual's right to personal property. The moral duty to be truthful helps safeguard not only business deals, but relationship foundations. Finally, we are told not to covet or lust after other people's spouses or possessions etc. This law examines the heart; for before a sin is birthed, it is first conceived in the heart and mind. In other words, if you begin to think right, you will begin to act right.

'In the Ten Commandments, Moses outlined a basis for morality which has lasted over 3,000 years,' explained an expert 'and been embraced by two-thirds of the world's population.'[9] Noah Webster (1758-1843), compiler of America's most influential dictionary wrote: 'The duties of men are summarily comprised in the Ten Commandments, consisting of two tablets; one comprehending the duties which we owe immediately to God – the other, the duties we owe to our fellow men.' Her Majesty Queen Elizabeth, the late Queen Mother said, "Many of the evils which beset us today would be avoided by strict adherence to the precepts of the Ten Commandments."[10] It is true to state: 'By associating the belief in one God with moral behaviour, the Ten Commandments establish a code of morality and justice for all – the ideal of Western civilisation.'[11] It may be true that every civilisation has had to develop moral foundations, but these hallmarks of the West became deep-seated in our culture because of Christianity. If we consider the non-Christian world, we discover today that millions of people still worship items which are made with man's hands, the author found this to be the case in India. We also find that in some nations, personal property is not respected. In the post-Christian West, we discover that the requirement to be truthful and forsake adultery has been disregarded by many and numerous people are victims of this moral debasement. Life gets tricky, when citizens cannot trust those that they are doing business with, let alone the person they live with.

Community: The Church has always provided a sense of community and in the history of Europe, and in the English speaking world, it was often at the very centre of life. When there was no radio, cinema or TV, and no constant stream of entertainment, the Church was a place to go and be. It became not only a place to worship, but a place to meet and greet. When one entered a village, the heartbeat was often found in the Church. An echo of this role is still felt in the small rural villages of England today, where the post office and the Church are still the nerve-centres of the community. The Church was also once the source of information, where citizens were warned of the Black Death, or in the positive, where Americans first held a democratic assembly.

Christianity united people with common values, unifying beliefs, sacred doctrines and hymns which educated, encouraged and most importantly brought people together. Still today, the sacred hymns of old are sung by the elderly and the youth. Christianity helped people to know that they belonged to a global community of faith and at home, it provided cohesion which brought strangers together and presented them with accepted values. Christianity helped the divided peoples of many lands to be united and to discover nationhood. The Archbishop of York said, "The Venerable Bede in his *Ecclesiastical History* tells not only of how the English were converted, but how that through corporate-discipleship, the Church played a major socialising and civilising role by uniting the English and conferring nationhood on them."[12] At the end of 2001, H.M. Queen Elizabeth II looked back upon the year in which the terrible terrorist attacks had taken place in America and said, "As so often in our lives at times of tragedy – just as on occasions of celebration and thanksgiving – we look to the Church to bring us together as a nation or as a community in commemoration and tribute. It is to the Church that we turn to give meaning to these moments of intense human experience through prayer, symbol and ceremony. For Christmas marks a moment to pause, to reflect and believe in the possibilities of rebirth and renewal. Christ's birth in Bethlehem so long ago remains a powerful symbol of hope for a better future. After all the tribulations of this year, this is surely more relevant than ever."[13]

Throughout history, the Church has played a central role in community life. The bells still ring out to celebrate a wedding and in times of war, they have celebrated military victory. In the West, the sense of community is rapidly breaking down and many people feel isolated from the rest of the world. Yet, the Christian Church still plays a pivotal role in providing a place to meet people from other backgrounds. In the Church one can find teenagers, young mothers, mature men and pensioners all studying the Bible in a small group, and sharing the reality of their world. Today in the Church we find groups for young mothers, retired people, teenagers and single people etc. Much of our population also turns to the Church throughout the journey of life; from the celebration of the birth of a new baby, to the mourning of a lost loved one. In addition, the Church is still a place where the overlooked, the isolated and the insignificant can find meaning. Within the Christian community, there has always been a long standing desire to help others. This has led to works which help widows, the poor, the homeless, strangers, migrants etc; as well as those seeking spiritual direction.

"The Bible has helped to shape the values which define our country," said British Prime Minister David Cameron. "Indeed, as Margaret Thatcher once said, 'we are a nation whose ideals are founded on the Bible.' Responsibility, hard work, charity, compassion, humility, self-sacrifice, love, pride in working for the common good and honouring the social obligations we have to one another, to our families and our communities these are the values we treasure. Yes, they are Christian values and we should not be afraid to acknowledge that."[13a]

In Britain, the Conservative Party charity spokesman Greg Clark said, "Britain's churches are literally at the centre of their communities – they know intimately the problems people face, and have a deep commitment and track record of taking action to help them."[14] Former Tory leader Iain Duncan Smith agrees that Christian projects are at the heart of our communities saying, "Throughout Britain the Church is doing excellent work to help people struggling with problems such as addictions, family breakdown and serious personal debt. In many of our toughest neighbourhoods it is Christian projects that transform lives when others have given up."[15]

However, a report showed that the Christian contribution to social welfare is underestimated. Francis Davis, Co-Director of the Centre for the Study of Faith in Society at the Von Hugel Institute revealed the British 'Government had underestimated the number of faith based charities operating in the country by as much as fifty percent, resulting in the "significant underestimation of the civic and volunteering and social welfare contribution that they make across the country." ' In 2008, the Archbishop of Canterbury, Dr Rowan Williams in regards to the report said, "It reveals a depressing level of misunderstanding of the scale and quality of contribution faith based organisations make to...our common good." Francis Davis went on to praise, "The contribution of the Church in social welfare, demonstrated by the high number of bishops engaged in civic activities and the number of churches that double up as cafes, post offices, youth clubs and even GPs to ensure that their local communities do not go without vital services."[16]

A New Awareness: All around the Western world from Europe to America, the Christian contribution is huge and often under the official radar. In the U.S., after Hurricane Katrina had devastated New Orleans, the Federal Emergency Management Agency (FEMA) was severely criticised for the slow response, yet Christian agencies were praised for their prompt and considerable contribution. Senator John McCain said that the faith based initiative is, "One of the more successful parts of the Bush Administration," and Barack Obama agreed. When Barack Obama visited a youth programme, he claimed that his faith inspired his work as a community organiser in Chicago and said, "In time, I came to see faith as being both a personal commitment to Christ and a commitment to my community; that while I could sit in Church and pray all I want, I wouldn't be fulfilling God's will unless I went out and did the Lord's work." He went on to pledge more federal support saying, "The challenges we face today...are simply too big for government to solve alone."[17] In 2008 secular France, President Sarkozy also witnessed the positive role that Christianity can play in society, and called 'for a more active role for religion in public life and greater recognition of Europe's Christian roots.' Challenging French protocol he was hoping for a more positive attitude towards belief that 'would value the hope faith brings and allow state subsidies for faith based groups.'[18] In Berlin, Germany, Federal Minister Dr Wolfgang Schäuble said, "Our culture and civilisation, our way of living and our attitudes to life are influenced by Christianity, and in this light, Christianity will also play an emphatic role in our country in the future, of that there is no doubt."[19] In addition, French anthropologist René Girard, one of the most influential intellectuals of contemporary culture, believes that a Christian Renaissance lies ahead. In the Italian book *Verità o Fede Debole. Dialogo su Cristianesimo e Relativismo*[20] the anthropologist states that: 'Religion conquers philosophy and surpasses it. Philosophies in fact are almost dead. Ideologies are virtually deceased; political theories are almost altogether spent. Confidence in the fact that science can replace religion has already been surmounted. There is in the world a new need for religion.' Looking forward he wrote: 'We will live in a world that will seem and be as Christian, as today, it seems scientific.' He also criticised the 'politically correct world' which considers 'the Judeo-Christian tradition as the only impure tradition, whereas all the others are exempt from any possible criticism.'[21]

Christianity and Culture: There is much that we take for granted about our understanding of family and community, and when we distance ourselves from current culture, we learn that Christianity helped set these ideals into our culture and henceforth into our hearts. But there is still an awareness of Christ's influence – in a recent poll, nearly three-quarters of all Britons said they believed the birth of Jesus Christ remains a 'significant' part of British culture.[22] In 2008, H.M. Queen Elizabeth II said, "I hope that, like me, you will be comforted by the example of Jesus of Nazareth who, often in circumstances of great adversity, managed to live an outgoing, unselfish and sacrificial life....He makes it clear that genuine human happiness and satisfaction lie more in giving than receiving; more in serving than in being served."[23] U.S. President John Quincy Adams said, "So great is my veneration for the Bible that the earlier my children begin to read it the more confident will be my hope that they will prove useful citizens of their country and respectable members of society. I have for many years made it a practice to read through the Bible once every year."[24]

"Although we are capable of great acts of kindness, history teaches us that we sometimes need saving from ourselves," said H.M. Queen Elizabeth II, "from our recklessness or our greed. God sent into the world a unique Person – neither a philosopher nor a general, important though they are, but a Saviour, with the power to forgive. Forgiveness lies at the heart of the Christian faith. It can heal broken families, it can restore friendships and it can reconcile divided communities. It is in forgiveness that we feel the power of God's love."[25]

Chapter Twenty-One

Spiritual Revival and the Development of Social Cohesion

"And because lawlessness will abound, the love of many will grow cold" (Matthew 24:12).

We often credit revivalists like Jonathan Edwards, George Whitefield, John Wesley and Evan Roberts etc., for the reviving and filling of churches, but we should never forget that when people are truly converted, they begin to clean up their lives too and this has had a major impact upon the development of our civilisation. In the West, there has often been an assumption based upon the evidence that Christianity was a good thing for society, as well as for the individual. In our history, 'Victorian Britons were a God-fearing Protestant nation...Christian duty was expressed through the high moral tone of public life and in the desire of the better-off to do good deeds. In everyday life, it meant that all classes tried to be respectable and moral. Duty took precedence over inclination, morality over pleasure.'[1]

Before the British Evangelical Revival (1739-1791) and John Wesley's ministry, the historian Lecky speaks of it as one of the most morally debased periods in the nation's history. In Britain and the U.S., we owe much to the Christian faith, for encouraging personal restraint, which has led to greater social cohesion. Unfaithful husbands became moral, thieves went honest, alcoholics spent their money on the family, addicts were freed and all the problems associated with it went into remission. The streets were safer, the poor found jobs, the problems of others became the burdens of the Church, and the Church took the burdens of society into the highest places of power and called for reform. Children were cared for, the elderly protected, morality developed, restraint was called for, the family home was promoted, motherhood was valued, and marriage was respected. The faith in the churches soon impacted every area of the lives of citizens; workers' rights were protected, fair wages expected, better living conditions demanded, healthcare required, education facilitated and representation commanded. As prudence grew, the new Christians could give of their time, and money to support charities and missions abroad. Many of the problems that had been ignored by society for years, were exposed, challenged and resolved. British Prime Minister W.E. Gladstone in the House of Commons in 1880 said, "It has been said that greater calamities are inflicted on mankind by intemperance than by the three great historical scourges – war, pestilence and famine. This is true for us."[2] Speaking of Christ's restraining hand the social commentator Frank Ballard explained in *The Mission Of Christianity*: 'His real nearness...shall sober the drunkard, restrain the libertine (morally unrestrained), heal the bitter spring of selfishness, comfort the sorrowing, guide the perplexed, rescue the despair smitten prodigal...in a word, save men.'[3]

Christianity helped shape and create an ordered legal society without which things would descend into anarchy. At the same time it was the fear of God that helped people choose godliness, which saved our nations from chaos and according to some historians, saved Britain from a French styled civil war. For William Wilberforce, an ordered society was not enough, he wanted a mannered society. His book which contrasted the *Prevailing Religious System with Real Christianity* was a bestseller, which helped lead to a complete change of social habits in Britain in the nineteenth century. Christianity has always played an important role in creating a healthy society; back in the second century, someone noted how Christianity affected people's behaviour: 'They marry and have children like every one else; but they do not kill their unwanted babies. They offer a shared table, but not a shared bed...they obey the appointed laws, and go beyond the laws in their own lives.'[4]

We Don't Believe in Sin Anymore: The Bible teaches that sin is an offence to God's righteousness, but it also reveals that it dramatically lowers the quality of life for the sinner and the lives of those around him or her. Sin destroys relationships, tears apart families, costs us our peace, steals our long-term happiness and gives birth to unnecessary pain. Sin brings with it loss of trust, falling self-worth, heartbreak, fear and anger etc., whilst degrading and devaluing humanity. However, there is a tendency in the twenty-first century for people to suggest that the West does not have a problem with sin – essentially we are all good people. Nevertheless the Bible says, 'All have sinned and fall short of the glory of God' (Romans 3:23). A post-Christian society may believe it is good, but behind the nice appearance are some troubling conclusions; without Christianity we have become transparently dysfunctional. 'What the twentieth century proved was what Nietzsche predicted: as societies move away from God, they don't get happier, they get unhappier; they don't get more loving, they get more selfish.'[5] "The better the society, the less law there will be," said legal scholar Grant Gilmore at Yale Law School in 1974. In the post-Christian West, laws have rapidly increased.[5a]

The following comes from the British Crime Survey, revealing crime over a twelve month period in England and Wales (53.3 million people).[6] Please note that though every statistic would vary for each developed nation (as there are numerous variables), the general amount of crime is similar in Western nations as a percentage of the total population.

10,912,000	Total crimes.
3,369,000	Non-vehicle related thefts.
2,731,000	Criminal damage.
2,420,000	Violent offences.
1,731,000	Vehicle related thefts.
733,000	Domestic burglaries.
311,000	Robbery offences.[7]

We can conclude that the criminal element is responsible for the serious crime, but we cannot with sincerity suggest that ten million crimes in one year was the accomplishment of just the full-time criminals. There were 2.4 million cases of violent offences, how many of them happened in the home or on the street after a night of drinking?

The following statistics reveal how we treat each other.

1,900,000	Lone parents.[8]
500,000	Elderly people suffering abuse.[9]
31%	Of children experience bullying.[10]
16%	Of women were sexually abused before age 12.[11]
7%	Of men were sexually abused before age 12.[12]
1 in 4	Women will experience domestic violence.[13]
1 in 6	Men will experience domestic violence.[14]
1 in 9	Pre-teenage children have suffered from abuse.[15]

The British Crime Survey estimated that 35 million yob crimes take place every year – that's one a second.[16]

The following is the British yearly post-script to the Sexual Revolution.

790,443	Sexually transmitted infections.[17]
190,000	Abortions.[18]
85,000	Rapes.[19] (Charities state far more go unreported).
41,868	Teenage pregnancies (under 18).[20]
72%	Of children from single parent families in poverty.[21]
23%	Of women report a sexual assault since age 16.[22]
30%	Of non-resident parents fail to support their children.[23]
18%	Of children have no contact with fathers.[24]
1 in 25	Dads are not the real father of their believed child.[25]

In the U.S., psychologists blamed a society rife with sexuality and violence for a forty percent increase in juvenile sex offenders which are 'younger and more violent.'[26]

How do we treat public servants?

21,845	Assaults on police officers every year.[27]
92%	Of teachers are verbally abused by pupils.[28]
49%	Of teachers are physically abused by pupils.[29]
58,000	Teachers experienced parental aggression.[30]
75,000	Health workers were victims of assaults by patients.[31]
1,200	Attacks on firefighters.[32]
79%	Of A&E nurses attacked or harassed.[33]
40%	Of all nurses attacked or harassed.[33]

How do we treat ourselves?

31,000,000	Prescriptions for antidepressants in one year.[34]
7,100,000	People are 'hazardous and harmful' drinkers.[35]
1,100,000	Other people are 'dependent drinkers.'[36]
4,000,000	People use an illicit drug each year.[37]
1,100,000	Are affected by an eating disorder.[38]
170,000	People attend hospital for self-poisoning.[39]
85%	Gain in mental health admissions due to cannabis.[40]

'If we say we have no sin, we deceive ourselves and the truth is not in us. If we confess our sins, He is faithful and just to forgive us our sins' (1 John 1:8-9).

It would be foolish to attempt to compare these statistics with another age, where crimes or personal troubles were swept under the carpet. However, it is worth considering that once Western culture expected people to conform to Christian values, today the opposite is often true in many areas – think about language, alcohol, sex, 'insignificant theft,' and keeping one's word etc. Once a healthy sense of the fear of God would help people to exercise self-restraint in a moment of madness, but today the culture says there is no God. '...Is it not because I held

My peace from of old that you do not fear Me?' (Isaiah 57:11). Thankfully, generations of Christian influence in law has created a legal system, which helps keep order because people fear the law and the consequences of breaking it. Politicians can make good laws, but God inspires people to choose to live righteously.

Nevertheless, our culture has a significant influence upon all citizens, including people of faith. As the culture has rejected Christian values, it becomes easier for all people, including religious people to follow the crowd, rather than be influenced by the central doctrines of their faith. After all, a Christian often has only 1 hour a week in a church and the other 167 hours a week are open to all other influences. In a year a Christian may spend just over 2 days in church, whilst the other 363 days are full of other influences, including a highly charged mass media, which often presents faith based values as irrelevant.

William Wilberforce saw the need for a great 'reformation of manners' as he understood that culture has to be changed, because culture is the dominant factor in people's lives. We should consider culture like the tide which comes in and out. It does not change everything in an instant, but over time, it reshapes the entire landscape – just look at the British coastline. Every religious person fails like all others, yet at the same time it is evident that when people make an honest profession of faith, they do at least attempt to reform their ways and contribute something back. 'A Bristol University survey showed that, overall, Christians are three-and-a-half times more likely to do something helpful for someone outside their immediate family than the general population.'[41] According to Faithworks, an estimated 370,000 Christian volunteers contribute services, donating around 65 million hours of their time each year in England alone.[42] "In total, there are almost thirty thousand faith based charities in this country," said British Prime Minister David Cameron, "not to mention the thousands of people who step forward as individuals, as families, as communities, as organisations and yes, as churches and do extraordinary things to help build a bigger, richer, stronger, more prosperous and more generous society. And when it comes to the great humanitarian crises – like the famine in Horn of Africa – again you can count on faith based organisations. So it's right to recognise the huge contribution our faith communities make to our politics and to recognise the role of the Bible in inspiring many of their works."[42a]

The author's brother has researched hundreds of revivals and recorded his findings in several revival books, including *Revival Fires and Awakenings*. Mathew Backholer explains in his book that Church history often records a decrease in crime during times of revival. During the Welsh Revival he noted: 'In the Rhondda Valley and beyond, the magistrates were given white gloves (a symbol of purity) as there were so few cases to hear,' and 'white gloves were also handed out in Swansea County Court,' and 'Aberdare was almost entirely free from drunkenness.' In the capital Cardiff, 'the Mayor handed the chief constable a pair of white gloves in memory of there being no cases at all on the charge sheet on the last day of 1904.'[43] The decrease in crime and antisocial behaviour during Christian revival is a global phenomenon. In Mathew Backholer's book *150 Years of Revival* he researched many revivals, including one in twenty-first century India. A local Indian government official said, "I have seen the street outside my house. The people who used to stand around in the dark – drunk and swearing has reduced a lot. Many broken families have got together. Yes, many people have experienced change."[44]

On 20 June 1922, British Prime Minister David Lloyd George said, "I come from a country that owes more to the Methodism Movement, of which Wesley was the inspirer...than to any other movement in the whole of history. Its indirect influence is probably greater than even its direct influence. This is the story of all great religious reformations." In 2010, Dr Claire Strachan carried out detailed research into the social and economic contexts of Christian observance during the eighteenth and nineteenth centuries, and found that faith had a far greater impact on the social and political landscape than has been previously considered. Her research revealed that Christian revivals of this era led to rising confidence of the working classes, which impacted their behaviour, political beliefs and their relationships with their employers.[45]

If we consider all the Christian charities around the world, who give endlessly, they reveal to us that faith often gives a moral imperative to at least attempt to make the world a better place. The Christian faith has always encouraged self restraint and personal sacrifice for others, including concern for those outside of the immediate family. It also called for a sense of Christian duty in the government and at work. Christianity helped create social cohesion, as a culture of respect drove citizens to treat others as they wanted to be treated, and when they failed, Jesus' teaching encouraged repentance, forgiveness and the restoration of relationships. Today, Christian values though under attack, are still influencing our nations and are often called family values. One journalist wrote: 'British values such as neighbourliness, civic pride and concern for others spring directly from Christianity. The Christian ethical tradition was also crucial in marginalising corruption in public life and securing equal treatment for all classes of people before the law.'[46]

Liberty and Virtue: Around the world there are many religions and all have some form of moral code for their followers. The gift of modern Christianity to the world is that it challenges people to live better lives because they can be better people. In other parts of the world where other religions are dominant, there are often harsh punishments for those who fail, and strict laws to restrict and limit the roles of women and 'infidels' (unbelievers). In Cairo, Egypt, the author sat down with Dr Rev. Menes Abdul Noor, a humble Billy Graham type figure of the Middle East, who leads the nation's largest church. His story is one of spreading the Christian faith and values in the region through church planting, writing, radio and TV. Walking into his church is like entering into a different country; inside there is a sense of freedom, where men speak of human rights and unveiled women talk over their next career move. All of this is in stark contrast to the strict Islamic culture that one witnesses in the lives of many Egyptians in Cairo everyday. Former president of Youth For Christ International said, "Menes Abdul Noor stands as a bright and shining light in the midst of one of the most difficult societies in the world."[47] Christians in the Middle East, from Syria to Iraq, are perhaps the greatest illustration of how the values of the Christian faith shape society. The contrast between the Christian enclaves and the rest of the region are remarkable, yet this liberty does not come at the price of virtue.

Christian values were never designed as a social straightjacket upon society, but as a source of empowerment against the self-destructive element within us all, which if embedded into culture becomes a source of abuse. An example can be found in the post-Christian culture of the West where people search for meaning and value in materialism or promiscuity etc. Christianity desires that each individual should possess personal dignity, self-respect and that this should be extended to one's neighbour. Quality of life significantly increases in a society where people respect themselves and each other. However, in a culture that has rejected much of its Christian heritage, a British government adviser made reference to the decline of Christian values, and decay in society. Mr Campbell said, "When you look at the sort of slow, stealthy liberalisation of society (and we've all stood by passively and allowed it to happen), eroding many of the Christian principles on which the country's laws, education and relationships were built...governments unfortunately have presided over the steady erosion of society's principles...and we're asking ourselves now why are we here? It's because we failed to ensure that society's moved forward on the principles that made it great."[48]

Liberty and the Arts: When we consider the question of quality of life, we must understand that Christianity asks us to deny those aspects of our character which are harmful to ourselves and others, but at the same time it replaces it with a new view of who we are in Christ, and new ways to express our faith and belief. It also gives culture and society opportunities to express their faith corporately through the arts. One journalist wrote: 'The Church continues to play a largely beneficent role in the arts ecology of Britain. It maintains and restores the legacy of Church architecture – an important collection of beautiful buildings whatever your beliefs. And churches up and down the country offer, as any working musician will testify, a fantastic programme of recitals and concerts of both secular and religious pieces, often for free or for a low ticket price. Areas where there is little access to live classical music are having that provision met almost entirely by the Church. The more enlightened churches are still commissioning work, from paintings to sculptures and music. We should celebrate the Christian legacy in Western art and society – and stop the Dawkins army from denying us the possibility of drawing inspiration from faith to create the art of the future.'[49]

Chapter Twenty-Two

Empires and Superpowers

'And in the days of these kings, shall the God of heaven set up a kingdom which shall never be destroyed; and the kingdom shall not be left to other people; but it shall break in pieces and consume all these kingdoms and it shall stand forever' (Daniel 2:44).

The prophet Daniel in chapter two of his book symbolically calls forth four empires which would rise up and rule, beginning in his lifetime. His prophecy was fulfilled in the Babylonian Empire, the Medo-Persian Empire, the Greek Empire and the Roman Empire. However, after these powers another great kingdom would arise, which would consume and outlive all other empires – he was speaking of the kingdom of God.

The history of the world is the story of superpowers and empires, and how they exercised their might, spreading their values, by means fair or foul. Christianity arrived at a time when Roman roads, a common language and a regional hegemony made its diffusion rapid. In one sense, empire became a vehicle from which Christianity could spread to the world – directly or indirectly. In 43AD, the Romans colonised a tiny archipelago off the North-West coast of Europe; inadvertently they brought with them Christianity. One thousand, eight hundred and seventy-five years later, the inhabitants of these islands were ruling one quarter of the world's population and spreading Christianity as they went. In the meantime, many powers and empires had come and gone, but the prophecy of Daniel was still working as the final Kingdom was spreading, using the vehicles that each age made available. As we consider how Christianity made the modern world, we must also consider the vehicles that were used within that creation. There are many players on the stage, but for the last two hundred years, when the modern world emerged and advanced rapidly, the most powerful of these nations have been English speaking and Protestant.

Superpowers and God: 'Therefore that God, the Author and giver of felicity, because He alone is the true God, Himself gives earthly kingdoms both to good and bad,' so argued Augustine of Hippo (354-430) in *De Civitate Dei Contra Paganos*.[1] In the Old

Testament there is a consistent study of how God raises up nations, peoples and leaders to use them to His own ends. This however, is often overlooked by many contemporary Christians who are familiar with the Roman Empire of the New Testament, but unfamiliar with the empires of the Old Testament.

One of the greatest examples of God using the leader of a superpower is that of Cyrus of Persia. The Bible indicates that God raised up this man to bring the Jewish people back to their land. The famous first century historian Josephus explains that when Cyrus learnt of the two hundred year old prophecy of Isaiah 44:28 concerning him, that he 'called for the most eminent Jews that were in Babylon....and gave them leave to go back to their own country and to rebuild their city Jerusalem, and the temple of God.'[2] In the British museum we learn more: the Cyrus Cylinder explicates that in his pagan worldview, Cyrus became afraid of all gods therefore he 'resettled all the gods...in their former chapels.' In the Bible, Daniel was the prophet who foretold the fall of Babylon, which led to this era of restoration. His account in chapter five of his book is confirmed by the Greek historian Herodotus (484-425BC) who reasserted, 'The Persians who were posted with this intent made their way into Babylon by the channel of the Euphrates, which had now sunk to about the height of the middle of a man's thigh.'

The prophet Daniel believed in his day God raised up nations and peoples to His own ends; if we choose to believe the same (Acts 1:7, 17:26), then perhaps a case could be made for God using the flawed European empires in the 15th-18th centuries, the British Empire in the 19th century, the American superpower in the 20th and perhaps even the restored Chinese power in the 21st century where Christianity is now booming?

The British Empire: The British built histories largest and most influential empire, and in J.R. Seeley's famous words did so 'in a fit of absence of mind.'[3] From humble beginnings, to its demise, the British ended up ruling almost one third of the entire planet's surface, with one quarter of the world under British rule at one time, at its peak. The contemporary Briton will almost certainly envision empire and empire builders in a negative light, but to do so is to fundamentally misunderstand the worldview of previous generations. When Britons of another age heard of the burning of widows in India or of warring tribes in Africa, or of cannibalism in the Pacific, many believed it was their God-given destiny to help. Winston Churchill had no doubt that empire could be a tool for good: 'To give peace to warring tribes, to administer justice where all was violence, to strike the chains off the slave, to draw the richness from the soil, to plant the earliest seeds of commerce and learning.'[4] Perhaps what Winston Churchill was suggesting that the greatest case for empire is one of order and development, in an age where there was little worldwide. But all of this cannot take place without one terrible word – intervention. American administrations have battled with the same word when considering Rwanda, Sierra Leone and Somalia etc. Is it right to act, when, why and how, and...how long will it take? An Oxfam report looked at twenty-three African nations which had wars between 1990 and 2005 and estimated the cost to the people of Africa was $300 billion. It stated: 'The price that Africa is paying could...provide education, water and prevention and treatment for tuberculosis and malaria. Literally thousands of hospitals, schools, and roads could have been built.'[5] Many in the West have asked, "Is it truly moral for us to do nothing as this continues?" The British asked the same question, as they evaluated the world during their pre-eminence.

However, the greatest of intentions can lead to the worst of disasters. In the story of British intervention in Africa, perhaps there is none as famous as the story of the Zulu Kingdom. When the author visited the historic sites and museums in various countries in Southern Africa, it became clear that other African tribes believed the Zulus had the will and means to bring total annihilation to them. Within the Zulu Kingdom at the battlefield of Isandlwana,[6] the natives managed to bring a stunning victory against the British; but after the battle the Zulus mutilated the dead, castrated the young and placed the genitalia of the fallen into the mouths of the deceased. For the British, this was a perfect illustration of the need to bring order, civilisation and Christianity to 'the uncivilised world.' Today, the decedents of the Zulu live in peace with neighbouring tribes, sharing a common nationality and often the same Christian faith. In fact, at the base of the battlefield of Isandlwana there now resides a Christian church. If a Victorian could see Zulu-Natal of today, perhaps they might well suggest that their vision was fulfilled.

Self-Interest: There is of course no nation that acts without first considering its own interests and it would be foolhardy to be naïve about national motives; yet within the context of domestic and international affairs, Christians showed they were able to influence politics in the hope of creating a better world. Human nature pulls at us to believe that the worst of all motives are always in action for it is easier to be sceptical; but to do this would show how modern cynicism has been allowed to replace historical fact.

A Protestant Empire: The Portuguese and Spanish were the first reprehensible European empire builders, but they did take Christianity to South America etc. Spain's authority had come from the Pope to 'occupy such islands and lands...as you have discovered and are about to discover.' In England, many began to argue that in response it 'had a religious duty to build a Protestant empire.'[7] The most prolific of these visionaries was the Rev. Richard Hakluyt (1552-1616) who was ordained in 1578. As he pondered the future of England he was shown the verses Psalm 107:23-24 – 'Those who go down to the sea in ships, who do business on great waters, they shall see the works of the Lord and His wonders in the deep.' For the Rev. Hakluyt, this was a sign from God that the English should build a seafaring empire;[8] little did he know that one day the British would sing, 'Rule Britannia, Britannia Rules the Waves!'

Richard Hakluyt thus began to work tirelessly to promote the idea of English settlements in North America and his vision from the Bible never left him; the memorial to him at Bristol Cathedral makes reference to the verses which were his inspiration. With this biblical grounding the English began their expansion by undermining Spanish strength, which would lead to the decisive confrontation and defeat of the Spanish Armada in 1588. English enlargement continued over the years, which brought conflict with many. Over time England grew to become a great world power and those in authority recognised God for this blessing. In Westminster Abbey, England, there is a thirty-three feet high memorial to Prime Minister William Pit the Elder (1708-1778) which gives credit to God for the supremacy of Britain. 'During whose administration and in the reigns of George II and George III, Divine Providence exalted Great Britain to a height of prosperity and glory unknown to any former age.' The continued battles with France ended with French defeat at Trafalgar (1805) and after the Battle of Waterloo (1815), Napoleon (1769-1821) was humiliated, living under British guard on a tiny island in the British Empire. The Royal Navy therefore found themselves in control of the oceans and seas of the world. With unchallenged sea power, the British presided over Pax Britannica (Latin for 'the British Peace' beginning after the 1815 Battle of Waterloo), a hundred years of relative peace, expanded trade, prosperity and progress, with law, order and stability, where Protestant Christianity and British values thrived and spread globally.

With the triumph of British military might and the advances since the Industrial Revolution, Britain became the wealthiest nation on earth and the inscription over the front portico of the Royal Exchange (the former London Stock Exchange) made reference to the source of this wealth – 'The earth is the Lord's and the fullness thereof' (Psalm 24:1). During the reign of Queen Victoria (1819-1901) the British empire reached its peak, ruling at one time a quarter of the world's population. Now the British had made the Roman Empire look small many asked, 'What is the secret of its greatness?' The answer according to Queen Victoria can now be found in Britain's National Portrait Gallery. Visitors can make their way to room twenty-three, where the 1863 painting by Thomas Jones Barker resides. 'The Secret of England's Greatness' was purchased for the gallery in 1974; it shows a humble Queen Victoria presenting a Bible to an African chief, in the audience chamber at Windsor Castle. History reveals that this was not the only time that such an undertaking took place. On 20 November 1896, a visiting dignitary asked the Queen, "What made England great?" Queen Victoria held a Bible and declared, "That book accounts for the supremacy of England!" British Prime Minister W. E. Gladstone (1809-1898) must have agreed saying, "I have known ninety-five of the world's great men in my time and of these eighty-seven were followers of the Bible. The Bible is stamped with a Specialty of Origin, and an immeasurable distance separates it from all competitors."[9] In 1901 in Canada, this sentiment was echoed once again, as a statue to the now late Victoria was unveiled. The speaker talked of the people of Britain and the Queen being comforted "from the secret of Britain's greatness – the Bible."[10]

Christian Superpowers? The problem with our perception of superpowers is that it is very easy to magnify their mistakes and minimise their achievements. As Gibbon wrote in *The Decline and Fall of the Roman Empire*, 'There exists in human nature a strong propensity to depreciate the advantages, and to magnify the evils of the present times.' Antagonists of any superpower could easily publish a catalogue of crimes, failures and flops, and proponents could equally build a case for the opposite. In this book we are not examining the record of superpowers, but rather considering the Christian influence within these powers. In the history of the British Empire there are many prime examples of how it was often checked and chastised by Christianity. William Wilberforce and David Livingstone are perhaps two of the greatest examples of how Christianity used empire as a vehicle for advancing Christian values. These men were able to see the evil within and without, and had the ability to motivate the masses to bring change. Britain and her empire were invariably shaped by the Christian ethos and this influence was spread in two ways – the direct and indirect.

Direct Christian Influence: The direct Christian influence within the British Empire is that which can be clearly determined and studied. For example, British Christians became successful at influencing politics by mobilising the vast streams of Christian opinion and by working with believers in key positions of power. They managed to end the slave trade and protect workers' rights etc., because they found how to work the system for the means of advancing Christian values. The direct influence of Christians is found in historical documents, from ending the burning of widows in India, to promoting education and healthcare, to advancing human rights at home and abroad.

An Imperative Duty: When David Livingstone mapped the unknown regions of Africa, he did so believing that British influence could end the terrors of slavery and bring legitimate commerce to the continent. After having the opportunity to redeem some local slaves, he had a personal vision of British Christians redeeming the continent; "I have a strong desire to commence a system of colonisation among the honest poor; I would give £2000 or £3000 for the purpose. Colonisation from such a country as ours ought to be one of hope, not of despair. It ought not to be looked on as the last shift a family can come to, but the performance of an imperative duty to our blood, our country, our religion and to human-kind...in no part of the world I have been in, does the prospect seem so inviting and promise so much influence."[11]

David Livingstone's vision was for a sacrificial fatherly form of colonisation, with Western Christians arriving in Africa to give, expecting nothing in return. However, when political colonisation came and Western businessmen arrived seeking to profit from Africa, at the expense of the locals, Livingstone's vision soon died; and in response it was British Christians who reported back to Britain what was happening and called for justice. The author found in the National Museum in Botswana, that in 1895, Cecil Rhodes attempted to gain control of the territory and Prime Minister Chamberlain showed little interest in helping. In response, Christians in England fought to give the locals a voice where it most mattered – in the British parliament. The museum explains how the local leaders 'gained much public sympathy throughout Britain through public meetings organised by missionaries like W.C. Willoughby, forcing Chamberlain to reconsider.'[12] Lonely Planet's guide to Botswana continues: 'As a last resort they turned to the London Missionary Society (LMS) which in turn took the matter to the British public...pressure mounted and the government was forced to concede.'[13]

Indirect Christian Influence: The indirect Christian influence of the British Empire is that which cannot be immediately traced back to the faith, but by further study reveals its Christian roots. The British established political, economical, financial and scientific hegemony around the world, and by doing so they unintentionally replicated the undertide of Christian values and exported them to other civilisations.

When Britons decipher their history they discover that for over a thousand years the Christian faith was redefining their values and beliefs – this ultimately expressed itself in British civilisation. Their politics and law etc., became infused with the Judeo-Christian ethic. By exporting this civilisation to much of the world – a British legal system, a British educational system and as independence arrived, a British political system, the empire itself was carbon copying the Christian influence within British life into her colonies. In Britain, Christians had fought for a solid legal framework which would protect their rights; as British law penetrated India, these rights were slowly transferred to Indian citizens. It is of no small significance that Gandhi (1869-1948) and others that won Indian independence were lawyers trained in the British legal profession. As another example, for many years in England there was a strong Christian voice that helped create parliamentary democracy; upon independence, the rights that believers had fought for at home, were immediately transferred to every Indian. The historian Niall Ferguson wrote: 'Without the influence of British imperial rule, it is hard to believe that the institutions of parliamentary democracy would have been adopted by the majority of states in the world, as they are today. India, the world's largest democracy, owes more than it is fashionable to acknowledge to British rule. Its elite schools, its universities, its civil service, its army, its press and its parliamentary system all still have discernable British models.'[14]

Around The World In One Empire: "I have made the earth ...and have given it to whom it seemed proper to Me...now I have given all these lands to Nebuchadnezzar the King of Babylon...all nations shall serve him" (Jeremiah 27:5-7).

The most remarkable thing about the British Empire was its sheer size. If politics allowed and overland transport was available, it would be possible to travel North West from Singapore through Asia, into the Middle East to Israel and South into Africa, all the way down to the tip of South Africa, without ever leaving soil that was at one time administered by the British! If we allowed sea voyages as well, we could sail from New Zealand to Australia, then hit Singapore to take the overland route; from the Cape in South Africa we head North into the Caribbean and former British North America. In Canada, we head West to the coast, then sail through the old colonies in the Pacific, back to where we started in New Zealand! In all of these countries that the British administered, traces can be found of the direct and indirect Christian influence.

It is popular to decry missionaries for a perceived complicity with the sins of empires, but this is not the testimony of the citizens of colonies. The author discovered a publication in Malawi from the government which showed the direct and indirect influence of Christian missionaries, it stated: 'David Livingstone was an extraordinary man. If the Victorian British public took him to their hearts as a missionary, explorer / hero and modest family man, the Africans saw him as a saviour, a man of iron will and unflinching bravery, a medicine man who gave his life for the betterment of the African.'[15] They also credited him as being the informal founder of their nation: Livingstone is 'often credited with laying the groundwork for the country that was to become Malawi...he was in turn, followed by a stream of missionaries and businessmen.'[16] On the author's visit to the tiny landlocked nation of Swaziland in Southern Africa, he found once again an example of how Christianity used empire as a vehicle to spread itself. The Swaziland national anthem proudly declares: "O Lord our God, bestower of the blessings of the Swazi: we give Thee thanks for all our good fortune; we offer thanks and praise for our king and for our fair land, its hills and rivers. Thy blessings be on all rulers of our country; might and power are Thine alone; we pray Thee to grant us wisdom without deceit or malice. Establish and fortify us, Lord Eternal."[17] The Island of Zanzibar is perhaps an interesting illustration of how British Christian morals and the means of the state found themselves infused. After the British had outlawed slavery, the Islamic world continued trading slaves and the two cultures collided. The former was forced to concede when the Royal Navy was called upon to use its military might to destroy the crumbling network of the slave trade around the world. The expert James Walvin notes in *Black Ivory*: 'Between 1820 and 1870 the Royal Navy seized almost 1,600 ships and freed 150,000 slaves.' Today one third of the world's population still live in nations where their political institutions, society and even geographic boundaries were shaped by Britain – which was in turn transformed by Christians. These British institutions were forged in the heat of Christian influence and exported to the world via empire. They may appear secular, but in fact, the Christian spirit and ethic is often at their source.

American Superpower: Benjamin Franklin (1706-1790) helped draw up the Declaration of Independence and the Constitution; he did so believing in a God who raises powers and nations. "God governs in the affairs of man. And if a sparrow cannot fall to the ground without His notice, is it probable that an empire can rise without His aid? We have been assured in the Sacred Writings that except the Lord build the house, they labour in vain that build it. I firmly believe this. I also believe that, without His concurring aid, we shall succeed in this political building no better than the builders of Babel."[18]

The British Empire began with Richard Hakluyt's call, inspired by Psalm 107:23-24 to go out in ships and build a Protestant empire, beginning in North America. Later when Victorians in Britain saw the empire double in size, they believed that their global standing was not down to chance or good luck, but rather many believed they had been made powerful by God to fulfil a specific Christian purpose on earth. The Christianisation of Africa, parts of Asia and the Pacific are in many ways, their interpretation of that purpose. In the same way, the American superpower began with a distinct Christian purpose.

The Mayflower pilgrims undertook their mission 'for the glory of God and the advancement of the Christian faith' planting the first colony in the Northern parts of Virginia. They were not the first Europeans to arrive in North America, but the Mayflower Compact did become the first basis of English written law in the North American colonies. Just as the British believed they were called by God for such a time as this, so too many in America believed that the rising of the American nation was to fulfil a specific Christian purpose on earth. The vision of the English colonists was to build a Christian civilisation which would glorify God and spread the values of the gospel. In the first charter granted to Virginia, the vision was laid bare – 'We, greatly commending, and graciously accepting of, their desires for the furtherance of so noble a work, which may, by the Providence of Almighty God, hereafter tend to the glory of his divine majesty, in propagating of Christian religion to such people, as yet live in darkness and miserable ignorance of the true knowledge and worship of God.'[19] After independence in 1776, America rose as a power which cherished liberty, but was content to build a sea of freedom at home, apart from the rest of the world, which continued until 1941. President John Quincy Adams said, "The people of the North American union and of its constituent States, were associated bodies of civilized men and Christians in a state of nature...they were bound by the laws of God, which they all, and by the laws of the gospel, which they nearly all, acknowledged as the rules of their conduct."[20]

A Christian Nation: During this period, as America grew, the influence of Christianity was felt in every area. George

Washington (1732-1799), the first president of the United States said, "It is impossible to rightly govern the world without God and the Bible." President John Quincy Adams (1767-1848) said, "The first and almost only book deserving of universal distinction is the Bible. I speak as a man of the world, to the men of the world and I say to you, search the Scriptures!" President Andrew Jackson (1767-1845) said, "That book, sir, is the rock on which our republic rests." U.S. President Grant (1822-1885) continued this faith in the Bible, with his belief that Christianity is the source of American freedom saying, "The Bible is the sheet-anchor of our liberties."[21] Perhaps these sentiments can be best summed up by James Madison (1751-1836) the fourth president of the United States who said, "We have staked the whole future of American civilization, not upon the power of government, far from it. We've staked the future of all our political institutions upon our capacity...to sustain ourselves according to the Ten Commandments of God."[22]

Nevertheless, there have always been Americans who have been opposed to the idea of the U.S. being a Christian nation. Charles Carroll (1737-1832), a signatory of the Declaration of Independence wrote to James McHenry (1753-1816), the U.S. Secretary of War – 'Without morals a republic cannot subsist any length of time; they therefore who are decrying the Christian religion, whose morality is so sublime and pure...are undermining the solid foundation of morals, the best security for the duration of free governments.'[23] In 1799, Jedidiah Morse (1761-1826), a historian of the American Revolution said, "To the kindly influence of Christianity we owe that degree of civil freedom and political and social happiness which mankind now enjoys. All efforts made to destroy the foundations of our holy religion ultimately tend to the subversion also of our political freedom and happiness."[24] Two hundred years later these battles continue, despite this nearly two-thirds of the population still believe the U.S. was founded as a Christian nation. All fifty State Constitutions refer to God or a higher power, and a poll from the First Amendment Center showed 65% of Americans believe the founders intended the U.S. to be a Christian nation, and 55% polled thought the U.S. Constitution itself establishes America as a Christian nation.[25] In another poll, 90% of respondents voted to keep the phrase 'under God' in the Pledge of Allegiance.[26] *Time* magazine wrote: 'Americans remain, to the continuing bafflement of other Westerners, stubbornly religious – a consistent 85% tell pollsters at the Pew Research Center that religion is an important part of their life. And for the most part, they don't separate religion from the political sphere. In those same polls, 70% of Americans say they want their president to be a person of faith.'[27]

A New Protestant Global Power: The role of the United States in the world changed dramatically during the Second World War. The Arsenal of Democracy radio broadcast marked the decline of the isolationist and non-interventionist foreign policy of the United States. President Franklin D. Roosevelt (1882-1945) said, "Some of us like to believe that even if Great Britain falls (to Nazi Germany), we are still safe, because of the broad expanse of the Atlantic and of the Pacific…if Great Britain goes down, the Axis powers will control the continents of Europe, Asia, Africa, Australia and the high seas, and they will be in a position to bring enormous military and naval resources against this hemisphere."[28] The American public responded and Winston Churchill was hailed as a hero, as the leader of 'the spearhead of resistance to world conquest.' All of a sudden, the U.S. and Great Britain began to focus on their mutual values – these two nations share a common language, a belief in democracy, the rule of law, freedom of speech and of the press etc. In addition they both have a long history of Protestant Christian belief which gave them both a sense of duty towards the world, infused with a concern for justice and human rights.

The British believed their empire had made the world a better place by removing vile dictators, failed governments and inhuman customs all over the world. The legacy of schools, hospitals, churches, legal institutions and modern infrastructure is their testimony. But now as the British Empire was crumbling under the cost of WWII, America joined with Britain and then led the world to defy the awful alternatives which wanted to replace British rule. The mantle of global leadership had changed hands and so too had the sense of Christian vision. In the twentieth century, America rose to become the primary agent to defy and dismantle the most horrific regimes that the world has ever witnessed. Fascism, in its forms in Italy and Germany was crushed. In Asia, the rape of China and other nations was halted as the violent empire of Japan was stopped and re-shaped. By the late 1980s, the dark shadow of Communism was forced back until finally the Soviet Union collapsed. Many in America felt that all of these experiences were the expression of their destiny to spread democracy and liberty to the ends of the earth. In the twenty-first century, the spiritual sentiment that America has a destiny to end tyranny found itself expressed clearly in the second inaugural address of President G.W. Bush: "It is the policy of the United States to seek and support the growth of democratic movements and institutions in every nation and culture, with the ultimate goal of ending tyranny in our world."[29]

America's concern for spreading political and religious liberty around the world must be understood in the light that nations which practice these freedoms for all do not constitute a threat to the peace of the wider world. Senator John McCain said, "Our nation was founded on Judeo-Christian values and principles," and, "our Judeo-Christian principles dictate that we do what we can to help people who are oppressed throughout the world...we can't right every wrong, but we can do what America has done throughout our history, and that is be a beacon of hope and liberty and freedom for everyone in the world – as Ronald Reagan used to quote (from Matthew 5:14), 'a shining city on a hill.' "[30]

During President Abraham Lincoln's second inaugural address, using 'only 701 words, Lincoln quoted the Bible four times, named God fourteen times and invoked prayer three times.'[31] President Barack Obama selected the same Bible for his inauguration which Lincoln used in 1861. In Obama's speech he quoted 1 Corinthians 13:11, "It is time 'to set aside childish things' " saying, "The time has come to reaffirm our enduring spirit, to choose our better history to carry forward that precious gift, that noble idea passed on from generation to generation, the God-given promise that all are equal, all are free, and all deserve a chance to pursue their full measure of happiness...This is the source of our confidence – the knowledge that God calls on us to shape an uncertain destiny...and with our eyes fixed on the horizon and God's grace upon us, we carried forth that great gift of freedom and delivered it safely to future generations."[32]

Christian Vision: Americans just like the British before them have been filled with Protestant zeal for evangelism at home and mission work abroad. In 1740, in British America, the English revivalist George Whitefield preached the gospel on the Boston Common during the height of the Great Awakening (1735-1760). Two hundred and ten years later, on 23 April, a crowd of 50,000 came out to listen to another preacher sharing the same message and values. The preacher was Billy Graham. By the end of the twentieth century, Americans had assembled the largest mission force which the world had ever known. One quarter of the global mission force can still be attributed to American Christians, as well as the financial backing of much of the new indigenous mission movement.

China: Zhong Guo or Middle Kingdom as it is called by its citizens, is proud of its five thousand years of civilisation, and during 500AD-1500AD China was the world's leading power. Chinese inventions include paper, the first printing press, gunpowder and the compass. But of course, things went terribly wrong. European nations later overtook China and between 1840-1940, the nation experienced what it calls The Century of Humiliation. Beginning with the British, the Chinese were time and again defeated by Western powers and made to concede to their wishes. Then the Japanese arrived. In December 1937 Nanking fell – soldiers were ordered to 'kill all captives' and around 300,000 non-combatants were butchered. China was brought to its knees. After World War II, the early Communist era filled the power-vacuum, but brought unending suffering to the Chinese people, as forty million people starved from failed land reforms, and the Cultural Revolution left the nation bereft of its best and brightest. By the 1980s China began to slowly open up to the world and reform – the result is a superpower awakening. Napoleon rightly said of China, "When the sleeping dragon awakes, she will shake the world." The Beijing Olympic Games of 2008 were designed to send a clear message to the world – China is back. It has the world's largest population, the largest army, the fastest growing major economy, a U.N. veto, nuclear weapons and has a vision to put a human on Mars.

On the author's visit to China, he visited many of the sites associated with the influence of Christianity upon the nation and was able to witness the breakneck speed of its development. But back when China was struggling to keep up with the modern world, it was Christian missionaries who brought the best of the

West to their nation. David Bonavia, an expert on China wrote: 'The most important religious influence on modern China has been Christianity, not principally through conversions, but through scientific and political ideas that were brought to China by missionaries. Western medicine, Western ethical concept, Western music, sport and ideas about democracy – all to a large extent imported by the missionaries.'[33] It should come as no surprise then, that Sun Yatsen (1866-1924), the Father of the Nation and founder of the republic of China was a Christian whose ambitions seemed to be more Western. The source of these Western aspirations can be traced back to his education in a British Christian school. Sadly though, China's first modern political leader died without realising the dream of a strong, united modern China. Others rose to power and the nation turned away from the path to democracy. However, the Christian missionary endeavour continued.

In Asia, those who flock to Christianity do so for many reasons. In India, the author found that many of the new converts come from 'the untouchable' cast. These new believers appreciate the elevation of status that is found in being 'created in the image of God.' But in China, many of the Christian converts (as is the case in Singapore, Hong Kong and South Korea) are highly educated. For many in China, Christianity is considered as the 'religion of progress, modernity, business and science' – the source of Western strength and pre-eminence. The early missionaries may not have had immediate success in converting the masses in China, but after they were forced to leave in the 1950s, something began happening underground.

Decades after Christian missionary work was deemed largely 'unsuccessful,' the Chinese Church began to emerge as one of the strongest and largest in the world. Protestantism has been growing faster in China than any other belief system, yet finding accurate statistics, whilst the Chinese Church is persecuted, is a problem. Officially, the state approved Three-Self Patriotic Movement estimates that China currently has sixteen million Protestants and three million Catholics. But this is an inaccurate picture of the entire Church.

A few years ago, the author received a presentation of the underground Church in China from a British Christian organisation. They brought back first-hand accounts of the phenomenal growth of Christianity in the country; which included the story of a nineteen year old girl, who after conversion shared the message with friends and family, and within a year became the de-facto senior pastor of a congregation several hundred strong. This explosive church growth is happening all over the country. According to the president of the China Christian Council, one of the greatest problems that the Three-Self Patriotic Movement faces is that, "Christianity is growing too fast...we cannot catch up with the growth of the quantity of the believers," said Gao Fend. The concern is that there is a dire shortage of pastors, teachers and Bibles.[34] By the late 1990s, Chinese house Church leaders said there were at least eighty million Christians in the House Church Movement alone.[35]

David Aikman, former Beijing Bureau Chief for *Time* magazine estimated there is 'a growth rate of 7 percent annually'[36] and if this substantial expansion continues 'Christians will constitute 20 to 30 percent of China's population within three decades.'[37] Years later China Aid reported: 'Ye Xiaowen, Director of China's State Administration for Religious Affairs (SARA), claimed behind closed doors in 2006 that the combined total (of all Christians) is closer to 130 million.'[38] Zhao Xiao, a former Communist Party official and convert to Christianity speaking to the *Economist* agreed there are up to 130 million Christians in China saying, "If you want to know what China will be like in the future, you have to consider the future of Christianity in China."[39] How these Christians will exercise their influence could be one of the defining factors in the shaping of modern China. David Aikman 'discovered that there are deputy provincial governors, judges and lawyers in China who are Christians, and that legal experts were working hard behind the scenes to try to implement laws of religious freedom and the larger concept of the rule of law.' In addition 'there are Christian entrepreneurs at every level of Chinese society,' and, 'Christian actors, singers...and journalists' etc. The list goes on from students to scholars, soldiers to officials and mentions that Christian schools, orphanages and hospitals are all over China.[40]

Will China Be Christianised? Caution is needed when we attempt to measure the size of the Chinese Church, yet one thing is certain Christianity is booming in China. If these figures are accurate and if growth continues at these rates, China could be walking down the same path as South Korea, ending up with a significant percentage of the population being Christian – enough to shape China's destiny. China is already the Bible printing capital of the world and they are already planning the largest mission force in history.[41]

The Christian Influence: It appears that Christianity has its greatest impact upon a nation when two factors are taken into account. The first is the substantial mobilisation of the Christian community by great leaders to change the social landscape and culture – such as happened in Britain with John Wesley or William Booth. The second is when devout Christians enter into public life and exercise huge influence upon policy, based upon their fundamental Christian values – such as William Wilberforce and Lord Shaftesbury. This has already happened in Britain, America and recently in South Korea; only time will tell if this will be the case in China.

The Future: China is increasingly important and the *Global Trends Report*[42] by the U.S. National Intelligence Council predicts that U.S. economic, military and political dominance will continue to decline. Therefore the shared values between China and the U.S. will be crucial for world peace and prosperity.

Christianity could aid in bringing China and the West together because the values the West cherishes may be embraced by millions of Chinese Christians – leading to the shared heritage faith brings to cultures. "The very concept of freedom, including religious freedom, has ancient Christian roots," said former U.S. federal judge Ken Starr, "contrary to popular perceptions, the precursors for modern ideas of liberty are rooted in Jewish scripture and the writings of early Christians such as St Paul, Tertullian and Lactantius. Notions of universal human dignity and freedom were developed by medieval scholastics and Protestant reformers, and were first codified in the American founding. In the late second and early third centuries, Tertullian became the first thinker in history to use the phrase 'religious liberty,' and, furthermore, to argue that religious liberty is a human right belonging to all people regardless of class or creed. A hundred years after Tertullian's invention of the concept, it formed the basis of the Edict of Milan of 313, which granted religious freedom to all sects throughout the Roman Empire.'[43]

Chapter Twenty-Three

Capitalism – Creating Wealthy, Productive Nations

'Now it shall come to pass, if you diligently obey the voice of the Lord your God...that the Lord your God will set you high above the nations of the earth. And all these blessings shall come upon you and overtake you' (Deuteronomy 28:1-2).

By the beginning of the twentieth century it was becoming obvious that a few nations had dominated the last three centuries of global economic and scientific progress. Whilst millions of people were living in inefficient, non-productive failed states which had maintained a body of poverty for generations, the Christian West was experiencing progress which was unparalleled in human history. It was especially evident that Protestant Christian nations since their creation were at the fore of progress. Great Britain had dominated the nineteenth century and pioneered the industrial age in the eighteenth, Germany was growing and the U.S. was fast becoming a giant who would later own much of the twentieth century.

Political economist Professor Max Weber believed he knew why the Protestant nations were so successful. In his book *The Protestant Ethic and the Spirit of Capitalism* he concluded that the economic dominance of the Protestant nations was to be credited to the Protestant work ethic. He noted that capitalism emerged when the Protestant work ethic encouraged the masses to engage in enterprise and trade which led to the creation of wealth. Weber's ideas found an affinity amongst those who witnessed the Protestant nations succeeding, whilst other nations were failing. William Petty, Montesquieu, Henry Thomas Buckle, John Keats and other experts have noted the link between Protestantism and the development of commercialism. Examples of the call to the Protestant work ethic can be found in the teachings of many Protestant leaders.

The teaching of the Reformation including the priesthood of all believers encouraged the faithful to consider their career as a way of serving God. Martin Luther revealed that the farmer was serving God just as the priest was; therefore, if the farmer pursued his best he was honouring God. William Hogarth (1697-1764) used art to encourage hard work, thrift and honesty. In

1747, he embodied the Protestant work ethic in twelve engravings which reveal the life of two apprentices – the hard working man succeeds, the lazy man's life ends in failure. John Wesley (1703-1791) encouraged each individual to pursue his personal best by scorning idleness and encouraging work. He wrote *Early Rising* which called people into action with hard work and thrift. Sir Thomas Foxwell Buxton (1786-1845) was an evangelical reformer and one of his famous sayings was, "Laziness grows on people; it begins in cobwebs and ends in iron chains." Proverbs 10:4 states: 'He who has a slack hand becomes poor, but the hand of the diligent makes rich.'

Sociologists believe these types of writings are a practical formulation of the Protestant work ethic, which led to the economic dominance of the Protestant nations. Christian exhortation to work hard, led to unplanned and uncoordinated mass action which created capitalism. Capitalism motivated the individual to achieve his personal best in all fields, knowing that his labour would be rewarded with better standards of living. As individuals pursued their most proficient attainment, these Christian nations created unparalleled advancement and productivity. Christian nations with a heritage of non-conformity were also lands that cherished liberty, for freedom was essential for the development of capitalism. In a free nation, everyone can benefit from higher standards of living, as entrepreneurs create wealth and jobs for all; in a tyranny the few benefit from the labour of all. If people are not free, then there is no reason to work hard because the state could confiscate all without question. But in free nations people can maximize their rewards by achieving their true productivity.

The Protestant work ethic was most notable in the U.K., Germany, Holland and the U.S. It inspired citizens to be successful, creating a climate in which being wealthy was not a sin, after all, the poor needed help whilst the well-off could help others. *Time* magazine named Niall Ferguson of Harvard and Oxford, as one of the world's hundred most influential people;[1] in his book *Empire* he revealed, 'Between 1757 and 1947 British per-capita gross domestic product increased in real terms by 347 percent'[2] and, 'by 1880 Britain's share of the world's manufacturing production was 23 percent.'[3] 'Thanks to the unrivalled productivity of her shipyards, Britain owned roughly a third of the world's merchant tonnage. At no other time in history has one power so completely dominated the world's oceans as Britain did during the mid-nineteenth century...if the British wished to abolish the slave trade, they simply sent the navy.'[4]

Britain for most of the eighteenth and nineteenth centuries was, according to Niall Ferguson, 'the most successful economy in the world.'[5] One needs to bear in mind that a nation which covers a flyspeck of the earth's surface should never have, according to any logic, become for over a century the world's most successful economy. The earth's total surface area is 510,065,284 km²; Britain's total area is 242,900 km², making it 79th in the world's nations sorted by area. The U.S. is the fourth largest nation, with 9,629,091 km².[6] Britain's repositioning in global standing during the twentieth century (according to her size and population) was inevitable – it was her rise to the status of economic superpower which seems inconceivable.

Throughout the last three hundred years the link between Protestant Christianity and the impact upon the world by Protestant nation states is remarkable. Pioneering Protestant nations during the eighteenth and nineteenth centuries made their impact around the globe whilst other nations were asleep. Holland once packed a punch far above its own size, Great Britain dominated the world despite being a tiny island off mainland Europe, Germany became an industrious nation and the United States with a very small percentage of the world's population has dominated the globe since WWII.

In the Catholic world poverty and godliness were often presented as co-heirs of spirituality, but for Protestants, they began to believe wealth could be a sign that God was blessing their hard labour. Traditionally this led to other developed nations with a Catholic heritage, such as Italy and France to have a laid-back attitude pertaining to work. In Catholic nations some have suggested that, "We feel uncomfortable with wealth." French President Sarkozy tried to change this culture and reform France's stagnant economy with slogans like, "Work more to earn more." In the Protestant nations Christians often have the opposite view to Catholic nations, believing that only by being wealthy will they be in a position to help others. It was citizens of wealthy Christian nations who had the money to send out missionaries, as well as starting schools and hospitals around the globe. Large numbers of schools and hospitals worldwide are still run and paid for by Christians.

The rise of the U.S. expanded after her Civil War (1861-1865), but it was the twentieth century which is considered as America's century – for Europe bankrupted itself fighting. The allies spent their money in America buying weapons to win and necessities to survive two world wars, and after WWII, the U.S. loaned many nations the money to rebuild, and it was this transfer of wealth in the first half of the twentieth century which played a role in helping her to become an economic and military giant. Britain began the twentieth century as the World's Banker and was bankrupted twice fighting Germany. Only the U.S. walked away from war with significant economic and militarily growth. The U.S. set up bases and global supply industries for its military during the war, and Coca-Cola is just one company which became a world player when the U.S. government helped it build factories around the world to supply the troops. When the troops went home, these factories supplied the locals. After 1945, Europe was struggling to get back on her feet, whilst the U.S. turned its industry from military production to making goods for consumers, and soon it was flooding the world with its products. By the end of the century, the U.S. share of total output was 22 percent[7] and her economy is still the largest the world has ever known. The U.S. is another great example of the Protestant work ethic in action. Stephen McDowell, President of the Providence Foundation said, "Our economic philosophy, principles of individual enterprise, benefiting from the fruit of your labour and the concept of wanting to labour hard are all rooted in the Bible."[8]

Capitalism, as it evolved from the 1980s onwards has changed dramatically from its foundations, which initially sought to provide equal access for all to the market, and by doing so, enabled prices to lower for all, especially with mass production. Dr Michael Schluter wrote: 'Capitalism, it is argued, rests largely on Christian values. According to its early proponents like Adam Smith, it takes account of the sinfulness of the human heart. So rather than rely on the state to allocate resources and fix prices where human greed can too easily play a part, impersonal markets determine these outcomes. The greed of any individual is constrained, in effect, by the enterprise of others through the mechanism of the market. Indeed, biblical teaching assumes free markets for exchange of goods and services, providing only that the conduct of markets is just and fair and that traders do not hoard food in periods of shortage. In addition, for human beings to reflect fully the image of their Maker, they must have the opportunity to exercise responsibility, to make choices, to experience liberty.'[9] The BBC's *The Protestant Revolution* examined this process in action by showing how Protestant Christianity 'developed modern work and business practices as well as providing the intellectual and financial impetus to launch the Industrial Revolution.'[10] Christians not only helped create capitalism, but they led the West to put people's rights before profit, thus bringing in good business practices. The historian Tristram Hunt noted, "Our modern world owes a profound debt to Protestantism."

There are many opponents of capitalism and balancing global wealth to benefit all will be a constant challenge for all generations. However, it's worth considering that Western style capitalism has done more to bring millions of Chinese people out of poverty in the last twenty years, than two hundred years of charity. The same was true of Britain in the past; previously the individual could spend more than half a week's wages on the most basic food – today in Britain the average wage is amongst the highest in the world. In Britain during the twentieth century, capitalism's excesses were curbed by creating an economic climate which encouraged entrepreneurs to produce wealth and jobs, whilst at the same time having regulations to protect workers' rights and to redistribute wealth to the needy. Paul Collier, Professor of Economics at Oxford University suggests that in the last thirty years, one billion people have been lifted out of poverty by countries adopting the capitalist-inspired trading system.[11]

However, in the twenty-first century, the near collapse of the global banking system, through greed and unsustainable debt, which fuelled unrelenting reckless consumption, shows how very far capitalism has gone from the spirit of the hard working thrifty Christian pioneers. Also, since the 1980s most people feel like powerless spectators in economies run by capitalist leaders of multinationals, who have rejected traditional values to embrace a culture of pushing down wages whilst demanding more. This had led to the relative impoverishment of the masses, by transferring wealth from the poor and middle classes, to create the new capitalists 'aristocracy' at the top. An Oxfam study in 2014 found that 85 global billionaires now own the equivalent wealth of 3.5 billion people – that's half the world's population![12] Another Oxfam study found in Britain that five of our richest families own more wealth than the poorest 12.6 million.[13]

Following the Protestant Model: In the twenty-first century there are those who study wealthy non-Christian nations around the world, hoping to find ways to discredit the Christian influence in creating capitalism. We must remember that the nations which developed capitalism were Christian. The influence of Christianity in developing an economic model that was successful should not be discredited because other nations followed its example. Put simply, if it works, copy it!

In the 1950s book *Asia and the West*, Maurice Zinkin of the Indian Civil Service explained that in traditional Asia the trader was of low rank, whilst in the West people embraced trade because of their faith. He wrote that Christian 'traders feel that their business is honourable. It is work approved by God. (This attitude is found especially in Protestant countries). By contrast, in traditional India the merchant ranked below the teacher and soldier. In China he ranked below the peasant and artisan.'[14] First we discover that non-Christian nations had to embrace a secular form of the Protestant work ethic and second, they had to learn from the West's technical expertise. The historian J.A. Williamson wrote of Japan: 'They realised that they must adopt Western methods or go under. In 1867-8...they sent picked bodies of young men to Europe to study engineering, manufacturing and war. They engaged European instructors to teach them the same things in Japan.'[15] Then the Japanese government sent out the famous Iwakura Mission diplomatic team in 1871, to gather information from all the major Western powers on education, technology and economic structures etc., in order to begin the modernisation of Japan. With this knowledge Japan built the world's first non-Christian industrial state and they used their new-found power for evil. After World War II, Japan was given a new peaceful constitution by the Protestant United States and it modelled its new economy largely on the American structure. Malaysia, Hong Kong,

Singapore, India, South Africa, as well as Christian Canada, Australia and New Zealand were all shaped by Protestant Britain. South Korea's rapid economic rise also coincided with the rapid rise of Christianity within its population. The United States prolific investment into every country possible, can also explain much of the growth around the world.

China and India: When a scholar from one of China's premier academic research institutes, the Chinese Academy of Social Sciences was asked to research why the West had emerged with pre-eminence over the world, they examined, "Everything we could from the historical, political, economic and cultural perspective." Their final conclusion was that "the Christian moral foundation of social and cultural life was what made possible the emergence of capitalism and then the successful transition to democratic politics." They finished by saying, "We don't have any doubt about this."[16] Today in China, after the failure of Communism's economic model, the nation is following the economic model the Protestant nations developed. If China can sustain her growth, she is set to be the world's largest economic superpower by 2022.[17] India is also one of the rising economic powers of this century, with her strength in technology and services, whilst China's is manufacturing. However, it is going to take possibly a hundred years of rapid development in these great nations to provide living standards for everyone of their citizens, such as are now experienced in the West. In China 2008, the average wage was 'only about £1,000'[18] and a fifth of the population – more than 300 million people, lived on less than a dollar a day, whilst 0.4% of the Chinese possess 70% of the nation's wealth.'[19] India as well, still has countless millions of citizens who live in terrible poverty and per-capita income remains far below the developed world. China and India's economies will be massive because their populations are huge, but the challenges ahead for these developing nations are immense. These examples teach us something; in the twenty-first century the economic model which developed in the Protestant nations will be duplicated because it succeeded whilst other models failed. Being Protestant is not a requirement of following the example of these nations. The rising economic giants of the twenty-first century may well be non-Christian by historic religious tradition, but they will be following the economic model which Christian nations developed.

Chapter Twenty-Four

The Industrial Revolution and Compassionate Capitalism

'As for every man to whom God has given riches and wealth and given him power to eat of it, to receive his heritage and rejoice in his labour – this is the gift of God...God keeps him busy with the joy of his heart' (Ecclesiastes 5:19-20).

The Industrial Revolution was a major shift of technological, 'socioeconomic and cultural conditions in the eighteenth century. It began in Great Britain and spread throughout Europe, America and later the world. During that time, an economy based on manual labour was replaced by one dominated by industry and manufactured machinery. It began with the mechanisation of the textile industries, the development of iron-making techniques and the increased use of refined coal. Trade expansion was enabled by the introduction of canals, improved roads and railways. The introduction of steam power and powered machinery, mainly in textile manufacturing, underpinned the dramatic increases in production capacity. The development of all metal machine tools in the first two decades of the nineteenth century facilitated the manufacture of more production machines for manufacturing in other industries.'[1]

Non-Conformist Pioneers: In British history non-Anglican Bible-believing Christians were often known as non-conformists, because they rejected the established expression of religion and often politics too. Their views did not win them any friends in the public sector and this often led to Christians being excluded from universities, forcing many of them out of this route to traditional positions of power. These believers put their energy into manufacturing and industry which led to them being the forerunners of much of today's science and technology.

Before the Industrial Revolution the world looked backward hoping that one day they would rediscover the glory of Rome. The Father of Humanism, Francesco Petrarca (1304-1374), believed the Roman Empire would rise again in some form and restore classical cultural purity. However, after this revolution every great nation aspired to amplify this British achievement. The Industrial Revolution was not a project which came from government; it was a movement which emerged from Protestant Britain's hard working citizens. The fundamental 'Triangle' of the Industrial Revolution was textiles, steam power and iron founding. Cotton spinning led to cotton mills, and steam power led to powered machines and semi-automated factories.

One third of the fundamental 'Triangle' of the Industrial Revolution was invented by the Christian, Abraham Darby (1678-1717), who invented coke smelting which furthered the mass production of brass and iron goods. Darby founded the world's first metallurgy laboratory at his Baptist Hills Brass Works factory. His son, Abraham Darby II (1711-1763) built upon his father's achievements and the industrial development of his area exploded. In the next few years there were several world changing developments, including the first cast-iron railways, the first cast-iron bridge and the first steam locomotive designed by Richard Trevithick (1771-1833).

Another third of the fundamental 'Triangle' was transformed by the Christian James Watt (1736-1819), whose improved steam engine was the key innovation which made the Industrial Revolution possible. Without his work, we would have no modern world! It led to locomotives, steam boats and powered factories. He also created a base from which generations of inventors could build from, with new efficient engines. With his business partner Boulton, he manufactured steam engines and by 1823 they had made 1,164 engines which helped make Protestant Britain the world's first industrialised nation and the Workshop of the World. The final part of the fundamental 'Triangle' was textiles. Author and devout Anglican Christian, Samuel Johnson (1709-1784) financed the world's first mill to spin cotton in 1741, which was created by the Christians, John Watt (1700-1766) and Lewis Paul. The idea was perfected by others and famously spread by Richard Arkwright (1733-1792), who was once a partner with non-conformist Christian and pioneer industrialist Jedediah Strutt (1726-1797).

The Spread: In America, Moses Brown (1738-1836), a Christian abolitionist, decided to start his own textile industry. He hired Samuel Slater (1768-1835), an Englishman, who is today known as the Father of the American Industrial Revolution, because he brought British textile technology to America, which quickly spread. When Slater died, his Bible was found with many of his favourite passages referenced.[2]

From Survival To Success: Most of human history has been a battle for human survival, as individuals attempted to provide for themselves, without becoming casualties of famine or other lack. But in Christian nations, new farming techniques helped change the world by abundantly providing for our basic needs in a cheap and productive way. In Britain, between the seventeenth and mid-nineteenth centuries, there was immense growth in farming production, known today as the Agricultural Revolution. Previous to this point the population always grew, but because there was not enough food and poor hygiene, it shrunk again. The new agricultural technology and methodology supplied demand, and allowed population growth to continue. With less workers required and larger populations, people began to invest their energies outside of farming and created demands for goods, which fuelled the Industrial Revolution.

In 1731, Jethro Tull (1674-1741) published *The New Horse Hoeing Husbandry*; at that time seeds were distributed into furrows by hand, but his essay on the *Principles of Tillage and Nutrition* introduced new innovations in thought and technology, which helped lead to productive farming techniques. He was baptised in St Bartholomew's Church, Berkshire and his grave humbly states his achievements in agriculture.

In Virginia, U.S., Cyrus McCormick (1809-1884) designed a harvesting machine which rapidly increased reaping. Labour intensive manual cutting was replaced by a horse-drawn mechanical cutter, which was the forefather of today's industrial farming machines. Previously ninety percent of the population had to farm to survive, but today it's only two percent. McCormick saw his work as a holy calling, inseparable from his walk with God. In 1845 he would write: 'Business is not inconsistent with Christianity; but the latter ought to be a help to the former.' Freed from the soil, Americans were then, and are now, able to focus on other things like industry, transportation, science and full-time Christian service.[3] Improved farming skills and McCormick's time and money saving devices helped more Americans move from survival, to success. With a flourishing business, McCormick used his wealth for God, helping to found the Moody Bible Institute and McCormick Seminary.

Commerce and Christianity: British trade and industry rapidly expanded at the beginning of the railway era and during this time, employers were willing to exploit many in their thirst for profit, but Richard Tangye (1833-1906) was not one of them. Tangye and other Christian capitalists proved by example that wealth and power could be used in the service of mankind, not at the cost of humanity. Richard Tangye and his brothers were engineers who employed thousands of people, and pioneered many great works. He became the head of one of the biggest engineering firms in the world and it was to him that the famous engineer Brunel turned to for help to launch the huge Great Eastern paddle steamer. He believed that Christian employers should set an example to others and share the blessing of wealth; with this in mind he did much to help the lot of the downtrodden worker. In *Yarns on Social Pioneers* by author Ernest Hayes it explains he 'proved a pioneer in improving the conditions of industry, humanising the relations between employer and employee by providing social amenities, education classes, shorter working hours and a system of co-partnership or profit sharing.'[4]

Sweetening The Workers' Lives: George Cadbury (1839-1922) was the son who turned a tea and coffee business into a chocolate empire. When the Cadbury brothers inherited their father's business, the company was in very bad shape. All was in decline, but despite this they felt the workers were not getting paid properly: "If we can't afford to pay our workers a decent wage, we had better shut the place entirely," said George and his brother agreed. Other business men mocked them, suggesting that better wages and more free time would lead to collapse. But they believed that instead of exploiting people, Christian principles should be applied in the work place, which would help create an environment where workers played a part in shaping a successful company, in which all benefited from progress. Things did not go well for a season, but the breakthrough came when the company started to sell a pure cocoa drink and very soon new premises were needed. But instead of building a new factory, the brothers wanted to build a new community! Their plan was to build an estate, with beautiful modern homes, recreation grounds, open work facilities, with plenty of light and air. "It would be the ruin of them," many thought, but the brothers went further, introducing canteens, games rooms, restrooms, guards for machinery, and the factory had a doctor, dentist and nurse ready to help! The factory was a first of its kind: "It is stupid people who only make money," said George Cadbury, "the central doctrine of Christianity is that men and women, rich or poor are infinitely valuable and their lives should not be squandered or exploited. From this it follows that the work of men and women should be well paid."[5] When the Cadbury's chocolate drink was first sold, the brothers hoped it would stop people becoming alcoholics. The *Times Newspaper* of 19 January 1863 said, "The use of strong drink produces more idleness, crime, disease want and misery than all other causes put together."[6] People did not believe it was possible to have happy workers and a thriving business, but the brothers showed that capitalism with Christianity can be good for all. The rights which workers expect as standard today were denied not too long ago, and it was often Christians who set the standard and legislation had to follow.

Joseph Rowntree (1836-1925) was another Christian philanthropist with an edge in business. He was left the family business which had a handful of workers and by specialising in confectionary it grew, and by the early 1900s, there were over four thousand workers. His faith was not in words, but action. His Trust explained: 'He worked to improve adult literacy, and to safeguard democracy and political fair play. Acutely aware of the social conditions many of his factory workers lived in, he was keen to improve the quality of civil life for all through the provision of affordable, decent housing, recreational facilities and opportunities for self-improvement.'[7] Joseph Rowntree learnt the secret of being successful in business whilst providing a fair deal for his workforce. He was a person who believed in getting to the root of social problems at home, and by doing so, health would spring throughout the whole system. When he died in 1925, he left behind a renowned brand, a healthy workforce and a Christian legacy for other business leaders to follow.

Henry Heinz: In the U.S., an industrialist who manufactured and sold processed foods built a global business which reflected his Christian values. Henry Heinz (1844-1919) left twenty-six factories behind him, with over six and a half thousand employees, in more than two hundred premises, which broke new ground in the food industry. Heinz was one of the first in the U.S. to make staff welfare a priority; he included free life insurance, free hospital and dental treatment, educational facilities, dining rooms, dressing rooms and even swimming pools. The road to success was full of hazards and failure, but Heinz built a food empire which would stretch around the world. On his visits to England, he made sure he saw the sites associated with his Christian faith, from Wesley's churches, to Bunyan's grave. He also supported Christian endeavours around the world, including the creation of Sunday schools in Japan and beyond! His Last Will and Testament started with 'a confession of my faith in Jesus Christ as my Saviour.'[8]

Sporting Around: Arnold Hills (1857-1927) was a wealthy London shipbuilder. As a Christian, he was deeply concerned about the way alcoholism was ruining the lives of many – how could a family survive with an abusive father who wasted all their money on drink? He encouraged his workers to sign the pledge to become teetotallers, but he also wanted to give them something healthy to replace the drink. He invested sums of money into creating the work's football pitch and in 1895, he founded the Thames Ironworks Football team; two years later he paid for a new stadium. 'For the team, it was the first step that would take them to world fame and cup-winning glory as West Ham United.'[9]

Creating Wealth: In Protestant Christian nations, a culture was created in which entrepreneurs were given the liberty and licence to succeed. By doing so, they not only created wealth for themselves, but they provided jobs for others, income for the government and investment. Without their skills, the jobs and industries that they created would never have existed. Without their success, many people would have been unemployed. Without employment, workers would have no money to purchase goods and other businesses would go bust. Without the wealth they created, the government would not receive their taxes and investment in education, healthcare and infrastructure etc., would not take place.

The Christian capitalists mentioned here are just a few of many who discovered that by applying Christian principles to the work place, they could balance the creation of wealth, with the rights of the individual. It was Cadbury, Rowntree, Heinz, Hills and others like them who helped set the gold standard in the workplace, not because of compulsion of law, but because of the compulsion of Christ's love. Their examples helped strengthen the argument for changing the law, because they proved that new requirements would not force businesses to close down, but in fact it would strengthen them. A healthy workforce, they proved, could lead to a healthy business. Today, the basic rights of the worker which are now compulsory in the West are still vigorously denied in much of the developing world. Perhaps this will make us stop and think, and be thankful for the leaders who pioneered change, the politicians who fought for new laws and the Christian heritage that made it possible.

A Global Industrial Vision: In the last 300 years, Britain and more recently the U.S., have taken their industrial know-how to the world. The English language itself became known as the language of progress and technology, and the world queued to learn it. 'The ancient Chinese did not lack ingenuity and talent,' wrote one commentator, 'but their philosophies enforced fatalism, not aspiration. To the religions of the Indian subcontinent, reality was an illusion to be dispelled and life a cycle to be transcended.' But in Christian nations the faith itself became an agent of progress. It's hard to imagine the planet three hundred years ago, when the West still knew little about entire continents; but the British believed it was their God-given purpose to take 'Christianity, commerce and civilisation' to every corner of the planet. Consider this – during British rule in India, five times the amount of rail roads were laid compared to her neighbours – the Indian rail and primary road system, including the famous yellow taxi, is all part of the British legacy. Globally, the British brought the rule of law, so that it would be safe for development to begin; roads and transport routes followed – then business could flourish. With wealth and security came an expansion of missionary schools, hospitals and churches etc. All across Africa, to Malaysia and Singapore etc., despite many failings, their vision was often realised and the foundations of many modern nations were laid. The vision of the U.S. is often considered as 'Democracy, capitalism and (by NGO's) Christianity' and they too have had success. Despite the obvious human flaws and the hidden secular agendas, the believers in these two nations thought it was their Christian duty to shape the world, hopefully for the better because God had destined them to have the power to do so. Some would point to the faults of the Christian powers as a reason to question this, but when we consider these things we must ask ourselves – what was the alternatives to these powers? Was Napoleon's France, Nazi Germany or the Japanese Empire a better force than the British Empire? Would the Communist Soviet Union have been a better force than the U.S.? The mistakes of superpowers should not be overlooked, but if we consider what could have been, our perspective soon changes.

Loss of Compassionate Capitalism: During the 1970s/80s, the West's philosophy on capitalism went through a major shift. The thrift and traditional values associated with the West were slowly replaced by exuberant consumerism peddled by unreasonable debt. This era revealed a major shift of values from the Christian pioneers of industry, from those who made products which added value, created jobs and enhanced life, to those who put profit before people. This led to the creation of many new billionaires who now hoard the world's wealth, whilst their workers struggle to keep roofs over their heads.[10]

There is a moral question that needs to be asked of capitalism; how much money does one person need? How many billions, or homes, cars etc., does one person need, when billions struggle on with so little? When the State tried to answer this problem in history, it failed miserably, because it must be asked in the conscience of an individual's heart. In British history, the answer came by Christian capitalists who realised they could produce wealth, whilst paying a decent wage; then to top it off, they gave much of their wealth away, and found true riches of the soul and spirit! Nevertheless, when we ask what has gone wrong with capitalism, we're not truly addressing the core of the issue. The real question is what went wrong inside of us? An economy in its simplest form is the combined economic decisions of the people of that economy. Sadly, the heart of compassionate capitalism, which many Christian pioneers embraced, has often been lost in consumerism, the lust for profits by corporate giants and the titans of globalisation. Yet all is not amiss, the spirit of these early pioneers of industry has not been fully swept away, as there is pressure to encourage each generation to create wealth for the good of humanity, not at the price-tag thereof.

Chapter Twenty-Five

A Fair Deal – Justice Not Charity

'Proclaim liberty throughout all the land to all its inhabitants. It shall be a jubilee for you...he shall be released in the year of Jubilee – he and his children with him' (Leviticus 25:10, 54).

It took hundreds of years for Western countries to develop into free democratic nations, which respect human rights and personal liberty. Corruption, civil wars, failed reforms, incompetent governments and conflict with other nations all hindered this process. It should come as no surprise then, that the very things which hindered the West's development are also working havoc in some nations of the developing world today. Corruption, civil war, failed land reforms and conflict with other nations are some of the reasons why some third world nations have failed to develop whilst others (which gained independence at the same time) are now successful.

By the late 1990s, the wealthy newly independent nations had, by economic prudence, been able to invest, trade and pay-off their debts, but in many countries, corruption wasted the money and many nations have were spiralling out of control. The situation in these countries became tragic, the money was now gone – with little to show for it and the international community wanted their debts paid. This led to huge amounts of the GDP of developing nations being used to service debt interest to the rich. At the same time the international rules for trading seemed to favour the rich. Politics aside, the reality led to millions of people being without an education, healthcare, or even a regular meal. Many families have no access to clean drinking water, sanitation or a home that meets basic needs. In the midst of this crisis two voices were raised. One said these nations had wasted their loans and must repay them, and by doing so they would learn fiscal responsibility; whilst another voice said it was time to stop letting the poorest people in the world, pay with their lives, for the failures of their governments – in other words it's time to cancel the debt and give them a fair deal.

American author Tony Campolo wrote: 'Christians in England, working together across denominational lines, have seriously influenced international policies regarding Third World debts.

When the heads of the G8 nations held a summit in the city of Birmingham in 1998, Christians mobilised tens of thousands of church members to hold a prayer vigil in front of the convention hall where the meetings were held. Clare Short, who was then Britain's secretary of State for international development, told me that it was that church-sponsored prayer vigil that moved the world leaders to make the first efforts toward debt cancellation.[1]

In 2005, British Prime Minister Tony Blair said, "As churches and faith organisations, you also play a significant role in the campaign against international poverty and injustice. Here too you are often direct providers of services. I pay tribute to the wide array of Christian and faith based charities which work across the developing world, in difficult and often dangerous circumstances to bring relief, compassion and hope."[2] Two hundred years earlier, Christians had pioneered the birth of modern campaigning which included celebrity endorsements and logo's. They managed to end the slave trade and slavery itself; now in the twenty-first century, celebrities, churches and charities would follow the same model. They were calling the G8 to give the Third World a chance by cancelling the debt and it truly was an international effort with many calling for justice.

In 2005 there was an unprecedented level of campaigning from the One Campaign in the U.S., which included film stars to Christian leaders, to Make Poverty History[3] in the U.K., with celebrity filled concerts to Church leaders mobilising the faithful. Church leaders amongst others had helped keep these issues alive for several decades and 80 percent of the activists who joined the Make Poverty History campaign were from churches;[4] and now joining hands with concerned celebrities, the campaign went mass-media, as celebrities used their gifts to mobilise the media to draw attention to the cause. A turning point in the campaign came when the eight most powerful leaders in the world came to Britain. Scotland was the host of the G8 and the U.K. held the presidency of the European Union. Prime Minister Tony Blair and Chancellor Gordon Brown were forerunners in shaping the forum. Tony Blair told the broadcaster Fern Britton that the inspiration of the Christian faith, and the solidarity of large numbers of Christians encouraged him to increase development aid and cancel the debt.[5] Later, the serving British Prime Minister Gordon Brown, known as the 'son of the manse'[6] said, "Churches and Christian charities have been Britain's conscience on causes from debt cancellation to child poverty."[7] At the G8, action was promised from debt cancellation, to aid increases, from trade to HIV; this time people called for justice not charity. Four years later, a report confirmed that an estimated 34 million more children now attended school and perhaps three million lives were saved through treatment. But France and especially Italy have failed to keep their commitments. Whilst the U.S., Canada and Japan were, whilst Britain and Germany were trying for more ambitious targets.[8]

Later, when the G20 leaders met in London in 2009, Britain's most prominent religious leaders urged them not to forget their promises to the poorest people in the world. In addition, one of the major Christian projects which is working towards global justice is Micah Challenge, which represents people in over forty nations, who are taking the challenge of Micah 6:8 seriously. Micah Challenge is a global Christian campaign helping the poor and challenging world leaders to 'halve absolute global poverty by 2015.'[9] British Prime Minister Gordon Brown, speaking of the project said, "Micah Challenge is harnessing that faith to unite Christians globally from across Church denominations to deepen that commitment to people living in poverty through prayer, service and advocacy...you (the Church) are already making a huge difference."[10]

In 2010, the serving British Prime Minister Gordon Brown said, "This year we have particular reason to celebrate as 2010 will see...the fifth anniversary of the Gleneagles G8 summit where Christians of every denomination were instrumental in the securing greater justice for the poor. The Christian churches are the conscience of our country, always ready to bear witness to the truth and to remind us of our responsibilities to what the Bible calls 'the least of these.' "[11] The war against poverty will continue, but as U.N. Secretary-General Ban Ki-Moon said, "Christians are 'good allies' in the fight to end global poverty."[12]

Chapter Twenty-Six

The Foundations of Modern Democracy

'He looked for justice, but behold oppression; for righteousness, but behold a cry for help' (Isaiah 5:7).

It's two am in the morning. The sound of unison footsteps marching up the stairs is unmistakable. The noise of their vehicles arriving has paralysed the neighbourhood with fear for decades, and every time the residents hope that they've come for someone else. For many years, we've all heard people being dragged down the stairs screaming for their very lives, but no-one ever tries to help. The last twenty years have been a nightmare. Every person has his or her job, but it does not matter if they like it or not. It's the system that counts, not the person. Industry has been derailed by disenfranchised workers and lack of investment; this has led to shortages and the breakdown of infrastructure. But no-one complains, well, not openly. Even in secret we fear telling our closest friends and family, just in case they tell the authorities and we get taken away. My daughter had to wait for two hours in a queue to get a loaf of bread yesterday, she was quicker than usual. I sometimes envy local leaders, corruption gives them the right to get all they want, but it comes at our cost. Here only the few benefit whilst the majority suffer. My wife died of a terrible disease last year and her sickness was caused by the chemicals she used at work, but we can't demand action or call people to account, and others are still using the same chemicals and falling sick. I came home once to find that many items from my flat had been stolen, they had been commandeered by the government. The local official decided they'd look better in his house than mine. Who do you go to when your leaders are the ones who oppress you? We received a letter three months ago, stating that our building would be knocked down and we had to move to a new flat; it turned out to be half the size of ours. Someone is making lots of money, and it always comes at the expense of our labour and suffering. But I've seen worse; I saw a man gun-downed in the street – but it wasn't a criminal gang, it was local officials. We never read about it in the papers, no criminal investigation began and no-one was charged. Life is cheap here.

For my entire life I've never had a voice. There is no where I can go to complain, no department where I can ask for justice. The rule of law is very simple; it's one rule for them, another for us. I've never been able to remove my government; I've never had a vote. Everyday they tell us we are the greatest nation on earth and we have all we need, but I'm hungry, cold and impoverished. I tried praying once, but I gave that up when my son told me to stop. He told me his friend was a Christian, who was sent to a prison camp for doing the very same thing. Human rights, what are they? I can't even pray without fear. I remember going to church when I was a child, but it was closed by the government. As I silently sign this note for posterity, I want you to know the Christian nations that have democracy are almost right. They may not be perfect, but they are not paralysed with fear, corruption and state criminality like my country. I've never had rights or known liberty. Next time you feel free, remember me, my life and my death – for they are now outside my door.

Liberty and Accountability: Democracy is not just crossing a box in an election, it is the right for every citizen to question the state, demonstrate against wrong, call for action and exercise their rights without fear. Democracy gives citizens the right to have a say about everything which affects their lives and when their government makes a mistake or commits a crime, the people can keep them accountable. For Christians, democracy gives them the right to worship God and practice their religion without state interference, and it lays a foundation for national justice – something which the Old Testament prophets often spoke of. Today, free people can bring change without violence and can remove a government with the click of a pen, instead of the blow of a sword. In a democracy the end of a government is a natural timely event, but in a dictatorship it can be a matter of life and death, bloody revolution or even genocide. Democracy is liberty for the people and accountability for their leaders.

Only in nations with a long Christian history did the blueprint for the modern democratic state develop; no other new foundation led to liberty! Why in a world of 7 billion plus people and over 194 nations and 61 territories, did the modern democratic state only emerge through Christian nations? It's one thing for respected cultures to see beauty in the system and copy it – it's another to develop it. Today, thankfully the world has been turning democratic, but does it realise that democracy was often shaped by Christians who fought for our rights, because they believed in the doctrine of the fundamental equality of all?

Western democracy is a political system in which the supreme power lies in the body of citizens, who elect officials to represent them in government. Competing political parties are formed through the rights of freedom of assembly and speech, and regular elections give voters a chance to elect suitable candidates. The historian J.A. Williamson wrote: 'Unless those in power remember that they will one day be in opposition and behave with tolerance to the views of the minority, the result will be a succession of tyrannies, each bent on uprooting all the works of its predecessor, and each bring the destruction of liberty a step nearer, for the only outcome is a dictatorship or civil war.'[1]

Democracy is 'rule by the people' from the Greek demos, 'people,' and kratos, 'rule or power' – thus we speak of people power. In a democratic state, the government's power over the people is limited and it is kept accountable by them. A free press can expose their failings and reveal corruption, and regular elections force a legal and peaceful change of government. Indirectly, the voter participates in ruling the state.

The word democracy was coined in ancient Greece; Athenian democracy was a classical direct democratic system developed in the Greek city-state of Athens, but it did not last. Aristotle's Constitution of Athens laid claim for every citizen, rich or poor to fully participate in government, but there's a twist, it is estimated that only ten percent of the population were actually citizens![2] Unfortunately, most people 'did not qualify' for citizenship and many who did, were not wealthy enough to spend the time needed to be involved with the politics of ancient Athens. The system imploded after a relatively short experiment.

The modern democratic state was founded on the cornerstone of Western Christian civilisation, with the belief that if God made all equal, then some are not more equal than others. The development of democracy in England and the U.S. was a slow process of the gradual transition of power from the crown or state to the people. Throughout the story of the development of the modern democratic state, we will often find Bible-believing

Christians playing a prominent role in forcing a corrupt leader to concede power and rights to the majority. The famous preacher Charles Spurgeon (1834-1892) said, "There is not a land beneath the sun where there is an open Bible and a preached gospel, where a tyrant long can hold his place. Let the Bible be opened to be read by all men, and no tyrant can long rule in peace. England owes her freedom to the Bible."[3]

The Bible: The first chapter of the Bible announces a phrase which determines God's pronouncement of the equality of all mankind, because all are created in His image. God said, "Let them rule" (Genesis 1:26). At the heart of Western democracy is the Christian understanding that all are equal, and our equality comes from the ultimate authority – God. As this is the case, no one person or group has the right to rule in spite of and at the cost of the people. In the case of ancient Israel, it was not God's original intent for one flawed person to rule over all as a king.

The ancient Hebrews emerged from the family of Abraham and as a family, the patriarch – the male head of the family or tribe, led. This headship passed through the generations, until Jacob led his family into Egypt, and as Joseph was forgotten, the people were subjugated and became a slave nation. In Egypt, the chiefs of the families became the elders of the nation, and it was to these that Moses presented his vision of deliverance from slavery. Moses did not grab power, he went to the elders of the people and they entrusted him with the authority to lead (Exodus 4:29-31, 18:17-16, 24:1). After Israel's deliverance from Egypt, Moses established the first basis of law for the Jews, which included a strict moral code, restricting the authority of any future leader, establishing that kings are subject to the law and must rule for the good of the people (Deuteronomy 17:16-20). After the period of establishing the nation, through the leadership of Moses and Joshua, who also began to rule by consent (Joshua 1:16-18), and both of whom sought a pure theocracy – the nation fragmented. Once again the elders of the families guided their own, until national emergencies led to them investing their authority in the Judges because of their prophetic gifting. 'The elders of Gilead went to get Jephthah from the land of Tob. Then they said to Jephthah, "Come and be our commander" ' (Judges 11:5-6). The people later chose to be ruled by kings, against the wishes of God, who warned them how a king would demand much from them (1 Samuel 8:10-20).

"Just as our language and culture is steeped in the Bible, so too is our politics," said British Prime Minister David Cameron, "from human rights and equality to our constitutional monarchy and parliamentary democracy, from the role of the church in the first forms of welfare provision...The Bible runs through our political history in a way that is often not properly recognised. The history and existence of a constitutional monarchy owes much to a Bible in which kings were anointed and sanctified with the authority of God, and in which there was a clear emphasis on the respect for royal power and the need to maintain political order. Jesus said, 'Render to Caesar the things that are Caesar's and to God the things that are God's.' And yet at the same time, the Judeo-Christian roots of the Bible also provide the foundations for protest, and for the evolution of our freedom and democracy. The Torah placed the first limits on royal power and the knowledge that God created man in his own image was, if you like, a game changer for the cause of human dignity and equality. In the ancient world this equity was inconceivable. In Athens for example, full and equal rights were the preserve of adult, free born men. But when each and every individual is related to a Power above all of us, and when every human being is of equal and infinite importance, created in the very image of God we get the irrepressible foundation for equality and human rights, a foundation that has seen the Bible at the forefront of the emergence of democracy, the abolition of slavery and the emancipation of women – even if not every church has always got the point. Crucially the translation of the Bible into English made all this accessible to many who had previously been unable to comprehend the Latin versions."[3a]

The Bible's message of equality was the essential ingredient in the establishment of the modern Western democracy. German philosopher Jürgen Habermas, one of the world's leading intellectuals said, "For the normative self-understanding of modernity, Christianity has functioned as more than just a precursor or catalyst. Universalistic egalitarianism, from which sprang the ideals of freedom and a collective life in solidarity, the autonomous conduct of life and emancipation, the individual morality of conscience, human rights and democracy, is the direct legacy of the Judaic ethic of justice, and the Christian ethic of love. This legacy, substantially unchanged, has been the object of a continual critical re-appropriation and reinterpretation. Up to this very day there is no alternative to it. And in light of the current challenges of a post-national constellation, we must draw sustenance now, as in the past, from this substance. Everything else is idle post-modern talk."[3b]

Magna Carta: In the English speaking world no document has been as much of a foundation to safeguard our basic civil liberties as the Magna Carta, which is Latin for Great Charter. Its author was a Christian. Archbishop Stephen Langton's (1150-1228) contribution to Christianity is very large. During the years 1244-1248, Cardinal Hugo De Sancto Caro (1200-1263) designed a systematic division of the Bible, but it was Langton who is believed to be the first one to divide the Bible into defined chapters, and his arrangement of books and chapters remains in use today. In his ministry in England, he was disgusted at the tyranny of the absolute ruler. The king was making very poor, ill judged decisions which affected all, but no-one could call him to account. Something had to be done and it was the Archbishop of Canterbury, who became the architect of a binding 'Charter of Liberties' to protect the barons, the Church and others from unreasonable demands from the Crown. Having continued trouble with the king, 'Langton searched the archives of the nation and produced the charter of Henry I, which...stipulated what privileges the prelates and barons respectively might claim for their order.'[4] The barons of England were angry at the king, and the Archbishop of Canterbury became their leader and it was he, more than any other who forced King John to accept Magna Carta in 1215. The complex document dealt with what a king could do and could not do to his subjects, what money and service he could demand, how judges should administer law, the rights of the Church, townspeople, merchants, and a setting down of standards and weights. One portion read: 'No freeman shall be seized or imprisoned except by the lawful judgment of his equals or by the law of the land. To no-one will we sell (into slavery), to no-one deny the right of justice.'

At the core of the freedom charter, was the Christian faith, which inspired, infused and shaped the entire document, and the first chapter of liberty would begin with the freedom to worship unhindered. 'First, that we have granted to God, and by this present charter have confirmed for us and our heirs in perpetuity, that the English Church shall be free, and shall have its rights undiminished, and its liberties unimpaired...we have also granted to all free men of our realm, for us and our heirs for ever, all the liberties written out below, to have and to keep for them and their heirs, of us and our heirs.'[5] King John abhorred yielding power and appealed to the Pope, who annulled Magna Carta, but the Archbishop's diplomacy continued, until with revision, it was accepted. By this success Langton secured a victory for England over the Monarch.

Magna Carta was the first major and permanent limitation of a Monarchs power; power had flowed from the Monarch to the barons, who now helped to keep the ruler accountable. After this those covered in law by the charter should be provided a trial by a jury of one's peers, and new taxes without the permission of national representatives was forbidden. The foundation of the mother of parliaments has its genesis in the restriction of the power of kings written into Magna Carta. The British National Archives notes: 'Magna Carta is an example of what citizens could force the Crown to concede.'[6] Magna Carta is also priceless in the heritage of the U.S., for the founding fathers turned to it in their quest for liberty, and in 1948 its qualities inspired some of the articles of the Universal Declaration of Human Rights. The best preserved copy of Magna Carta can be found in Chapter House, in Salisbury Cathedral, England.

If the history of the development of modern democracy is a slow transition of power flowing from the Monarch or state to the people, then Magna Carta is the source of that Nile. The Great Charter did not provide democracy for the masses, but it was a first step in the bleed of power from the top down. Magna Carta was a fine example of what a Christian leader could force the Crown to concede, and at its heart was a belief in liberty which drew directly from the Christian faith. When the English speaking world traces the origins of its liberty, it always finds its way to Magna Carta and the author of that document was a Christian. No wonder then that the Scientist Thomas Huxley (1825-1895) said, "The Bible has been the Magna Carta of the poor and oppressed. The human race is not in a position to dispense with it."[7]

First Elected Parliament: The modern idea of a democratic representative parliament began in England in the thirteenth century and it sprang out of the Curia Regis, which is Latin meaning Royal Council or King's Court. The Curis Regis in England was a council of leaders who advised the king, but as they struggled over power with the king, it slowly evolved into a parliament. The first English parliament of 1258 was followed by De Montfort's parliament, instigated by Simon de Montfort (1208-1265) without royal approval. It became the first elected parliament because he sent out representatives to each county, asking for the first time for two elected representatives. This was the first directly elected parliament of the modern world and it is as important as Magna Carta. As a founding father of modern democracy, a relief of De Montfort can be found in the U.S. House of Representatives.

The Church Saves Magna Carta's Freedom: Magna Carta guaranteed much freedom for those under its jurisdiction, but the king was beginning to ignore those guaranteed liberties and in response to this in 1279, the Archbishop of Canterbury ordered that Magna Carta be posted on the doors of every cathedral, and promised to use his power against those who would limit their legal rights. The king had no choice but to take notice and the Church became the stage-post for the first major demonstration against the power of the Crown, and the Monarch had to concede.

Parliament Established 1295: Following the De Montfort's example, the Model Parliament of 1295 received representatives from counties and boroughs, as well as Christian leaders and the aristocracy. In 1295, parliament was truly established when it received royal approval. Edward I of England (1272-1307) summoned this parliament with the echoes of democracy, 'What touches all should be approved of all, and it is also clear that common dangers should be met by measures agreed upon in common.'

The Peasants' Revolt 1381 and the Rev. John Ball: Life for the poor of England was cruel in 1381. Christians believe all governments are given a commission by God to serve, provide and protect their people, but instead in England by 1381, the people were abandoned, abused and taxed beyond ability. The Black Death of 1348, the epidemic form of bubonic plague killed nearly half the people of Western Europe, and England was still suffering great social and economic trouble because of it. As the people of England were attempting to find some hope in a terrible time, the government came down upon them with a crushing blow. A third poll tax was levied against them and one's ability to pay was not taken into account; a flat rate of one shilling per person was called for, even for the poorest. During the summer of 1381, the people of England proved for the first time that the Monarch and government could not treat them like animals, as it was rocked by an event called The Peasants Revolt. The peasants believed it was their God-given right to ask for justice and it was a Christian preacher who spurred them on to believe that all are created equal in God's sight; therefore all should be treated fairly.

The Rev. John Ball (1338-1381) was a devout preacher of righteousness, one who was feared by the bishops, but loved by the common folk. Rev. Ball had no parish of his own and so preached in the fields to all who would listen, and thousands ate his every word. His sermons were intertwined with a message of hope for the troubles of the common people. He used the Holy Bible to defend the people's rights and expressed the need for equality. John Ball said, "In the beginning we were all created equal,[8] if God willed that there should be serfs (peasants), He would have said so at the beginning of the world. We were formed in Christ's likeness and they treat us like animals. Matters cannot go on well until all things are held in common." He also fought against rank and class by saying, "When Adam delved and Eve span, who was then the gentleman?"

King Richard II (1377-1399) had become king at the age of ten and just four years later this mass popular uprising took place. The peasants marched to London in their thousands and King Richard defused the situation by promising reforms; but they were betrayed and when they dispersed, the army was let loose and thousands were slaughtered. The ring leader, the Rev. John Ball, 'declared himself as a disciple of Wycliffe,'[9] but in reality John was perhaps only inspired by Wycliffe without knowing him personally. The authorities did not care and Wycliffe was arrested for they wanted to call him to account for the whole reform movement. As for the Rev. John Ball, he was to be made an example of; he was hung, drawn and quartered. The process included being hung till he was nearly dead, cut down and disembowelled whilst still alive, and then finally chopped into four quarters and stuck on spikes for all to see.

The Peasants' Revolt set a new precedent for mass demonstrations and it was a warning to unjust governments. This event proved that the highest offices of power could be rocked by the people, if they were encouraged and united by Christian leaders who were prepared to make huge personal sacrifices in great causes. It was this precedent that Wilberforce, Martin Luther King Jr., Tutu and many others would replicate.

The chaotic Peasants' Revolt changed history and every mass movement from the Chartist movement, to modern day rallies all find courage from this revolt, and its leader and inspiration was a Christian preacher who died for his message of biblical equality. The Peasants' Revolt may have been crushed but it did not die out. John Wycliffe, the Christian reformer became the inspiration for a movement called Lollardism, but against his wishes they turned his ideas political. The Lollards were at times open air preachers and reformers who proclaimed 'that landlords had duties to perform towards the poor.'[10] Later the Lollards secretly read the Bible and continued underground for many years, as they sought religious freedom and reform in the nation. They suffered much for their faith, especially by the clergy who believed in all of the Pope's teaching; but now many remember them as freedom fighters and bearers of light in a dark age, who continued the struggle for liberty which the revolt had stood for. They were one group amongst many who believed in a theology of freedom, and afterward a major theologian who would expand upon similar ideas and make them mainstream.

The Theology of Liberty: During the sixteenth and seventeenth centuries, two major doctrines were pulling at the hearts of Christian believers as they dealt with corrupt governments. One of these doctrines was the Divine Right of the king, who it was taught, was ordained by God and those who opposed the king's will, opposed God Himself. John Calvin (1509-1564) helped set the scene for another doctrine, where one with the blessing of God and under proper authority can oppose tyranny. His thoughts began in 1 Samuel where a free people chose against the warnings of God, the tyranny of a king. Calvin wrote: 'Well, a formerly free people who sought royal dominance and subjected themselves willingly to it and thus gave up their liberty really deserves no better.'[11] Scottish reformer John Knox (1514-1572) expressed that it was the duty of God's people to see that Christ is truly preached and if the government hinders this, then it had to be resisted. Professor D.F. Kelly in *The Emergence of Liberty in the Modern World* stated: 'Knox, unlike Calvin, actually taught the right and duty of the common people to undertake revolution against the ruling authorities...to stamp out idolatry.'[12]

As the Theology of Liberty was developed by many biblical minds, some Christian leaders were beginning to consider that the king had made a covenant before God to lead righteously and justly, and if the ruler became tyrannical, he had broken his covenant with God, and consequently the people had a duty to remove him. These ideas developed differently in various nations and it was a complicated theological process, which was exacerbated by the conflict between Catholic and Protestants. In Scotland, Protestant anger led to the downfall of Mary Queen of Scots (1542-1587). The sermon at the inauguration of James VI (1566-1625) was preached by John Knox. James VI was educated by the harsh George Buchanan (1506-1582), and it was this man who instilled in him the new Protestant understanding that the source of all political power is invested in the people, and that it is lawful for the people to punish tyrants. But in 1603, James became King of England, Scotland and Ireland. In 1637, the Theology of Liberty was put to the test in Scotland again, when the English civil authorities attempted to force an unbiblical liturgy upon the Scots. Author R. Hetherington in 1878 explained: 'The attempt provoked an instantaneous and determined resistance.'[13] People from all walks of life found themselves united in a holy covenant before God to protect their liberties from an ungodly king. The King's attempt to use force failed and almost bankrupted him; this led to Charles I (1600-1649) going cap-in-hand to a parliament full of Christians who were already angry at him.

When the author visited Geneva, Switzerland, he was able to visit the Reformation Monument in which Christian leaders who celebrated liberty were honoured for their contributions to freedom. Nearby is the Cathedral where Calvin preached and in the small road adjacent is a plaque which marks the exact spot where his residence once stood. Many of his great ideas flourished and spread around Europe from this enclave in Geneva. We must never forget that during this era, Christian theologians had tremendous influence on public thought and they helped developed a deeper understanding of the Theology of Liberty, in which the king had made a covenant before God and if that covenant was broken, the people could remove him.

John Locke (1632-1704), spoke of similar ideas to the Theology of Liberty, in a different context; he called it, Popular Sovereignty. His *Two Treatise on Civil Government* for many is more of a biblical exegesis than philosophy. In it he argues that individuals give up many rights to the state and their liberty, life and property should therefore be guaranteed. If this does not take place, the rights of the people were being abused and they could legitimately overthrow the government. He draws much of his theories on human liberty and good government from the Bible itself, quoting from Holy Scripture over one thousand and five hundred times! Within this context, it is very easy to see how his work has been perceived as a secular understanding of the Theology of Liberty, with John Knox's theology near its heart.

The political philosopher Professor John N. Gray wrote: 'John Locke, the 17th Century English thinker who founded the modern theory of rights, believed rights were grounded in our duties to God. For him, human freedom was divinely ordained. That's why he believed we didn't have the right to commit suicide, or to sell ourselves into slavery. In Locke's view, we always remained God's creatures. Nowadays many believers in rights are indifferent or hostile to religion. The fact remains that human rights originated in monotheism – the belief that there's only one God, who creates a single moral law for all human beings. And there's a sense in which human rights still depend on some sort of religious commitment. For unless these rights are grounded in something beyond the human world, they can only be a human invention.'[13a]

English Civil War – Empowering Parliament (1642 and 1649): England's King Charles I was a firm believer that the Monarch was God's representative on earth and should not be made subject to man-made laws. He played with parliament as if it was a toy and when it suited him, he had the power to call and dismiss it. Within four years of his reign, he had summoned and dissolved parliament three times, and then he made the decision to rule without parliament. During his reign, Archbishop Laud began to renew persecution of the Puritans and without parliament sitting none was able to keep the king accountable. The Puritans were Christians who believed that the Bible taught the equality of all men; they did not think the Monarch could reign supreme without any accountability, and they had developed their own persuasion of the Theology of Liberty. It was this belief which led them into a confrontation with the king, as he consistently dissolved parliament at his own whim, and his tendency to lean towards the Pope's doctrines caused great problems. The dispute between parliament and the Monarch finally came to conflict when the English Civil War broke out in 1642. It lasted for three years; some people sided with the Crown and their faith in the Divine Right of Kings, whilst the others were led by the Puritan Cromwell, who had now fully grasped his own version of the Theology of Liberty. To serve God freely, Cromwell had to confront and even remove the king!

For Cromwell, individual freedom and his Christian faith were one and the same; he called the people to fight for, "The maintenance of our civil liberties as men and our religious liberties as Christians." The actions of the king were in strict defiance of Deuteronomy 17:16-20, which is a code of conduct which calls leaders to financial integrity, personal morality and confirms that all leaders, including the king must be in total subjection to the law. Cromwell won the war and the king was imprisoned and finally executed. The Monarchy was revived when Charles II took over the reins of the kingdom, but because of Cromwell the power-balance in England was changed forever. From that time on, the Monarch was in subjection to the law, just as Deuteronomy 17 demanded.

Oliver Cromwell delivered England from the tyranny of absolute Monarchy, but he was unable to evolve a new suitable system to replace it. He had dissolved the past, but had not been able to see and embrace the future. In 1658 Cromwell died, his conduct in Ireland stained his reputation, but we should never forget his achievements. Cromwell helped create several colleges, schools and Durham University. He also wanted to establish a national art gallery and there were numerous social reforms, and many cruel sports were outlawed. He founded the first modern disciplined army; helped double the English Navy and most importantly empowered parliament. Reflecting on Charles I, the historian John Adamson noted that the cause of freedom is far outside of the kings control; 'Charles I was standing, Canute-like, against historical tides which were outside mere kingly control: the rise of parliamentary authority and the belief in individual liberty guaranteed by common law.'[14]

Cromwell is a forerunner of civil liberties and parliamentary democracy. His greatest legacy was to permanently limit the power of the Monarch and to empower parliament. Before Cromwell, the Monarch could treat parliament like a child, after him, if the Crown did not listen to the concerns of the people, they could be dethroned! This power was proved when parliament removed James II (1633-1701). Cromwell's Theology of Liberty changed secular ideology forever.

Unjust Laws: In 1670, William Penn (1644-1718) was tried for preaching an 'illegal' sermon which violated England's unjust Conventicle Acts – which aimed to monopolise religion. Despite clearly breaking the law, the jury refused to convict him for his preaching and they were arrested. Sarah Palin, former Governor of Alaska noted how the life of this Christian hero changed the law not only in England, but also set the precedent for the U.S. 'Whereas, by refusing to apply what they determined was an unjust law, the Penn jury not only served justice, but provided a basis for the U.S. Constitution's First Amendment rights of freedom of speech, religion, and peaceable assembly...their later release and exoneration established forever the English and American legal doctrine that it is the right and responsibility of the trial jury to decide on matters of law and fact. Whereas, the Sixth and Seventh Amendments are included in the Bill of Rights to preserve the right to trial by jury, which in turn conveys upon the jury the responsibility to defend, with its verdict, all other individual rights enumerated or implied by the U.S. Constitution, including its Amendments.'[15]

Habeas Corpus Act 1679: Habeas Corpus is considered by many as one of the most important legal documents in the history of the English speaking world. Upon this foundation, citizens of Britain, Australia, Canada, New Zealand and the U.S. feel confident that their individual freedom is safeguarded against arbitrary state action. Habeas Corpus gives people a basic civil right of protection against illegal imprisonment. The writ ordered that prisoners must have their case brought before a judge, in order to receive a fair trial. The authorities should have 'Habeas Corpus' – 'have the body' of evidence before imprisonment. The prisoner should be charged with a crime within three days or released. Winston Churchill wrote of the importance of Habeas Corpus: 'No Englishman, however great or however humble, could be imprisoned for more than a few days without grounds being shown against him in open court according to the settled law of the land.'[16] This Act has ancient origins and has been updated many times. It is always central to world events; it was suspended during the American Civil War, as well as during WWII, and it keeps hitting the headlines today because of the conflict between safeguarding human rights in the light of modern terrorism.

The First Parliamentary Democracy – English Bill of Rights: Between the years 1688-1689, the first modern parliamentary democracy was truly birthed. The power of the Monarch was formally limited and the English Bill of Rights became one of the most important documents of liberty – for it shaped the infancy of modern democracy.

King James II ruled for three years and was at the centre of the battle between Protestantism and Catholicism. The Bible-believing Protestants supported the political rights of parliament, individual freedom and religious liberty, whilst traditional Catholic leaders appeared to support the 'Divine Right' of the Crown. The Glorious Revolution of 1688 saw the overthrow of James II of England, by many including the substantial number of Christian parliamentarians.

William III of Orange (1650-1702), was invited to be the new king, under the condition that he defended England's Christian faith and all the nation's liberties. This led to the English Bill of Rights of 1689, which gave citizens certain rights and increased the influence of parliament. Cromwell, the Christian Puritan had proved that the Monarch could be made accountable to the people, but the overthrow of James II finally sealed the fate of the Crown – never again could they hold absolute power. From now on the power of the Monarch was greatly restricted. They could no longer maintain a standing army, levy taxes, or suspend laws without parliament's permission. The British

National Archives state: 'After the short-lived constitutional experiments that followed the Civil War, the supremacy of parliament was finally enshrined in the Bill of Rights passed in December 1689. The Bill of Rights firmly established the principles of frequent parliaments, free elections, and freedom of speech within parliament.'[17] Voltaire (1694-1778), the French atheist concluded: 'The civil wars of Rome ended in slavery and those of the English in liberty.'

The English Bill of Rights was a victory for Bible-believing Christians who were often oppressed in many generations. They now knew that by law, no Catholic Monarch could reign in England, and persecute Protestants and all non-conformist Christians for their faith in Christ. Without Cromwell's actions or the Theology of Liberty, which gave a licence for believers to end tyranny, and without the Christians who helped overthrow James II, we can only speculate if the English Bill of Rights and frequent parliaments etc., would have ever found their genesis in England. American Professor Wilkes wrote: 'The Glorious Revolution checked the power of the Monarchy, paved the way for the rise of cabinet government and parliamentary democracy, and resulted in the enactment of the English Bill of Rights – some of whose provisions (such as those forbidding cruel and unusual punishments, excessive fines, or excessive bail) later found their way into the American Bill of Rights' in the Federal Constitution.[18]

The Mother of Parliaments: The English Parliament is often called the mother of parliaments and Princeton historian Theodore K. Rabb helps to explain why: 'Parliament was now unmistakably supreme and no Monarch could flout its wishes or those of the landed classes it represented.'[19] 'From then on, the basic elements of electoral democracy, as we know them, gathered inexorable force in England. By 1700, nationwide political parties with distinct agendas were beginning to organise; there were contested elections that forced governments out of office...the momentum continued as the mother of parliaments spawned countless imitators over the next 300 years.'[20]

The Parliament of Great Britain: The English and Scottish parliaments were dissolved in 1707 by the Act of Union, which created the parliament of Great Britain. Whilst other nations were tearing each other apart, the Act of Union clarified the most successful union of nations in world history. This led to hundreds of years of peace between the inhabitants of the British mainland, and allowed them to create the world's largest empire, exporting their values to the world; (the last battle to be fought on British soil was the Battle of Culloden of 1746). The next great shift of power from the Sovereign to the people began in 1714. King George I was more interested in Europe and trusted power in Britain to a group of ministers. Robert Walpole (1676-1745) was the most important of these ministers and is now often called Britain's first Prime Minister. Walpole accepted 10 Downing Street as a gift from George II in 1732. However, Britain was changing quickly and new industrial towns were growing without representation, whilst rotten boroughs were being controlled by rich land owners.

Voltaire 1729: The French atheist Voltaire is considered by many as the embodiment of eighteenth century Enlightenment. For a while he was in exile in England, where he could gain firsthand experience of the nation which would be called The Mother of the Free in *Land of Hope and Glory*. In 1729, Voltaire returned to Paris where he expressed his views on his experiences in England, in a collection of essays in letter form entitled the *Philosophical Letters on the English*. He was impressed by England's support of religious freedom, freedom of speech and the development of England's constitutional Monarchy. He praised England's development of liberty, as far more respectful of human rights, which included religious freedom. His thoughts were not well received in France and Voltaire was forced to leave Paris, as copies of his work were burnt by angry mobs who despised comparing England's (Protestant Christian) progress, to be far superior to France's, where other agendas had been more influential.

The Rights of Man 1791: English born journalist and American Revolutionary leader Thomas Paine (1737-1809), was the son of a Bible-believing man. In 1791 he published *The Rights of Man*. Paine wrote: 'Government cannot be the property of any particular man or family, but of the whole community. It is wrong to say that God made the rich and poor. He made only male and female, and gave the earth for their inheritance.' Paine believed in God, but not in religious institutions. However, his father's faith and upbringing greatly influenced his opinions about justice[21] and Paine suggested that all men over twenty-one in Britain should be given the vote. The book was banned in Britain, but in France his life was imperilled – for French 'liberty' quickly became tyranny. Paine had defended the French Revolution, but in 1793 he only just escaped the guillotine because of a jailer's error.[22]

The Right For All Men To Choose Their Government: William Wilberforce was waging godly war on many fronts during his era. He believed in religious liberty and trusted that this would find its way into political liberty too. He was a major supporter of popular education which began in the churches and helped equip people to gain their rights. The knock-on effect of Christian education and the aspirations of equality flowed like an under-current throughout the disenfranchised citizens of the nation. Wilberforce, as a Christian spokesperson fully supported the need for parliamentary reform. If the earth was given to all people, for the benefit of all, why then were only the few enjoying its fruits? It was the Bible's teaching on the equality of man which forged a new spirit in this generation of people to fight for what was theirs by right – justice.

In 1832, most British people were still deprived of many of their rights of citizenship, especially the right to vote; the right to choose one's government was the privilege of the wealthy and the upper classes, but a battle was beginning which would make voting become a universal right for all. Ninety-eight percent of the common masses still had no representation in parliament, this left only two percent of the wealthiest men in the nation to vote for the government of their choice, and some parliamentary seats were controlled by a single aristocrat or by a wealthy clique. The basic rights of individuals were not being respected and men would work their whole lives without being able to vote for someone who would give voice to their concerns – this was unacceptable to many non-conformist Christians.

Joseph Sturge (1793-1859) was a fine example of a non-conformist Christian leader, who struggled not only as an abolitionist, but also in the cause of Chartism. The first working-class movement in Britain began in 1836 with The People's Charter. It demanded a universal right for all men to vote by ballot. Six million signatures were gathered over a four year period from across Great Britain, demanding that all men should be treated equally, so that any man should be able to stand for parliament and vote. In July 1839, Chartist supporters took the People's Charter to parliament. Only 46 voted in favour and 235 votes brought it to its knees. In response, some Chartists started to become radical; their actions led to unrest in the cities, riots and death. The police responded with great violence and the situation was getting out of hand. By November of that year the ringleaders were arrested and accused of high treason.

The Chartists movement was made up by people of all beliefs and persuasions, but the violence incorporated with its vision, lost it much support from the established Church. It is important to understand that some opposed these events because they were afraid they would lead to the horrors, crimes and instability which happened in France during the French Revolution. Violent turmoil and mass executions were not for England.

It must be remembered that the revivals of John Wesley's day have often been credited as the reason why England did not have another civil war and now, non-conformists in the spirit of Rev. John Ball, were fighting for more liberty, but the religious establishment often opposed it. *Time* magazine of 1951, considering these days noted that 'Roman Catholicism stood against the democratic tide.'[23] Yet at the same time, there had been a long history of Christian non-conformist tradition in Britain. This faith had helped people reject the establishment's view of religion and this set them up for a rejection of the states exclusive politics too.

The Christian leaders involved in these campaigns wanted to achieve rights, but without violence. The expert Richard Brown estimated that at least forty clergymen sympathised actively with the Chartist movement in Scotland and[24] Alexander Wilson, noted twenty-nine Christian Chartist churches.[25] This mass demonstration of people power could not be ignored and another stage of concessions was made to the demands of the people. Journalist W.T. Stead wrote in a newspaper in 1870: 'Democracy, as developed and developing in the nineteenth century, is inspired by Christianity and Christianity is the inspiration of God.'[26] In the same era, Ernest Jones said, "We say to you whatsoever ye would that men should do to you, do you even so to them. When you realise this, you have democracy. For democracy is but Christianity applied to the politics of our worldly life."[27] Christians were in addition active in politics, reforming parliament and opening democracy. Christian statesman W.E. Gladstone introduced a bill for parliamentary reform, but it was defeated. Later, Benjamin Disraeli introduced the Reform Act of 1867 to trump W.E. Gladstone, which gave the vote to working men and almost doubled the electorate. Following Acts of parliament helped redistribute power and promoted secret voting including the 1872 Ballot Act. The Representation of the People Act, in partnership with the Redistribution Act of 1885 opened the doors further, and by 1918 all men over twenty-one were given the right to vote. The class system, where all were not treated equally was being slowly taken to pieces. Now it was not only the rich and powerful who could decide the destiny of their nation, the individual's right to choose a good government had become a right of law.

The Suffragettes: The British Suffragettes movement (1897-1914), which demanded women's rights, especially the right to the vote, owes a great deal of debt to Christian women's campaigns in the U.S. Christian women were often pioneers, but the greatest change took place after WWI; women had run the country when men were fighting, so The Representation of the People Act of 1918 gave women over thirty the vote, as well as all disenfranchised men over twenty-one. Ten years later, the Equal Franchise Act eliminated the last piece of discrimination.

No British Revolution: In Europe, the most important event of the eighteenth century was the French Revolution. These events protruded a whirlwind of passion which reconfigured the political contours of Europe from the French Revolution of 1789, to the Russian Revolution of 1917. Virtually every state in Europe witnessed at least one forcible overthrow of government during this era and many ended in oppression, not liberty. Great Britain was the exception; there was no revolution during this era, yet the British found liberty and stability. Historians have often asked, 'Why was Britain different?' Perhaps an explanation to why Britain remained benign was that whereas in Europe the people looked to the authorities for justice, in Britain Christian leaders brought justice to the people. The historian Gertrude Himmelfarb, in her book *The Roads to Modernity* considered the role of many revolutions and concluded that British philosophies led to practical changes in society, rather than French ideas which led to instability and bloodshed. British Prime Minister Gordon Brown responding to the book wrote: 'It is Britain and British ideas that led the way into the modern world by focusing on benevolence, improvement in civic society and the moral sense as necessary for social progress. And because this comes alive not only in families, but through voluntary associations, churches and faith groups and then on into public service we, the British people, have consistently regarded a strong civic society as fundamental to our sense of ourselves – that moral space, a public realm in which duty constrains the pursuit of self interest.'[28] Instead of trying to kill their way out of the past, Protestant leaders in Britain like Wesley decided to build their way into the future. The French were revolutionary, the British were evolutionary. Whilst French philosophers were suspicious of charitable works, British Christian leaders transformed society by such works. Whilst French rationality led to anarchy, British Christianity led to stability. France had a revolution of bloodshed; Britain had a revolution of justice.

Christianity and Freedom: A limited summary cannot do justice to the story of the development of democracy in Britain, but it can give us an opportunity to understand some of the Christian influences. Archbishop Langton was the author of the Magna Carta, the source of all liberty in the English speaking world. The Rev. John Ball mobilised the masses to call for justice and demanded change, and in doing so set a precedent for mass action. Christian theologians developed a Theology of Liberty which equipped the masses to stop submitting to evil and to start resisting tyranny. Cromwell, the Christian made parliament supreme and reduced the king's power. Later Christian politicians helped remove another king, which led to the English Bill of Rights, and to the creation of modern parliamentary democracy. Christian leaders were always at the fore of these significant events which created democracy, and from here on the next step was to extend these rights to others. *The Rights of Man* drew inspiration from its author's Christian upbringing and the belief in our universal equality before God, inspired people from all backgrounds to claim their rights and call for change. On one hand, Christians inspired people to higher ambitions; on the other hand, they helped the political process move forward by direct action. A British broadcaster agreed that in the nineteenth century evangelicals (like Wilberforce) helped 'reform the electoral system.'[29] In the history of our liberty the direct involvement of Christianity can often be traced, but it's also worth considering that the indirect involvement of Christianity cannot. For in nations with a Christian heritage this faith helped create a culture, set the scene and laid the foundations for a civilisation in which all the great advances could be made. In the twenty-first century, David Pollock from a secular viewpoint considers the Christian fabric that is still interwoven in Britain's democracy: 'The disadvantage of this benign evolution of a modern democracy is that our unwritten constitution remains a residual theocracy, with many laws enshrining religious privilege – though there is little positive discrimination against non-believers.'[30]

The role of Christianity in creating a culture of freedom was recognised by Britain's community cohesion minister Mr Dhanda, a Sikh, as he told MPs that Christianity has had a significant impact in securing people's rights and freedoms. He added, "Christian campaigners had worked hard in the past to secure freedom of speech and religion," and that "the Christian tradition has had a significant impact on the way these freedoms have been shaped." Upon reflection the U.K. government stated that Britain should celebrate 'the role of Christianity in the country's heritage and culture.'[31]

Two thousand years ago the first century Roman poet Juvenal asked, "Who will guard the guardians?" Non-conformist Christianity in Britain over time gave a direct answer – it showed us that people should not cower in fear of their government, but that government should fear the voice of the people. Democracy is not a perfect, nor a biblically mandated form of government, but it seems the best form of government which relies on human leadership – because at the heart of democracy is public accountability. Winston Churchill, understanding the problem of human government, said with tongue-in-cheek, "Democracy is the worse form of government, except for all those others that have been tried!" For the Christian, without an accountable government, without the right to protest, or air our grievances – without the right to vote for other leaders which represent our concerns, the government could take away all our freedoms, including religious liberty. In addition, an accountable government has a greater chance of being just, which the Old Testament explains is of the utmost concern to God.

The creation of the modern democratic state began stage by stage, with the gradual flow of power and rights from the political authority to the people; at one significant point in history, the story of democracy in the English speaking world split in two different directions. Two rivers of freedom, both finding their genesis from the same source, forged out different paths to the same destination. We speak of course of Great Britain and the United States. Referring to the shared Christian liberties and concern for the world, author Ernest Protheroe *In Empire's Cause* states: 'Politically the United States are severed from Britain' but they share the same values, 'They treasure the same Bible, they read the same Shakespeare and they are imbued with the same lofty conception of duty to humanity.'[32] Obama on a visit to Britain spoke of the two nation's shared history and the role of 'English tradition' in shaping the U.S. Constitution. He said, "We've been through two world wars together...we speak a common language. We share a belief in rule of law and due process."[33]

Forgotten History: It appears that the Anglophone world has forgotten or dismissed the non-conformist Christian legacy in shaping modern democracy and for this reason, it has over-glorified ancient democracies. Athenian democracy was the first great democratic experiment to which we owe a great deal, yet we have forgotten its cruelty. In Athenian democracy 90% of the population had no voting rights. Women had no votes (being considered almost as possessions of men), and one third of the population of Athens were slaves. In addition, you only obtained voting rights if you met the age restriction, and your birth place and that of your parents were taken into account. Finally, perhaps only 3% of those eligible to vote were able (financially etc.) to attend regular assembly.[34] The few who did attend to cast their votes, showed how deeply they valued human liberty – the heart of modern democracy – as their presence was only made possible because their slaves were forced to earn their living for them. The historian Bettany Hughes said, "We've taken the world of the ancient Greeks and we've whitewashed it. We've turned it into a kind of fantasy. We look back at ancient

Athens and see what we want to see, not what was actually going on."[35]

Athenian democracy which only lasted around 150 years led to war, bloodshed and dominance of their neighbours. Professor Simon Goldhill said, "In its Athenian form, democracy is a military state, where every able bodied citizen was a member of the armed forces and not only that, but they voted themselves into war...you may think of Athens as a place where people wander around in white sheets saying, 'What is justice?' but actually, it's a warrior state."[36] The Athenians dispossessed entire populations of other Greek city states, and by the end of their experiment, they threw away many of their freedoms and engaged in torture and mass-murder, with Socrates as their most famous victim. Professor Barry Strauss said, "It's difficult for us to admit that the golden age of Greece was actually an age of blood."[37] Though we owe much to ancient Greece, we should not forget the Christian legacy in shaping modern democracy because of cultural bias. The heritage of Greece is great, yet it would be unjust for us to disinherit Christian pioneers by crediting Greece with far more than is historically accurate. In addition, we should recall that the legacy of this civilisation, like that of the Church, is both good and bad. Professor Simon Goldhill speaking of Socrates said, "One should never forget that his most important pupil, Plato, was the theorist to whom Stalin and Hitler turned in order to justify their totalitarian states."[38]

Shami Chakrabarti, the director of Liberty, a civil liberties campaign group said, "It is a matter of historical fact that the struggle for democracy in Britain has been instinctively linked with the struggle for religious tolerance and freedom."[39] Columnist Peter Hitchnes wrote: 'Why is there such a fury against religion now? Because religion is the one reliable force that stands in the way of the power of the strong over the weak. The one reliable force that forms the foundation of the concept of the rule of law. The one reliable force that restrains the hand of the man of power. In an age of power worship, the Christian religion has become the principal obstacle to the desire of earthly utopians for absolute power.'[40]

Chapter Twenty-Seven

American Democracy

'So the Lord said to Moses, "Gather to Me seventy men of the elders of Israel...and they shall bear the burden of the people with you" ' (Numbers 11:16-17).

In the United States, democracy developed by the gradual flow of power from the authorities to the people. An explosion of democracy took place after the Declaration of Independence, but still it would take time for every citizen to be considered equal enough to vote. The first elections began at the beginning of the colonial era. Historian J.A. Williamson in *The British Empire and Commonwealth* states: 'In 1619, the company conferred upon the colonist the privileges of free-born Englishmen.' The English governor 'was instructed to hold elections...governor, council and assembly thus became the colonial counterpart of Kings, Lords and Commons at home.'[1] However, this was still not modern democracy because 'the freeman who elected the members were the owners of estates; their employees were not 'free' in this sense and had no votes.'[2]

In the first parliament in England in 1265, only landowners could vote and the colonies were following this precedent. In other words, to have a vote one had to be a white male landowner and this continued long after independence. The U.S., like England itself, did not become a full modern democracy, with universal suffrage until the early twentieth century. The U.S. National Archives state: 'When the Constitution took effect in 1789, it did not "secure the blessings of liberty" to all people. The expansion of rights and liberties has been achieved over time, as people once excluded from the protections of the Constitution asserted their rights set forth in the Declaration of Independence. These Americans have fostered movements resulting in laws, Supreme Court decisions, and constitutional amendments that have narrowed the gap between the ideal and the reality of American freedom. At the time of the first presidential election in 1789, only six percent of the population – white, male property owners – was eligible to vote. The Fifteenth Amendment extended the right to vote to former male slaves in 1870; American Indians gained the vote in 1924 and women gained the vote in 1920.'[3]

The Christian foundations of the U.S. are a continual source of agitation to those who would prefer it not to be, but to suggest that America does not have a Christian cornerstone is akin to suggesting Walt Disney founded his empire without the family audience in mind. President Thomas Woodrow Wilson (1856-1924) said, "America was born a Christian nation. America was born to exemplify that devotion to the elements of righteousness which are derived from the revelations of Holy Scripture."[4]

First English Colony: Jamestown was the first successful and permanent English colony in North America. 'They named it Jamestown, after James I, who was king of England at the time.'[5] Looking back upon the first great landing: 'It was a warm, clear day in April 1607, as an Anglican priest named Robert Hunt led a group of English colonists up a windswept dune to where they had erected a rough-hewn cross, carried over from England...lifting his eyes toward heaven, Hunt led them in a providential prayer.'[6]

As Englishmen, these settlers were heirs to English law and liberties. Parliament was truly established back in 1295 and they too wanted to claim their liberties in the New World. It was 30 July 1619 when a church became the setting for the first democratic assembly in North America; the first legislature of elected representatives in America was founded in God's house. President George W. Bush, speaking at the White House on the state visit of Queen Elizabeth II said, "The United Kingdom has written many of the greatest chapters in the history of human freedom. Nearly 800 years ago (1215), the Magna Carta placed the authority of the government under the rule of law. Eighty years later (1295), the first representative assembly of the English people met to debate public policies. Over the centuries, parliaments in Britain established principles that guide all modern democracies. And thinkers from Britain, like Locke and Smith and Burke showed the world that freedom was the natural right of every man, woman and child on earth. As liberty expanded in the British Isles, British explorers helped spread liberty to many lands, including our own. In May of 1607, a group of pioneers arrived on the shores of the James River, and founded the first permanent English settlement in North America. The settlers at Jamestown planted the seeds of freedom and democracy on American soil. And from those seeds sprung a nation that will always be proud to trace its roots back to our friends across the Atlantic."[7]

The Mayflower Pilgrims: A few years after the Jamestown settlers, a group of Puritans made a great voyage to set up another colony. The Mayflower Pilgrims left England seeking a new land where they would be free to express their Christian faith without interference from the state. In the Mayflower Compact they made an honest declaration of their Christian faith and purpose of the voyage. "In the name of God, Amen. We, whose names are underwritten, the loyal subjects of our dread sovereign Lord King James, by the grace of God, of England, France and Ireland, king, defender of the faith. Having undertaken for the glory of God, and advancement of the Christian faith, and the honour of our king and country, a voyage to plant the first colony in the northern parts of Virginia; do by these present, solemnly and mutually in the presence of God and one of another, covenant and combine ourselves together into a civil body politick (to engage in political activities), for our better ordering and preservation, and furtherance of the ends aforesaid; and by virtue hereof to enact, constitute, and frame, such just and equal laws, ordinances, acts, constitutions and offices, from time to time, as shall be thought most meet and convenient for the general good of the colony; unto which we promise all due submission and obedience. In witness whereof we have hereunto subscribed our names at Cape Cod the eleventh of November, in the reign of our sovereign Lord King James of England, France and Ireland, the eighteenth, and of Scotland the fifty-fourth. Anno Domini, 1620."[8]

The Mayflower Compact established the first basis of written law in the North American colonies. In *Mayflower Pilgrims* journalist E.J. Carpenter states: 'Here was the true root of our great republic, the first charter of a government established expressly for the glory of God and the advancement of the Christian faith.'[9] The first winter was terrible and half of the colony died, but after many years of struggle the North American colonies prospered and expanded. Author Michael J. McHugh explains: 'Few groups in human history have contributed more to the cause of virtuous liberty and civic equality than those Christians who first settled New England during the 1620s and 1630s.'[10] William Bradford (1590-1657) was a passenger on the

Mayflower and became the governor of the Plymouth colony. Writing about the pilgrim's hopes he declared: 'They had a great hope and inward zeal of laying some good foundation, or at least to make some way there unto, for the propagating and advancing of the gospel of the Kingdom of Christ in those remote parts of the world, yea though they should be but even a stepping stone unto others for the performing of so great a work.' But he was aware that not all wanted to live the Puritan life and when considering those who were not faithful to the Christian faith, he spoke of his own "grief and sorrow." In 1765, Stephen Hopkins looking back said, "That the first planters of these colonies were pious Christians; were faithful subjects; who, with a fortitude and perseverance little known and less considered, settled these wild countries by God's goodness, have maintained peace and practiced Christianity; and in all conditions and in every relation have demeaned themselves as loyal, as dutiful, and as faithful subjects ought."[11]

When the author was researching these events, he was made aware that in Nottinghamshire, England, there are several tours available where people can visit the churches and other places where these pilgrims dreamed of life in the New World. In London, Southampton and Plymouth there are also monuments erected in the places where the pilgrims left for the New World.[12] In Britain's Houses of Parliament, Queen Victoria's husband Prince Albert, insisted that the hallway between the House of Lords and House of Commons should be adorned with murals portraying scenes from Christian history, including the Pilgrim Fathers to remind British legislators that the Christian faith is the root from which all our liberties have grown.

The Lost 150+ Years: The media has a tendency to tell the story of America, beginning with the first landings and then jumping straight to the War of Independence ignoring much of what happened in-between. These are the 'missing years' of American history, which the average person knows very little about. Yet, these are the years that made certain that America would be an English speaking nation, with a Protestant faith and a legal system shaped by Judeo-Christian thought. The history of these 'missing years' are full of adventure, with Europeans sailing to the New World seeking out a fortune, to pirates sailing from the Caribbean along the East coast, to the battles between

France, Spain, Holland and England, all warring to settle the foundations of the New World. During the exploration of these years, we discover many surprises. For example, when Christians in England removed their king and created a republican government, there was an expectation that all settlers would welcome this change. In fact, 'Virginia and Maryland defied the Commonwealth and proclaimed the exiled Charles II as their king.'[13] Who could have imagined that settlers in North America would choose a king instead of a republican government? Three years passed before England acted and 'they obtained the surrender of Virginia and Maryland without any fighting.'[14] Events like these reveal that the story of America is far more complex than the immediate view would tell. However, during these years Protestant Christianity took root and became the most influential belief system which shaped the colonies, and the doctrine of the universal equality of all human beings, helped these settlers to eventually become masters of their own destiny.

Heirs of Magna Carta: In 1690 the colonies had a population of 250,000 who were almost exclusively British.[15] As time passed many other Europeans arrived, but each colony continued to be distinctly English in law and culture. As heirs of English Law, North Americans began to demand more rights for the individual against the Crown. The U.S. National Archives notes: 'As English men and women, the American colonists were heirs to the thirteenth-century English document, the Magna Carta, which established the principles that no one is above the law (not even the king), and that no one can take away certain rights.'[16] This belief sprung directly from the Christian influence in England, and now theology would play a central role in shaping America.

Theology of Liberty: In European history the doctrine of the Divine Right of the king had been damaged by those who believed in a Theology of Liberty. Throughout Scripture there are many examples of those who were civilly disobedient within Divine service – Moses, Daniel, Peter and Paul etc. Now in the English colonies of America many preachers began to interpret Galatians 5:1 not only as a spiritual freedom, but also to signify political self-determination. Romans 13, one of the cornerstones of the Divine Right theology, was reinterpreted to suggest that

God only ordains the general institution of government and therefore did not support corrupt or oppressive governments or laws. Consequently opposing such a government was fulfilling the will of God.

In 1776, when Congress appointed Benjamin Franklin, Thomas Jefferson and John Adams 'to bring in a device for a seal for the United States of America' – one of the popular ideas was an image of pharaoh's army drowning in the Red Sea, with the words, "Rebellion to Tyrants is Obedience to God." In 1898's *A History of American Christianity*, Leonard Woolsey Bacon wrote: 'The quickening of religious feeling, the deepening of religious conviction, the clearing and defining of theological opinions, that were incidental to the Great Awakening, were a preparation for more than thirty years of intense political and warlike agitation.'[17]

Now that Americans had their spiritual freedom, they wanted their political freedom too. From the foundation of the Magna Carta, to the grievances and interference of the British Crown (and with echoes of the American expression of the Theology of Liberty), all was summed up in The Declaration of Independence of July 4 1776, which proclaimed: 'We hold these truths to be self-evident, that all men are created equal, that they are endowed by their Creator with certain unalienable rights, that among these are life, liberty and the pursuit of happiness...That whenever any form of government becomes destructive of these ends, it is the right of the people to alter or to abolish it, and to institute new government...We therefore, the representatives of the United States of America, in general Congress, assembled, appealing to the Supreme Judge of the world...with a firm reliance on the protection of Divine Providence, we mutually pledge to each other our lives....'[18] Consequently, the source and authority of all law in the United States of America finds its genesis in having faith in a Creator, who endows unalienable rights, and maintains liberty by Divine Providence, who will in addition, be the Supreme Judge of the world.

The founding father's all had various religious views and yet, it is important to note that there was only one Person, which all the founding fathers would have been aware of, who is called both Creator and Judge in the Bible – Jesus Christ. 'God who created all things through Jesus Christ' (Ephesians 3:9). 'For by

Him all things were created' (Colossians 1:16). 'The Lord Jesus Christ, who will judge the living and the dead' (2 Timothy 4:1).

The United States of America was the first republic founded, in such plain terms, upon faith in the God of the Bible. It was God who granted these liberties to Americans and it was God alone, the founder's solemnly transcribed into law, who would maintain such liberties. Then to celebrate their liberties, the founding fathers offered official thanksgiving to the God of the Bible. In Philadelphia July 1776, the liberty bell was rung to announce the signing of the Declaration of Independence. Inscribed on the bell is Leviticus 25:10 – 'Proclaim liberty throughout the land and to all the inhabitants thereof.' During the inauguration of the first president, George Washington (1732-1799) called for a Bible on which he would take his oath adding, "So help me God," and he leant over and kissed the Bible. The second president of the U.S., John Adams (1735-1826) said, "The general principles on which the fathers achieved independence were the general principles of Christianity. I will avow that I then believed, and now believe, that those general principles of Christianity are as eternal and immutable as the existence and attributes of God."[19] In 1783, the signatories of the Treaty of Paris, which ended the Revolutionary War, insisted the treaty begin with the phrase, "In the name of the most holy and undivided Trinity."

In a recent poll 55 percent of Americans said they believed the U.S. Constitution itself established a Christian nation. Senator John McCain referring to it said, "I would probably have to say yes, that the Constitution established the United States of America as a Christian nation." Then, clarifying the legal status he said, "What I do mean to say is the United States of America was founded on the values of Judeo-Christian values, which were translated by our founding fathers, which is basically the rights of human dignity and human rights."[20]

The modern spirit of democracy found its fullest expression in the U.S., and the Constitution presented the aspiration of liberty; however the aspiration and the application were different. In 1789, out of a population of around 3,000,000 people, only 180,000 had a right to vote and of them only 38,818 actually voted. Just as England, the American expression of democracy would take time as rights and freedoms slowly flowed towards the individual after much struggle with the powers to be. On one hand, white males proclaimed liberty and on the other – slavery, oppression of the indigenous people and female inequality continued.

Natural Rights: English political philosopher John Locke is often credited with working out the first systematic theory of natural rights in modern times which helped America shape its future. However, what is often forgotten is that in his first treatise on government he cited the Bible in 1,349 references; in his second treatise he quoted it 157 times. His arguments are clothed in biblical text and surrounded with Judeo-Christian ethic and logic. It was not secular ideology that was the cornerstone of American Independence, but Christian liberty. No wonder then that President John Adams wrote that the fourth of July 'ought to be commemorated as the day of deliverance by solemn acts of devotion to God Almighty."[21] Richard Henry Lee (1732-1794), the leader of the American Revolution who proposed the resolution which called for independence, and a signatory of the Declaration said that the Declaration itself was copied from John Locke's *Two Treatises on Government,* which together cites the Bible more than 1,500 times! John Locke said, "The Holy Scripture is to me and always will be, the constant guide of my belief and I shall always hearken to it, as containing infallible truth relating to things of the highest concernment." He also revealed that everything he wrote about responsible government had a founding in the Bible saying, "I shall immediately quit and condemn any opinion of mine, as soon as I am shown that it is contrary to any revelation in the Holy Scripture."[22] Benjamin Rush (1745-1813) a signatory of the Declaration wrote: 'For this Divine Book above all others, constitutes the soul of republicanism.'[23]

The American Bill of Rights: Many of the fundamentals of American liberty were not at first protected by the U.S. Constitution. These included the right to a fair trial, liberty to assemble, freedom of speech and of the press. The American Bill of Rights protected these fundamental rights and privileges for Americans, and was added to the Constitution as the first ten amendments on 15 December 1791. George Mason (1725-1792) was the author of the Virginia Declaration of Rights, which formed the basis for the American Bill of Rights. Mason's final testimony to all was, 'My soul, I resign into the hands of my Almighty Creator, whose tender mercies are over all His works, who hateth nothing that He hath made, and to the justice and wisdom of whose dispensation I willingly and cheerfully submit, humbly hoping from His unbounded mercy and benevolence, through the merits of my blessed Saviour, a remission of my sins.'[24] James Madison (1751-1836) also helped shape the Bill of Rights and in 1812, as president he signed a federal bill which financially aided the Bible Society of Philadelphia in its goal of the mass distribution of the Bible.

Not Athenian Democracy: Greek ideas about democracy were an inspiration to many, yet in the U.S., citizens wanted to create a new form of government – a republic with a Judeo-Christian heritage. President James Madison said that ancient democracies, "Have ever been spectacles of turbulence and contention; have ever been found incompatible with personal security or the rights of property; and have, in general, been as short in their lives as they have been violent in their deaths."[25]

Fifty years after the inauguration of the first president, President John Quincy Adams (1767-1848) explained that America was not copying the democracies of the ancient world. "Experience of all former ages had shown that of all human governments, democracy was the most unstable, fluctuating and short-lived."[26] America's republic, according to this president was founded upon Christianity: "In the chain of human events, the birthday of the nation is indissolubly linked with the birthday of the Saviour. The Declaration of Independence laid the cornerstone of human government upon the first precepts of Christianity."[27] Consequently, the rights of the citizen would be protected, because this republic recognised God as the author of these rights. Benjamin Rush (1745-1813) wrote that the 'only means of establishing and perpetuating our republican forms of government is the universal education of our youth in the principles of Christianity by means of the Bible.'[28] Noah Webster wrote in the 1832 *History of the United States* that 'our citizens should early understand that the genuine source of correct republican principles is the Bible, particularly the New Testament, or the Christian religion.'[29] In 1851, Alexis de Tocqueville (1805-1859) a French political commentator wrote: 'The Americans combine the notions of Christianity and of liberty so intimately in their minds, that it is impossible to make them conceive the one without the other; and with them this conviction does not spring from that barren traditional faith which seems to vegetate in the soul rather than to live.'[30] Journalist Horace Greeley (1811-1872) wrote: 'It is impossible to enslave mentally or socially a Bible-reading people. The principles of the Bible are the groundwork of human freedom.'[31]

Voting Rights Extended: The years 1861-1865 are marked in history as the American Civil War which brought death to over 600,000 people. At its heart was the question of slavery, which was finally resolved by President Abraham Lincoln whose Emancipation Proclamation and Thirteenth Amendment outlawed slavery once and for all. In the late 1860/70s the freed male slaves were given the right to vote and the Nineteenth Amendment in 1920 gave women the vote too (due in large part to the Women's Christian Temperance Movement), and by 1924, American Indians gained the right. By 1965, the last disenfranchised Americans received their constitutional rights, when the National Voting Rights Act outlawed discriminatory voting practices. When one considers the entire story of American democracy, Christianity is ever present and believers are often at the fore. Abraham Lincoln (1809-1865), the president who is credited with saving the Union said, "I believe the Bible is the best gift God has ever given to man. All the good from the Saviour of the world is communicated to us through this book." President Herbert Hoover (1874-1964) said, "Democracy is the outgrowth of the religious conviction of the sacredness of every human life. On the religious side, its highest embodiment is the Bible; on the political side, the Constitution."[32]

Preserving Global Liberty and Democracy: In 1824, the Pennsylvania Supreme Court explained that, "No free government now exists in the world unless where Christianity is acknowledged and is the religion of the country."[33] Christianity helped create modern democracy, it also helped to preserve it. Billy Graham's evangelistic campaigns helped revive biblical faith in America and around the world, and as Christianity flourished, so did liberty. President George H.W. Bush, with other former Presidents Bill Clinton and Jimmy Carter explained how Christianity played a significant role in preserving democracy during the threats of Fascism and Communism. "In both World War II and the Cold War," Bush said, "Freedom's victory was far from foreordained. It would require vigilance in the face of laxity; courage in the face of appeasement; moral clarity in the face of relativism; and above all else, hope in the face of despair. These matters of state were never separate from the spiritual issues to which Graham had dedicated himself," Bush observed. "Graham's central role in restoring America's religious spirit contributed directly to democracy's survival internationally."[34]

In the Western world, the U.S. is still the most religious nation; the Church and state may be officially separate, but faith and politics have never been. It's a regular occurrence to hear a U.S. president quoting Scripture or publicly celebrating Christianity. As Rick Warren of Saddleback Church said, "We believe in the separation of Church and state, but we do not believe in the separation of faith and politics, because faith is just a worldview, and everybody has some kind of worldview."[35] "People often say that politicians shouldn't 'do God,' " said British Prime Minister David Cameron, "if by that they mean we shouldn't try to claim a direct line to God for one particular political party they could not be more right. But we shouldn't let our caution about that stand in the way of recognising both what our faith communities bring to our country...To me, Christianity, faith, religion, the Church and the Bible are all inherently involved in politics because so many political questions are moral questions."[35a] *Time* magazine wrote in the build-up towards the 2008 U.S. presidential election: 'It is a sign of how seriously Americans take religion that the first general-election meeting between Barack Obama and John McCain will take place not in a university auditorium, with network news anchors as moderators, but in the sanctuary of an Evangelical megachurch with a Southern Baptist pastor playing the role of interrogator.'[36] The Christian foundations of the U.S. are probably one of the most studied subjects in regards to the relationship between Church and state, and there are numerous works that deal thoroughly with this. For Christians, we celebrate the fact that Christianity was a direct influence in the creation and preservation of American liberty.

The Development of Democracy: In the West, Protestant Christianity is the forge which shaped modern democracy. 'According to the Judeo-Christian worldview, human beings were created by God and, as such, have never 'acquired' their basic rights from the state,' explained Creation Ministries International. 'The recognition by law of the intrinsic value of each human being did not exist in ancient times. Among the Romans, law protected social institutions such as the patriarchal family but it did not safeguard the basic rights of the individual, such as personal security, freedom of conscience, of speech, of assembly, of association, and so forth.'[37]

Modern democracy emerged through the gradual transition of rights from the crown or state, to the people. The year 1215 marked the first permanent transition of some power from the crown in England to a very few barons. Over time parliament emerged and gradually asserted its power over the Monarch, and as time went on, more people found representation. It took until the twentieth century for parliament to be elected by the entire adult population. Britain "hath been the temple as it were of liberty," said Lord Viscount Bolingbroke (1678-1751), as early as 1730, "Whilst her sacred fires have been extinguished in so many countries, here they have been religiously kept alive." Voltaire wrote: 'The English are jealous not only of their own liberty but even of that of other nations.'[38] The American experience was different and was still built upon England's experiment. Elections first began in the colonial era, later in 1789, only six percent of the white adult male population had a vote and it took until 1920 for the last female citizen to get the vote. However, discrimination against African Americans continued, including at times voting rights being denied; the Civil Rights Act of 1964 and the 1965 National Voting Rights Act finally turned the U.S. into a fully living democracy.

Revolution: In mainland Europe, many nations embraced democracy between the years 1789-1914, but true democracies were few and often failed. In France and Germany their democratic experiments often ended in total disaster. In 1789, one hundred years after the British set the essential elements of parliamentary democracy in place, the French Revolution broke out and the principles of democracy, citizenship and inalienable rights took hold. The Declaration of the Rights of Man and of the Citizens led to the National Convention which gave fifty percent of the population the right to vote, but it only sat in the years 1792-1795. France was then at war from 1793-1815.

Our perceived image of the French Revolution is one of a passionate charge to liberty; the reality however was somewhat different. We tend to believe that only corrupt aristocrats and clergy died during the Reign of Terror (1793-1794), but the BBC estimated that 55,000 people were killed by state terror during this period, and over seventy percent of these victims were the innocent poor. Most were murdered without a trial and the evidence of their guilt was often only their accusers 'intuition.' Saint Just (1767-1794) a major French revolutionary leader said, "The republic consists in the extermination of all who oppose it." "In other words," said the historian Simon Schama, "the point of the Revolution is slaughtering anyone who might disagree with the government at that moment in time."[39] Stalin, Hitler, Pol Pot and Mao all shared this conviction. Just over a decade after executing their king, the French then celebrated the ascension of an absolute dictator to the throne as emperor in 1804. Napoleon Bonaparte (1769-1821), called himself the embodiment of the Revolution, even though he himself was not French – being a son from the occupied island of Corsica. Beethoven (1770-1827) who had once dedicated his third symphony to Napoleon, identified the evolution from military genius to dictator and said, "Emperor Napoleon is nothing more than an ordinary mortal; he would trample on all human rights and become a tyrant."[40] Napoleon said he fought for the people, but his elitism took over. He said, "I have come to realise that men are not born to be free; liberty is a need felt by a small class of people whom nature has endowed with nobler minds than the mass of people."[41] The French historian Claude Ribbe, who was appointed to be a French human rights commissioner, broke with the hero tradition in his book Le Crime de Napoléon by listing the atrocities carried out during this age. Former French Prime Minister Dominique de Villepin said, "I was taught to think of Napoleon as a superstar. To mention his crimes against humanity has been a taboo."[42]

James H. Billington, the American Librarian of Congress, in his book Fire in the Minds of Men examined how the French Revolution became an inspiration for Communism, Nazism and all manner of totalitarian horrors. In 1940, three days after the fall of France, Hitler visited the tomb of his hero Napoleon calling it, "One of the proudest days of my life." Many have made comparisons between Napoleon and Hitler. Both were born outside of the nations which they would rule. Both wanted total control of Europe and they were obsessed with absolute power. The two had a powerful sense of self-belief and they lost confidence in everyone, believing in their own infallibility.

Napoleon proved in Spain he was prepared to commit crimes against humanity by deserting rules of engagement, with his troops torturing and mutilating prisoners. The French historian Michael Kerautret said, "It's a war of atrocities...not like the other campaigns."[43] Hitler shared the same contempt for life and millions died because of their ambitions. The Napoleonic Wars of 1803-1815, led to around three million military deaths and between one to three million civilian casualties. Napoleon said, "I have been nourished by reflecting on liberty, but I thrust it aside when it obstructed my path."[44]

In 1848 revolution broke out again in France and by 1852, the second republic came to a dark end. There was no stable democracy in France; it was governed between the years 1825-1900 through a republic, a dictatorship, a constitutional Monarchy and through no less than two empires. Looking back, the French Revolution was followed by terror at home, glorified dictatorship, brutal conquests abroad, warfare with every other major European power, restored Monarchy and further revolutions. Democracy found a home again, but WWI and later the French capitulation to Hitler ended any political stability. After liberation by the U.S., Britain, Canada etc., France was able to become democratic again. But first another republic crumbled. France utterly failed to create a stable, successful model democracy, which would last and could be emulated. However, after WWII the British and American models became the gold standard for the world. After the war France began to look to the English speaking world for direction. Prime Minister Guy Mollet secretly requested that France be allowed to join the British Commonwealth. The BBC reported: 'A secret document from 28 September 1956 records the surprisingly enthusiastic way the British' responded. The Prime Minister recommended that 'in the light of his talks with the French, "We should give immediate consideration to France joining the Commonwealth," and, "Monsieur Mollet had not thought there need be difficulty over France accepting the headship of her Majesty." '[45] In the end, the 1958 constitution was followed by France seeking unity with her other neighbours, finding stability within what is now the E.U. In Germany the state was only unified as a nation in 1871, after fracturing it emerged from the Holy Roman Empire. It saw WWI & WWII and then reunification in 1990 before democracy could truly flourish.

The Legacy of British and American Liberty: The British Empire and then the American superpower led the way into the modern world. Both nations were shaped by biblical Christianity. Therefore the modern world which they developed is flooded with the undercurrent of biblical values. But many would argue that the French Revolution begot liberty. In the name of liberty the French Revolution led to European instability; but in the cause of liberty the English speaking democracies led the world to an age of freedom and stability. The French Revolution provided the impetus to remove an old order creating anarchy, but the British and Americans designed a blueprint for Western liberty and durability. The French created chaos, but the heirs of Magna Carta set the example of freedom with order. The French destroyed the past, the British and Americans created the future. The French Revolution had talked a great talk, but it never truly walked the walk. In 1789, in the name of liberty France created what would soon become the world's first modern police state. In 1776, in the cause of liberty the Declaration of Independence led to the U.S. becoming what is today the world's longest and most successful modern republic. In 1689, in the cause of liberty the British created the mother of parliaments, setting in place the essential elements of all modern democracies. Many who fought for liberty in Britain and America contended for justice because they believed they were striving for God's will; whilst atheistic revolutionary leaders in France disposed of life without fear because in their own eyes they became as gods.

In 1989, British Prime Minister Margaret Thatcher was in France during the anniversary of the 1789 Fall of the Bastille. French reporters proud of their Revolution, which in their opinion led to liberty, asked for her thoughts. Margaret Thatcher responded, "It seems to me it resulted in a lot of headless bodies and a tyrant." But the French Revolution had advanced human rights they declared. Sternly she replied, "Certainly not, human rights began with Magna Carta in England in 1215."[46]

The Twentieth Century: In other areas of the world, democracy found a home. In the late nineteenth and early twentieth century the British Empire granted full democratic rights to Australia, Canada and New Zealand. Canadian Prime Minister Stephen Harper said, "Now I know it's unfashionable to refer to colonialism in anything other than negative terms...no part of the world is unscarred by the excesses of empires. But in the Canadian context, the actions of the British Empire were largely benign and occasionally brilliant."[47] In Australia, the Christian legacy in democracy is not forgotten – a poll revealed that two-thirds of Australians still believe Christian values should continue to influence the country's politics.[48] In Europe, WWI shook old empires and led to the creation of many nominally democratic nations. However, The Great Depression of the 1930s led to most of Europe falling into the hands of dictators including Italy, Spain and Portugal. At the end of WWII the freed territories could once again re-engage with democracy. The Christian West then turned occupied nations democratic including Japan, Italy, Austria, West Germany etc. After Nazi defeat, the old regimes of Poland, the Balkans and the Baltic's fell into the Soviet Union's hands and only had the chance to embrace democracy after the fall of the Soviet Union in 1991.

Since WWII, especially after the collapse of the Soviet Union outstanding numbers of democratic states have exploded onto the world scene. After Independence, many former British colonies and protectorates chose to build upon the legal and political heritage of Britain, and today from the world's largest democracy of India, to Papua New Guinea freedom is spreading. Political freedom which once began as a trickle would turn into an ocean of free humanity – from Britain to America, from Europe to Asia, Africa, Oceania and beyond. Today the U.S. is considered the leader of the free world. This nation which was shaped by Christianity is often counted as the primary agent for spreading the values of democracy and global liberty. Much of the democratic progress in the twentieth century can be traced back to the direct and indirect influence of the U.S., and the liberty of America can be traced back to the Christian influence. Simon Schama, the historian said, "Faith is what created America – it is what gave it her freedom."[49]

Chapter Twenty-Eight

The Founding Fathers of Modern Science

'In all matters of wisdom and understanding about which the king examined them, he found them ten times better than all' (Daniel 1:20).

It is commonly presented that the Christian faith has impeded scientific progress and therefore stunted the cause of humanity. On occasions this was true for the religious establishment, but when we consider the pioneers of scientific study, we discover that many of them were devout Christians. Many of the founding fathers of scientific progress were dedicated Christians, who were motivated by their faith in an orderly universe. As they discovered the foundations of science and technology, they believed they were reflecting the creative nature of God and serving Him by being innovators in various fields. The Bible is not a scientific text book, but the God who is revealed in the Bible is a rational Being who did not create a world of chaos, but of order and logic. Benjamin Rush (1745-1813), physician and signatory of the U.S. Declaration of Independence said, "The greatest discoveries in science have been made by Christian philosophers" and he noted that Christian nations were the pioneers: "There is the most knowledge in those countries where there is the most Christianity." Broadcaster Gailon Totheroh said, "Christian believers made up a Who's Who of the scientific revolution...sociologist Rodney Stark calculated that a great majority of early scientists were followers of Jesus Christ. More specifically, he found that about 96 percent of innovators from the mid-1500s to 1700s were Christian believers. And the great majority of those – 61 percent – were devout Christians."[1]

If the God of the Bible created the world, these Christian scientists knew they could search for logic and order in every area of creation. Through the application of reason, the very handiwork of God could be discovered. Concerning the Science museum in London, Professor Irvin Hexham wrote: 'Visitors to this museum need to be aware that almost without exception every scientist mentioned before the 19th century, such as Robert Boyle and many in the 19th century, like Michael Faraday, were Christians.'[2] At Yale in the U.S., faith and scientific knowledge grew side by side. Reporter Wendy Griffith said, "Yale's founders were told to create an institution where 'youth may be instructed in the arts and sciences, who through the blessing of Almighty God may be fit for employment both in the Church and civil state.' Historian Peter Marshall explained, 'There were Scriptures assigned to the students for each day, and the rules said that a student had to be ready to give evidence of his understanding of that Scripture.' "[3]

Professor Henry M. Morris (1918-2006) explained: 'Thousands of scientists of the past and present have been and are Bible-believing Christians. As a matter of fact, the most discerning historians and philosophers of science have recognised that the very existence of modern science had its origins in a culture at least nominally committed to a biblical basis, and at a time in history marked by a great return to biblical faith.'[4]

Scientific Method: Sir Francis Bacon (1561-1626), when considering the purpose of his life, established his threefold goals – the discovery of truth, service to one's nation and service to the Church. He showed loyalty to his Christian faith and its doctrines, and Bacon championed empiricism – the foundational doctrine that knowledge derives from observation and experience. He was also the Lord Chancellor of England, a philosopher, jurist and author of *The Advance of Learning* (1605) and *The New Atlantis* (1624). His work led to the creation of the Royal Society of London and his greatest legacy, the Scientific Method created a new paradigm for the world.

Modern Chemistry: Robert Boyle (1627-1691) is the father of modern chemistry. Both physics and chemistry are in his debt because of his numerous contributions, and he was a founder of the Royal Society of London. He also spent time and money on advancing the gospel at home and abroad.

The Greatest Scientist: Professor Henry M. Morris wrote: 'Most scholars who have studied the question have judged Sir Isaac Newton (1642-1727) to have been the greatest scientist who ever lived...his discoveries provided the solid framework within which the great scientific and industrial revolutions of the 18th century could develop.'[5] Isaac Newton testified of his faith: 'We account the Scriptures of God to be the most sublime philosophy. I find more sure marks of authenticity in the Bible than in any profane history whatsoever.'

Astronomy: Sir William Herschel (1738-1822) discovered infrared light and catalogued the stars, as well as discovering the planet Uranus. He said, "All human discoveries seem to be made only for the purpose of confirming more and more strongly the truths contained in the sacred Scriptures."

The Telegraph: The era of global communication took its first gigantic leap forward with the invention of the telegraph. The inventor Samuel F.B. Morse (1791-1872), had a genuine faith in the Divine inspiration of the Bible and the first message sent over the wire was, 'What has God wrought!' The telegraph revolutionised global communications, by 1880 the British Empire had the first global information highway. From Britain across to Asia, from Australia to Canada and to the corners of Africa there were 97,568 miles of cable in the world's oceans.[6] The planet's first global communication system shrank the world and allowed Britain to hear in hours of a crisis, which might have taken months to have known about in other generations. One Victorian commentator called it 'the annihilation of distance.'

Electricity: What would the world be like without electricity? How would the world communicate, how would our homes, industry and appliances work? "Very few men," said the scientific writer Sir William Bragg, "Have changed the face of the world as Faraday has done...of his discoveries none has had more consequences than that which he made in 1831...on this had been founded all those applications of electricity which form the muscles and nerves of our modern life."[7] Michael Faraday (1791-1867) was an English physicist and chemist who discovered electromagnetic induction and is acknowledged as one of the greatest physicists of all time. Faraday was a man comfortable with sharing his Christian faith; he publicly testified of Christ and believed his scientific explorations revealed the handiwork of his Creator. He came from poverty, worked hard to find an education and eventually outshone his teachers. He laid the foundations of the electronic age by achieving the production of electricity without a battery. 'Faraday's work took on new meaning when James Maxwell explained and applied Faraday's work to everyday life, in what is known simply as the Maxwell Equations.'[8] Dr Peter Master's revealed that his scientific understanding was vast: 'In 1846, Faraday, far ahead of his time, conceived an understanding of the nature of light, later taken up by James Clerk Maxwell and later still by Albert Einstein.'[9] Queen Victoria recognised his brilliance and gave Faraday a residence at Hampton Court, where in 1867 he died. He received ninety-seven distinctions from international academies of science, and left his mark as a devout Christian and founder of electrical science.

Encouraging Science: Charles Kingsley (1819-1875) was a famous preacher who said, "Go out...take a microscope, hammer, dredge and collecting box; find all you can, learn all you can; God speaks to us through physical facts."[10]

Father of Modern Electronics: Sir John Ambrose Fleming's (1848-1945) 'life spanned some of the greatest discoveries and advances in physics and electrical engineering', revealed *Men of Purpose*. 'Not only did he have a direct influence on many of these, but he was the outright inventor of a number of key innovations including: in 1904, the radio valve, which made possible the development of radio and television technology, and remained the vital component of radio circuits for almost half a century. For this breakthrough, Fleming has been called the Father of Modern Electronics.'[11] (The first image on TV was a Christian cross).[12] Sir John's Christian faith played a significant role throughout his whole life and he would often speak of the Bible's importance during his lectures in London. His retirement gave him the freedom to turn his energies into evangelistic zeal, and all he preached was to encourage others to trust in the authority of the Bible, and in His Lord and Saviour.

The Natural History Museum: This museum in Oxford was founded 'for the glory of God' by Sir Henry Acland (1815-1900) and was funded by the University Press' Bible account. Sir Henry Acland said, "It would provide the opportunity to obtain the knowledge of the great material design of which the Supreme Master-Worker has made us a constituent part." A debate took place within this museum between Richard Dawkins and Christian Oxford mathematics professor John Lennox, the author of *God's Undertaker: Has Science Buried God?* One journalist wrote of the book: It 'is to my mind an excoriating demolition of Dawkins' overreach from biology into religion as expressed in his book *The God Delusion* – all the more devastating because Lennox attacks him on the basis of science itself.' In the debate, it was reported that Richard Dawkins made a stunning admission that "a serious case could be made for a deistic God."[13]

Men of God and Science: The BBC has also recognised how Protestant Christianity lays at the heart of modern science. In the programme The Protestant Revolution, historian Tristram Hunt uncovered 'how a Protestant culture of inquiry and discovery drove on a new scientific age and also how religion lies at the heart of some of our most significant scientific discoveries.'[14] The historian focused on many key leaders in scientific discovery and explained how their faith was central to their search for scientific truth. It also suggested that faith is still very much alive within the scientific community, reporting a study which stated that 40% of scientists today believe in 'a God who answers prayer.' Professor Roger Trigg said, "Their belief in God gave them confidence that the physical world, in all its complexity and vast extent, could be understood. As a matter of historical fact, modern science has developed from an understanding of the world as God's ordered creation, with its own inherent rationality."[15] In his book *Men of Science Men of God* Professor Henry M. Morris notes a few of the contributions of Bible-believing scientists of the past. He includes the discipline they founded and developed, or their discovery etc. A part of that list follows on the next page; each person had a genuine belief in the Bible and had made a personal commitment to the Christian faith. Morris wrote: 'It was the reviving spirit of biblical faith associated with the Reformation and the Great Awakening that actually facilitated the rise of modern science, as many historians of science have shown. Many of the early scientists, in fact, were also clergymen.'[16]

The founding fathers of science were devout people. Lord Melvyn Bragg said, "Religion was the enabler and the protector of science in this country in its first century and beyond. Most of those scientists were unarguably religious, like Isaac Newton, who came into the Society in the 1660s. In the 18th century there was the dissenting Protestant Joseph Priestley, who made ground-breaking experiments in chemistry and electricity. In the 19th century, Faraday with fields of force which eventually led to much of the technology of the modern world. And into the 20th century with Arthur Eddington...All these men were Christian and deeply conversant with the King James Bible."[16a]

Achievement	Scientist
Scientific Astronomy	Johann Kepler (1517-1630)
Scientific Method	Francis Bacon (1561-1626)
Hydrostatics, Barometer	Blaise Pascal (1623-1662)
Statistics, Scientific Economics	William Petty (1623-1687)
Chemistry, Gas Dynamics	Robert Boyle (1627-1691)
Natural History	John Ray (1627-1705)
Stratigraphy	Nicolas Steno (1631-1686)
Dynamics, Calculus, Gravitation Law, Reflecting Telescope	Isaac Newton (1642-1727)
Ecology	William Derham (1657-1735)
Paleontology	John Woodward (1665-1728)
Taxonomy, Biological Classification System	Carolus Linneaus (1707-1778)
Mineralogy	Richard Kirwan (1733-1812)
Galactic Astronomy, Uranus	William Herschel (1738-1822)
Atomic Theory, Gas Law	John Dalton (1766-1844)
Comparative Anatomy	Georges Cuvier (1769-1832)
Chemical Synthetics	John Kidd (1775-1851)
Thermokinetics	Humphrey Davy (1778-1829)
Optical Mineralogy, Kaleidoscope	David Brewster (1781-1868)
Food Chemistry	William Prout (1785-1850)
Electro Magnetics, Field Theory, and Generator	Michael Faraday (1791-1867)
Telegraph	Samuel F.B. Morse (1791-1872)
Operations Research, Computer Science and Opthalmoscope	Charles Babbage (1792-1871)
Anemometer	William Whewell (1794-1866)
Electric motor, Galvanometer	Joseph Henry (1797-1878)
Oceanography, Hydrography	Matthew Maury (1806-1873)
Glaciology, Ichthyology	Louis Agassiz (1807-1873)
Thermodynamics	James Joule (1818-1889)
Fluid Mechanics	George Strokes (1819-1903)
Pathology	Rudolph Virchow (1821-1902)
Genetics	Gregor Mendel (1822-1884)
Sterilisation, Immunisation, Bacteriology, Biochemistry	Louis Pasteur (1822-1895)
Entomology of Living Insects	Henri Fabre (1823-1915)
Energetics, Absolute Temperatures and Atlantic Cable	Lord Kelvin (1824-1907)
Astral Spectrometry	William Huggins (1824-1910)
Non-Euclidean Geometrics	Bernhard Riemann (1826-1866)
Antiseptic Surgery	Joseph Lister (1827-1912)
Ionospheric Electricity	Balfour Stewart (1828-1887)
Electrodynamics and Statistical Thermodynamics	Joseph C. Maxwell (1831-1879)
Vector Analysis	P.G. Tait (1831-1901)
Electronics, Electron Tube, Thermionic Valve.[17]	John A. Fleming (1849-1945)

Faith Challenged: In the last two centuries, many have claimed that the expansion of scientific knowledge has made faith irrelevant, but how can this be the case when Christians were at the forefront of these discoveries? In the BBC programme Did Darwin Kill God? Philosopher Conor Cunningham said, "For most of the nineteenth century, science was almost a branch of religion, with Anglican clerics holding the top jobs at Oxford and Cambridge."[18] Darwin supported missionary work overseas and when he neared the end of his life, he showed both respect and honour to people of faith. By the end of the nineteenth century, after Darwin's ideas were published, Britain and America were more religious, more Christian and more devoted to Christianity than at the beginning. The growth of science and the regeneration of biblical Christianity happened at the same time. By the twentieth century, Christians were still working in the highest circles of scientific discovery. Arthur Eddington (1882-1944) was a Christian astrophysicist, who led arguably the most important scientific experiment of the twentieth century,[19] proving through his expedition Einstein's Theory of Relativity. Today, there are many scientists expanding our knowledge, but few could be called the founding father of a new field; for this reason the extensive contributions by Christians to the foundations of the entire fields of science is very significant. The question has to be asked, who are greater – the Christian founding fathers or the students who build upon their work?

Space: In 1968, the biggest TV audience in history watched mankind's first encounter with another world, as the crew of Apollo 8 reached lunar orbit. It was the first human journey to another world and its astronauts captured one of history's most influential images. Earthrise became one of the most reproduced photographs of all time and changed the way the world viewed itself. For the first time humans saw their planet 'whole and round and beautiful and small,' as the poet Archibald MacLeish (1892-1982) put it. On Christmas Eve, 1968, three astronauts undertook a live TV broadcast from the lunar orbit and in a awe-inspiring moment astronaut William Anders said, "For all the people on earth the crew of Apollo 8 has a message we would like to send you...In the beginning God created the heaven and the earth...and God said, "Let there be light," and there was light. And God saw the light, that it was good and God divided the light from the darkness." Astronaut Jim Lovell then continued, "And God called the light day and the darkness He called night. And the evening and the morning were the first day..." and the astronaut Frank Borman continued the reading.[20] Science had made the mission possible, but faith gave it tangible philosophical meaning. Science gave us the 'how,' but Christianity revealed 'why.' The success of the Apollo 8 mission paved the way for the Apollo 11 moon landing. Buzz Aldrin, pilot on the Apollo 11 moon landing and the second man ever to walk on the moon privately took communion on the lunar surface! Later he said, "It was interesting for me to think: the very first liquid ever poured on the moon and the very first food eaten there were the communion elements."[21] Astronaut James Irwin became the eighth person to walk on the moon. He said, "It was my experience in exploring the moon on the Apollo 15 mission that moved me to devote the rest of my life to spreading the good news of Jesus Christ."[22] Many have claimed Christianity is a great hinderance to the development of science, yet the U.S. remains the world's leader in science and technology, whilst at the same time, it is the Western world's most religious nation; and it should not be forgotten that many people working on U.S. space ambitions were also people of faith.

A Chemist and God: Henry Schaefer, professor at the U.S. University of Georgia, is a leader and much quoted pioneer in theoretical chemistry. Professor Schaefer, who is most comfortable explaining Molecular Quantum Mechanics, has also spent years explaining how his faith and science complement each other. In 1973, as a professor in California he became a Christian and was made aware that many believed faith was in conflict with science. "It was a problem for so many people that finally I decided to do a little research on whether it was true that scientists were not Christians. I discovered pretty quickly that essentially all the pioneers of the modern physical sciences were Christians. It was encouraging to me and I think even more encouraging to others." His conclusion like that of many others, is that there is an obvious nexus between the Christian faith and the growth of science.[23]

A Physicist and God: Sir John Polkinghorne of Cambridge University, is a British particle physicist and theologian, who is considered one of Britain's top scientists. He said, "When Scientists probe the structure of the world, at its deepest levels they find it is wonderfully, beautifully ordered. It's a world, if you like, shot through with science of mind and it's natural to ask whether that might be a Divine, capital M Mind, behind that marvellous order."[24] Richard Dawkins said of Polkinghorne that he is one of a number of "good scientists who are sincerely religious."

Christian Scientists: Owen Jay Gingerich, is the former research professor of astronomy and of the history of science at Harvard University. He said, "I don't think that science leads you to atheism, science could just as well lead you to God."[25] Gingerich is very active in the American Scientific Affiliation (ASA), which is a fellowship of scientists who share a common fidelity to the word of God and a commitment to integrity in the practice of science. The stated purpose of ASA is 'to investigate any area relating Christian faith and science,' and, 'to make known the results of such investigations for comment and criticism by the Christian community, and by the scientific community.' In Britain, The Faraday Institute for Science and Religion is an academic research enterprise based at St Edmund's College, Cambridge, where the Christian influence in science is promoted and discussed.

The Human Genome and the Future of Medicine: Many Christian scientific pioneers believed they were discovering 'the deep things of God,' and therefore opening the eyes of the world to the great mysteries of the omniscient One. Albert Einstein (1879-1955) once wrote: 'Science without religion is lame, religion without science is blind.'[26] It should therefore be expected that the passion of religious people and the expertise of science should continue to grow together.

U.S. Presidential Medal of Freedom holder Francis S. Collins, PhD, is the 'former director of the National Human Genome Research Institute at the National Institutes of Health. He led the successful effort to complete the Human Genome Project, a complex multidisciplinary scientific enterprise directed at mapping and sequencing all human DNA, and determining aspects of its function.'[27] Collins led a multinational team of two thousand four hundred scientists, that co-mapped the three billion biochemical letters of our genetic blueprint, a milestone that then serving President Bill Clinton and British Prime Minister

Tony Blair celebrated.[28] The U.S and Britain were the 'leading partners in the project'[29] and Tony Blair announced it was, "The first great technological triumph of the twenty-first century." During a visit to England, Collins explained how his Christian beliefs have influenced his life and work saying, "There really is no conflict between faith and reason." Before his conversion at the age of twenty-seven he had "never really looked at the evidence...atheism had only been a convenient pathway."[30] Now with over twenty-five years of experience as a scientist and a believer, he spoke to *Time* magazine saying, "Because I do believe in God's creative power in having brought it all into being in the first place, I find that studying the natural world is an opportunity to observe the majesty, the elegance, the intricacy of God's creation."[31] Historians will indeed consider this a turning point in human history, Bill Clinton continued, "Humankind is on the verge of gaining immense new power to heal. Genome science...will revolutionize the diagnosis, prevention and treatment of most, if not all, human diseases."[32]

"There is no necessary conflict between science and God," said Oxford Professor John Lennox, "the real conflict is between worldviews – atheism and theism. God is not the same kind of explanation as science is. God is the explanation of why there is a universe at all in which science can be done...atheism has become so dominant...and those who hold it often fail to see that atheism involves faith commitments."[33] Nevertheless, critics still proclaim that Christianity limits new science; but perhaps the faith is actually protecting humanity from itself. Christianity teaches all are created in the image of God and therefore all life demands respect. The slave trade and the holocaust took place because people were brainwashed to believe that these victims were not 'fully human.' Abortion continues today because of the same indoctrination. The revolution of genetics and biotechnology will have benefits, but still there are those who don't believe mankind is created in God's image – therefore that 'image' can be manipulated, exploited or is expendable. Christian values in science are fundamentally important to check those who are in danger of creating a Frankenstein future of genetically engineered people, a cloned under-class, a designer baby catalogue and a transhumanists age of genetic apartheid.

Chapter Twenty-Nine

Great Authors and Freedom Fighters

"Write the vision and make it plain...that he may run who reads it" (Habakkuk 2:2).

The Bible is the greatest, most influential book in the history of the world. It took over a thousand years to be written, by forty different authors and covers the full body of human experience. Never has any book been translated into so many languages and no other book has come close to its sales – it is the best selling book of all time and remains the best selling book of the year, every year. The Bible has impacted history and humanity like no other book. The stories contained within its pages have been cherished and taught for over two thousand years, and according to a Gallup poll, nearly two-thirds of Americans believe the Bible holds the answers to most if not all of life's basic questions. The Bible is the most important book in history and people have died for their faith in its message.

Hannibal Barcai (247-183BC), is perhaps the most famous son of free Carthage (Tunisia), but today when visiting one of the greatest cities of the ancient world, it feels little more than a lost suburb of Tunis. Of all the magnificent temples and metropolis, virtually nothing remains – Rome's carnage was complete. A short journey from Tunis took the author to the remains of Roman Carthage, where a small overgrown coliseum stands; its centre is dominated by a memorial to St Perpetua and St Felicitas who were martyred here. These two believers are like many others who suffered and died for their faith in the Holy Scriptures. The words of the Bible have inspired people even unto death; therefore it should come as no surprise that the Bible has also been the inspiration for much of the greatest literature in the world's history. No other book has influenced the world like the Holy Bible, because no other book has inspired so many to make the ultimate sacrifice for faith in its word.

The Holy Bible has not only inspired martyrs, but also became the motivation for many of the great authors and champions of liberty in the modern age. The secret these great authors and freedom fighters found is that the world's greatest story has already been told – it's the story of God in Christ reconciling the world unto Himself. The Scriptures, they discovered, contain the greatest mystery of all literature, but still reveal a message that a child can understand. British poet Sir Walter Scott (1771-1832) said on his deathbed, "Bring me the Book!" When asked, "What book?" he replied, "There is but one Book!" In 1864, Bishop Wordsworth made note that every great author has found inspiration from the Bible – 'Take the entire range of English literature; put together our best authors, who have written upon subjects not professedly religious or theological and we shall not find, I believe, in them all united, so much evidence of the Bible having been read and used, as we have found in Shakespeare alone.' Shakespeare's home church (still open) was Holy Trinity in Stratford-upon-Avon; in his writings he drew from forty-two books of the Bible, using around 1,300 biblical allusions.

The Father of English History: The Venerable Bede (672-735) was a monk who valued history and encouraged labour in the written word; he lived in an age where history and writing in England was virtually lost. The discipline of authorship was an important part of his life and his passion was revealed by his words, "It has always been my delight to learn or to teach or to write." His work covers a vast field of knowledge from theology to science, from music to metrics. He is best remembered as The Father of English History because of his great work, *The Ecclesiastical History of the English People*. The Father of English History contributed enormously to the knowledge of the English story; therefore The Age of Bede's Exhibition was built to commemorate his work. It contains Bede's narrative, quotes from his work, archaeological finds, models and original pieces of art. They state: 'Bede began his *Ecclesiastical History of the English People*, completed in 731, in the days of Roman Britain, when Christianity first arrived in this island, and traced the thread of Christianity through the departure of the Romans, the arrival of the Angles, Saxons and Jutes, and the development and eventual conversion of the early Anglo-Saxon Kingdoms.'[1]

To Neglect a King: St Hugh (1140-1200) was a friend to the friendless and an example to the most powerful. On his way to dine with the king he found a beggar lying dead by the roadside; changing his plans he stood the king up and decided to bury this poor man instead! The king was furious, but St Hugh's reply was, "I am occupied in the service of the King of kings." Born into wealth, he cared little for himself, as he constantly made appeals for justice against the corrupt clergy, nobles and the king. He helped the poor, cared for the sick and appealed for the rights of the forgotten. *Yarns on Christian Torchbearers* says of him: 'No man did more to restrain the undue power of the crown; yet Hugh was the personal friend of both Henry II and Richard I, who both valued his honesty. An old chronicler said, "It may be observed, that he who neglected kings to bury the dead, at his own burial was followed by kings." '[2]

John Wycliffe: During the Middle Ages, the Roman Catholic Church abounded with corruption, as people often sought office, not because of a call from God, but because of a lust for power and financial gain. That power was often abused and as time was spent, many called for reform and suffered greatly for their faith. The established Church itself had become the greatest hindrance to the faith that it once stood for. Salvation (they claimed) was now only found in the teaching of the Church, not in the Bible or in a personal faith in Christ, and salvation could be bought, sold, or withheld at Rome's pleasure. John Wycliffe (1330-1384) followed in the spirit of John the Baptist, for he was an English preacher who promoted a return to biblical Christianity. Famously he was called The Morning Star of the Reformation. Deeply disturbed by the rottenness and false teaching of Rome, he was a forerunner of the Protestant Reformation, called believers back to the Bible and set an example from which many others would learn and follow. He made the first English translation of the Bible from the Latin Vulgate, sent the gospel to the poor and unmasked the failed Papacy of his day, whilst exposing many false doctrines. We must never underestimate the fierce persecution that true believers experienced by the Roman Catholic Church as they fought for freedom of religious belief. An enemy wrote: 'John Wycliffe, the organ of the devil, the enemy of the Church, the idol of heretics, the image of hypocrites, the restorer of schism, the storehouse of lies.'[3]

St Julian of Norwich: The days of St Julian of Norwich (1342-1416) were very difficult, but the suffering she saw did not drive her from God; on the contrary, she believed that suffering drove her closer to a loving God. She trusted that the Christian faith does not pertain to legalism and obligation, but to an experience of God's personal and compassionate love lavished in personal joy. *Revelations of Divine Love* (1383) commanded her the role as the first known female author in the English language; the book found popularity and encouraged a revival of faith in England. It has been a motivational tool down the ages to inspire other generations to accept the Reformation and other renewing experiences.

The Printing Press: Around 1445, Germany's Johann Gutenberg (1400-1468) developed Europe's first printing press and the first book off the press was the Holy Bible. 'No event of any century has...done more to dispel the ignorance upon which erroneous teachers traded. Thenceforth the laborious work of multiplying copies of any book by hand was at an end.'[4]

Martin Luther: A monk named Tetzel arrived in Germany with a message from Rome – with great wrath, he threatened the people with extreme punishments from God for their wicked ways and warned them of judgment to come. But he was not a evangelical preacher, he was selling the forgiveness of sins! Out of terrible fear, people impoverished themselves to buy their pardon. Today many would know immediately that this person was a swindler, but in 1517, this was the official message of the Roman Catholic Church, for the Pope himself had authorised the sale of indulgences.

Martin Luther (1484-1546) grew up without any first-hand account of what was in the Bible. He felt the call to serve Christ, but discovered that the monks knew little about the Scriptures because they believed the Roman Catholic Church had already extracted all the teaching from the Bible, and summed them up in the rules, creeds and traditions of the Church. As the Church of Rome grew corrupt over the centuries, people's lives were dominated by the influence of its teachings: There was no salvation outside of their rules and normal people were second class citizens to the priests. They could not receive forgiveness directly from God and because they had no access to the Bible, they had to believe what they were told. Luther was shocked by the corruption of the Church and went back to God's word for inspiration. He discovered that the establishment had debased God's word, taught lies as truth and profaned the gospel. In 1517, he nailed his ninety-five thesis to the Wittenberg Church door which exposed many of these lies and soon the world changed. People found liberty in the truth revealed and eventually the shockwave led to the forming of Protestant Christianity, which looked to the Bible for the truth, not to the Pope or to the doctrines of Rome. Martin Luther suffered a great deal because of the persecution of Rome, but his actions led to the Reformation which changed Europe, shaped Britain and later gave the U.S. a Protestant identity.

William Tyndale: The Lord's servant, William Tyndale (1494-1536) believed that the state or the established church should not have a monopoly on knowledge as it could be abused. He became an outlaw, simply because he wanted to translate the Bible into English. He produced the first English New Testament which was really popular and because of the new medium of print, was readily available. As a religious reformer and scholar his work became famous as the cornerstone upon which the 1611 King James Version of the Bible rests. His work at empowering the people did not go down well with the religious authorities, who tracked him down, tricked him and had him tried for heresy; he was found guilty, strangled and burnt at the stake.

On the author's visit to the Thames Embankment near the Houses of Parliament in London, he visited the statue of William Tyndale, with his last words recorded for posterity, "Lord open the king of England's eyes." Within a year by the king's command, an English Bible was made available in every parish church of the land. The English Bible brought knowledge to those outside of the established authorities, and helped bring accountability and freedom of thought to the people. No longer did they have to trust the priest or person in authority, they could study for themselves and interpret the Bible themselves. It would take a very long time for the people to truly be free to share knowledge and thoughts, but those who went before William Tyndale and those who followed his example, laid the foundation for free speech and freedom of knowledge – and they often paid for this with their lives.

John Knox: There are many who contributed towards the free expression of religious belief, especially as the Church of Rome grew corrupt and persecuted those who interpreted the Holy Scriptures differently. John Knox (1514-1572) was a man who passionately believed that the truth of the Bible was more important than the teachings of Rome. He was a forerunner in the cause of freedom of religious belief and though persecuted, he stood before the highest authorities and challenged them. He is regarded as The Father of the Protestant Reformation in Scotland. In Edinburgh, the old inscription which was on his tomb revealed the warrior spirit: 'Here lies one who never feared the face of man.'[5]

Book of Martyrs: John Foxe (1516-1587) recorded for posterity the stories of persecuted Christians from the early apostles up until the mid-sixteenth century. His book, *Foxe's Book of Martyrs* is without rival; it is the only exhaustive reference work on the martyrdom and persecution of early Christians and is considered to be one of the most important Christian history books ever printed. If you want to know what happened to the apostles after Acts, turn to this book.

Freedom of Speech – Milton's Argument Against Censorship: John Milton (1608-1674) was a man empowered and shaped by his Christian faith. His greatest work *Paradise Lost* is an epic, generally considered as one of the greatest works in the English language. Milton was a friend of liberty, an enemy of tyranny and used his command of language to help empower parliament during the English Civil War. He wrote defending the actions of the people against a corrupt Monarch. We should never underestimate John Milton's contribution to developing democracy by defending the rights of the people through his work influencing public opinion. In all that he wrote he was influenced by the Bible and his own Christian upbringing. Milton argued against the Licensing Order of 1643; his argument against censorship is full of biblical and classical notes. His tract, *Areopagitica: A Speech of Mr John Milton for the Liberty of Unlicensed Printing to the Parliament of England* was published in 1644 at the height of the English Civil War. This plea still remains the classic argument in the English language for liberty of speech and writing. We have free speech and press because of Christians like Milton.

Christian Allegory: John Bunyan (1628-1688) is one of the literary giants of printing history; his great works include *Pilgrim's Progress* and *Grace Abounding*. The former is probably the second most read book in publishing history and has been translated into more languages than any other book, second only to the Bible. The world's most famous Christian allegory *Pilgrim's Progress* found its genesis when Bunyan was imprisoned and suffering greatly for his faith in Christ. The book charms the reader with an intense character driven plot, full of incidents which many can identify with, all welded together with piercing imagination. With tenderness Bunyan drew from his own suffering to draw a picture of the Christian walk which millions have loved.

Robinson Crusoe: In the land that time had forgotten, Robinson Crusoe was stranded on his island of despair and the account of his conversion to Christianity, records the spiritual journey that the author himself had been on: 'I took the Bible and beginning at the New Testament, I began seriously to read it...I cried out aloud, "Jesus thou Son of David...give me repentance!" This was the first time that I could say, in the true sense of the words, that I prayed in all my life; for I now prayed with a sense of my condition.' Daniel Defoe (1660-1731) is best remembered for his novel about Robinson Crusoe. 'Daniel Defoe is generally considered to be England's first true novelist. His book *Robinson Crusoe* (1719), the tale of a sailor shipwrecked alone on a deserted island, is a classic of English literature.'[6] Defoe printed many pamphlets which addressed deep concerns of his day and considered himself a freedom fighter, especially as a dissenter against the Anglican religious establishment. Some of his work got him a ticket to prison! His writings continued and soon he started a newspaper called *The Review*. Many have called Defoe The Father of Modern Journalism because his dedication to truth and willingness to suffer for the sake of free speech, gave him a loyal following and loyal enemies. His most famous work was inspired by a real-life story of a man abandoned on the Pacific Island of Aguas Buenas, who spent time 'reading the Bible and singing Psalms, and enjoyed a more peaceful and devout existence than at any other time in his life.'

The Week-Day Preacher: Have you ever seen a satirised newspaper cartoon that sums up a weeks debate into a funny sketch? Next time you see one, spare a thought for William Hogarth a brilliant painter, pictorial satirist and pioneer of sequential art. William Hogarth (1697-1764) knew that it was not only the preacher who could cut through the moral junk-yard and speak out against corruption, but as the trailblazer of modern newspaper cartoons, he acquired the skills which made people laugh and think at the same time. His artistic creations jabbed at inept culture and politics; often with brute force he would confront governmental corruption or complacency in the Church. Book of Days states: 'William Hogarth, our great pictorial moralist. Repulsive and painful as many of his subjects are, seldom exhibiting the pleasing or sunny side of human nature, their general fidelity and truthfulness commend themselves alike to the hearts of the most illiterate and the most refined, whilst the impressive, if at times coarsely-expressed, lessons which they inculcate, place the delineator in the foremost rank of those who have not inaptly been termed week-day preachers.'[7] In 1747, he created a series of twelve comic engravings entitled Industry and Idleness. This body of art was another example of the Protestant Work Ethic which follows two apprentices; one is lazy whose life ends in crime and the other industrious who makes good of himself. The engravings promote hard work, honesty, morality and are all followed by instructive texts from the Bible. He clearly believed that the written word of God compiled with great artistry, could challenge people to live better lives. He also painted several biblical scenes, including Moses Before Pharaoh's Daughter, The Good Samaritan and Paul Before Felix. William Hogarth was also concerned that the law did not protect people's intellectual property rights; in other words, people could copy his paintings and sell them without giving him anything. He helped pioneer copyright law, which protects people's intellectual rights, as parliament passed Hogarth's Act.

An English Dictionary: Dr Samuel Johnson (1709-1784) will be remembered as one of the greatest and most honourable figures in the history of English literature. In his generation he was England's best known literary critic, an essayist and compiler of the famous dictionary which standardised English spelling. He was also a committed Christian who was devoted to the veracity of his faith; his studies led him to trust the Scriptures and his search led to him becoming a great apologist for the faith.

Johann Wolfgang Von Goethe: Considered by many as Germany's most important writer, Goethe (1749-1832) said, "Let mental culture go on advancing, let the natural sciences progress in ever greater extent and depth, and the human mind widen itself as much as it desires; beyond the elevation and moral culture of Christianity, as it shines forth in the gospels, it will not go."

Lexicographer: Noah Webster (1758-1843), the Father of American Scholarship and Education compiled America's most comprehensive dictionary and filled it with references to the Bible. He wrote: "The Bible was America's basic textbook in all fields," and "education is useless without the Bible."

Enduring Classics: 'It is a truth universally acknowledged that a single man in possession of a good fortune must be in want of a wife.'[8] Jane Austen (1775-1817) was the daughter of an English vicar, whose work has been read by millions, and made into multiple films and dramas. Her novels with chaste characters, valued-centred families and bitter-sweet integrity have caused a longing for more virtuous days. Her work was only possible because of her upbringing within a Christian culture, where faith and values were considered pre-eminent over self-seeking, and where duty took precedence over pleasure. Engaging each person, her work charters all characters in life from trivial busybodies, unhappy spouses to superficial marriage suitors seeking personal gain. The prime obsession of many of her characters was to find the person with whom they would spend the rest of their lives and it was this desire, which drove her bitter-sweet narratives. Today in Hollywood, often it is the Christian who is mocked, but immoral and impolite behaviour is often shunned in Jane's work and characters with Christian values are honoured. In *Mansfield Park*, the overlooked young lady who is our heroine is shocked even to consider that her love rival questioned the importance of prayer – unbelief was unbelievable! In *Emma*, the main character is humbled as she discovers how manipulation of others could indeed rob them of their destiny and happiness. She is forced to re-evaluate a class system which considers some better because of wealth and by her conclusion she discovers how much she has taken for granted. *Pride and Prejudice*, probably Jane's most famous work reveals how our first judgment of others is often flawed. Her consistent emphasis upon duty before feeling, character above pleasure and the importance of personal restraint, dignity and honour reveals a depth of Christian romance. In Jane's writings, the Judeo-

Christian order pervades all and it is the characters which exemplified Christian values that are honoured. Throughout her novels she was not afraid to be honest about life, showing humanity's failings and the difficulty of single women in her day. She also reveals how romance can be self-destructive and trivialised into a self-centred search for financial gain. Jane Austen's gravestone in Winchester Cathedral, England reads: 'In memory of Jane Austen, youngest daughter of the late Revd George Austen. She departed this life...after a long illness supported with the patience and hopes of a Christian...the extraordinary endowments of her mind obtained the regard of all who knew her...her charity, devotion, faith and purity have rendered her soul acceptable in the sight of her Redeemer.'

The Brontë Sisters: Charlotte Brontë (1816-1855) was a great Christian author and the elder of the three Brontë sisters, including Emily and Anne. Their famous novels include *Jane Eyre* and *Wuthering Heights*, which are considered in English literature as enduring classics, and have been translated to the small and big screen. *Jane Eyre* written by Charlotte Brontë was enormously successful. The author uses Jane's early experiences to express how harsh, critical and joyless some expressions of established Christianity had become; how very different was the master of Jane Eyre's boarding school, to the graceful Master that Charlotte knew by faith. Her love for Christ was revealed in her poems: 'When death bestows the martyr's crown and calls me into Jesus' rest. Then for my ultimate reward. Then for the world-rejoicing word. The voice from Father-Spirit-Son: "Servant of God, well hast thou done!" '[9] Emily Jane Brontë (1818-1848) novelist and poet, is best recounted for her novel *Wuthering Heights* and her poems reveal her faith in eternal happiness with God. 'Oh! Not for them should we despair. The grave is drear, but they are not there; their dust is mingled with the sod. Their happy souls are gone to God!'[10]

Thomas Carlyle: Scottish historian Carlyle (1795-1881), who is most notable for his work on the French Revolution said, "The Bible is the truest utterance that ever came by alphabetic letters from the soul of man, through which, as through a window divinely opened, all men can look into the stillness of eternity, and discern in glimpses their far-distant, long-forgotten home."[11]

Charles Dickens: The Famous author Charles Dickens (1812-1870) wrote many novels including *A Christmas Carol* and *The Adventures of Oliver Twist* which criticised social injustice. He said, "The New Testament is the very best book that ever was or ever will be known in the world."[12]

John Ruskin: Critic and author Ruskin (1819-1900) said, "Whatever merit there is in anything that I have written is simply due to the fact that when I was a child my mother daily read me a part of the Bible and daily made me learn a part of it by heart."[13]

Charles Dana: Charles A. Dana (1819-1897) wrote: 'The grand old Book still stands and this old earth, the more its leaves are turned and pondered, the more it will sustain and illustrate the pages of the Sacred Word.'[14]

C.S. Lewis: The magnum opus of C.S. Lewis (1898-1963) has rocked the world. Children have been entertained by his imagination, adults have grown in faith through his books and sceptics have been challenged by his thought. It was Lewis' BBC radio broadcasts, where his practical and intellectual sound experiences of faith were communicated, which drove countless numbers of people to tune in on a regular basis. Today, most people recall his famous book *Mere Christianity* and his children's stories, including *The Lion, The Witch and the Wardrobe*, in which Aslan the lion king, like Christ, died and was raised again. Lewis made the cover of *Time* magazine in 1947 calling him, 'One of the most influential spokesmen for Christianity in the English-speaking world.'[15] Millions have been entertained, inspired, challenged and even shocked by his work.

Tolkien: J.R.R. Tolkien (1892-1973) was the famous author of *The Lord of the Rings* and is loved by millions of readers and cinema goers alike. As a major scholar of the English language, he was twice Professor of Anglo-Saxon (Old English) at Oxford University. Tolkien and C.S. Lewis were contemporaries and friends; Chris Armstrong from Christianity Today wrote: 'Tolkien and Lewis shared the belief that through myth and legend – for centuries the mode many cultures had used to communicate their deepest truths – a taste of the Christian gospel's 'True Myth' could be smuggled past the barriers and biases of secularised readers.'[16]

Inspiring Others: Before action, comes thought and the great authors and freedom fighters that we have just considered, are some of the Christian people who have left a legacy of thought, which led others to action. They made great contributions to our freedom of speech, liberty of thought and practical demonstration of our faith. They helped record the past, change their present and secure our free future. However, the great problem with Western freedom is that people do not know what to do with it; and it was writers like C.S. Lewis who led the way, by showing that our purpose in the present is to be found in the faith of our past – in an individual relationship with the Lord Jesus Christ.

The Bible: The Bible has been the inspiration for many of the greatest authors and even movements in history. After being found reading the Bible, President Abraham Lincoln said to his sceptical friend Joshua Speed, "Take all of this book upon reason that you can and the balance on faith, and you will live and die a happier and better man."[17] President Woodrow Wilson (1856-1924) said, "I am sorry for the men who do not read the Bible every day. I wonder why they deprive themselves of the strength...it is the word of God...the key to your own heart and happiness."[17a]

"The Bible is a book that has not just shaped our country, but shaped the world," said British Prime Minister David Cameron. "The King James Bible has bequeathed a body of language that permeates every aspect of our culture and heritage from everyday phrases to our greatest works of literature, music and art...Along with Shakespeare, the King James Bible is a high point of the English language creating arresting phrases that move, challenge and inspire...From Milton to Morrison and Coleridge to Cormac McCarthy the Bible supports the plot, context, language and sometimes even the characters in some of our greatest literature. Tennyson makes over four hundred Biblical references in his poems and makes allusions to forty-two different books of the Bible...our language and culture is steeped in the Bible."[18]

Chapter Thirty

Great Explorers and Adventurers

"Send men to spy out the land" (Numbers 13:2).

The central African interior in the early nineteenth century was for the Western explorer what mars is to us today – unexplored, difficult to reach and fraught with danger. If an adventurer could reach the African interior what would one find – an ancient city, a forgotten civilisation, unknown wildlife or cannibalism? Even more worrying, when the missionary started the journey, would they ever return? For one missionary, his exploration of Africa would fill immense gaps in Western knowledge of Central and Southern Africa as he became the first European to cross the width of Southern Africa. He also discovered the great waterfall which he named after his Queen, Victoria. In the spirit of Indiana Jones, this real life adventurer travelled back to Britain to publicise his findings, report the terrors of slavery and set out for greater missions. He encouraged Queen Victoria and the British Empire to take the responsibility for ending slavery in the areas he had explored, and hoped to make a great chapter in Africa's history by opening the way for Christianity and commerce to enter Africa's interior. Later on in life, his great quest as well as the souls of men, was to search for the source of the world's longest river; at 4,150 miles the River Nile's fame spread around the globe. Around the world his stories aroused great interest and after being unheard of for some time, the U.S. *New York Herald* reporter Henry Stanley was sent out to find him. Against all the odds, Stanley met this explorer near Lake Tanganyika in October 1871 and greeted him with the most famous introduction in Western history, "Dr Livingstone I presume!"

The author has travelled in the footsteps of David Livingstone (1813-1873) and visited many of the homes, mission stations and places of discovery which were important in this missionary's life. The total overland journey in Africa consisted of 22,000km, 96 percent on public transport. The experience of travel, especially in central Africa is exhausting and consists of battles against pitiful roads, inadequate food and conflict to keep healthy. It also provides some of the greatest experiences and memories that one can imagine – the golden Island of Zanzibar, the overwhelming Victoria Falls and the ruins of his mission stations to name a few. With the benefit of one hundred and thirty years of development since his death, this experience proves that Livingstone was indeed a man unequalled in his generation.

David Livingstone achieved worldwide fame as one of the greatest European missionary explorers of Africa. He was the first to record and walk across Southern and Central Africa, including modern day Botswana, Zambia, Mozambique, Malawi, Tanzania and other nations. He started working in a mill in Scotland aged ten, but studied to become a missionary doctor. BBC History says of him, 'Livingstone became convinced of his mission to reach new peoples in the interior of Africa and introduce them to Christianity, as well as freeing them from slavery.'[1] After the journalist Henry Stanley left to report his findings to an anxious world, Livingstone wrote: 'My Jesus, my King, my life, my all, I again dedicate my whole life to Thee.' David Livingstone wore himself out as a missionary explorer and many diseases ravaged his body till finally, at four in the morning he was found kneeling by his bed – he had died whilst in prayer. The locals took out his heart, buried it in Africa and prepared the body to be sent back to England. London came to a stop in April 1874, as Livingstone was buried with kings in London's Westminster Abbey – his inscription states: 'David Livingstone. Missionary, Traveller, Philanthropist. His body is in Britain but his heart was buried under a tree in Africa – a custom reserved for those of a high rank.'

Navigating the Rapids of Canada: Egerton Young (1840-1909) took up the challenge of taking the gospel to the Indians in the North West of Canada. The locals were disturbed by the appearance of a white man, whose life was in constant threat because of the troubles between the inhabitants of the land – "I'm not the enemy of your people," was his declaration.[2] Young travelled hundreds of miles on the trail and by canoe; he battled fierce thunderstorms, torrents of rain, a cyclone and freezing water with rapids to take the gospel where no-one else would go. He led many Indians to the Lord, translated parts of the Bible into their language and taught many to read God's word. On one occasion small-pox broke out in a white settlement, which was quickly isolated to protect all the others. But this could lead to the starvation and death of every inhabitant – in a daring and successful mission, Egerton's Christian Indians took up the challenge of taking the much needed food and medicine to them over water, a route which only the Indians were capable of manoeuvring. The success of the mission saved many and true Christianity brought the two often warring peoples together through love and sacrifice.

Ending Slavery Abroad: General Charles Gordon (1833-1885) became a British celebrity and a national hero for his adventures in China, and for his endeavour to end slavery in the Sudan. He was a man of renown, but he never had confidence in self: 'I have less confidence in the flesh than ever, thank God, though it is a painful struggle and makes one long for the time when, this our earthly tabernacle, shall be dissolved; but may His will be done.'[3] He was born into a military family and as a young man saw action in the Crimean War (1853-1856). He inspired a generation at home by his extraordinary exploits in China, where he transformed a peasant force into a disciplined victorious army. On his return to England the public named him Chinese Gordon, for his exploits played a key role in Chinese history and helped save the Chinese Empire.

As an evangelical Christian Gordon believed his life should be used in the service of Jesus Christ and humanity, just as William Wilberforce had done previously. Wilberforce, another committed Christian had pioneered a change in British law which outlawed the slave trade and now the British government were dedicating vast amounts of its resources, including their army and navy, to force slave traders around the world out of business. 'By 1840 no fewer than 425 slave ships had been intercepted by the Royal Navy...nearly all of them were condemned.'[4] The British were shocked to discover the overwhelming influence of the slave trade in Sudan; the river Nile was full of slave traffic and nearly 70% of the population of Khartoum were slaves.[5] General Gordon arrived in the Sudan with a vision to eradicate the slave trade; his victories brought liberty to many and put traders out of business. He said, "No honour belongs to me, I am only the instrument God uses to accomplish His purpose."[6]

Gordon became a great explorer and visited the Holy Land searching for biblical sites, and it was he who discovered a tomb, which some believe to be the garden tomb and 'the place of the skull.' When the author visited Jerusalem, he toured this site which is also known as 'Gordon's Tomb,' and most believers who visit this area will see this empty tomb. Early in 1884, a leading newspaper said of him: 'General Gordon is without doubt the finest captain of irregular forces living.' Around the same time Prime Minister W.E. Gladstone said of him, "General Gordon is no common man. It is no exaggeration to say he is a hero. It is no exaggeration to say he is a Christian hero."[7]

Nevertheless, in the Sudan, a new force was arising which wanted to bring war to the entire Muslim world. Muhammad Ahmad Al-Mahdi declared himself the Mahdi (Muslim Messiah), raised a large fighting force, inciting them to Islamic Jihad and claimed he would unite the whole Muslim world under his name. Gordon was called to the Sudan to evacuate the Muslim Egyptian forces from Khartoum, which was soon under siege, but Gordon was committed to stay and help. At home, many did not want the British to get involved in the Sudan and as politicians debated, a relief force was withheld and the rebel army advanced. In 1885, Gordon could have saved himself but he refused to abandon the people in their hopeless situation. The Mahdi's army stormed into the city, overcame the Egyptian soldiers and killed Gordon; one eminent historian wrote: 'The Mahdi was in many ways a Victorian Osama Bin Laden, a renegade Islamic fundamentalist whose murder of General Gordon was '9/11' in miniature.'[8]

Queen Victoria was deeply disturbed that the British relief force was held back on purpose – it arrived two days after the fall of Khartoum, and the British public held Gladstone and his government accountable. The BBC programme *Clash of Worlds*,[9] featuring General Gordon's story revealed that after the Mahdi's victory, slavery was immediately re-introduced, as well as Islamic Shariah law; which included in the Sudan lashes for any women with their hair uncovered, and women caught in adultery were buried up to their necks in the sand and horses were run over them. This Islamist leader created a state of terror and destroyed the economy; so finally, Victoria's government sent her army to liberate the entire nation from the extremist government and free those forced back into slavery. Absorbing Sudan into the British Empire was never going to bring any financial gain to the nation, and it was an example of a costly endeavour, motivated by the nation's belief in a moral duty to help the most vulnerable in the world. But trying to square this belief, with the reality of the battlefield is troublesome. Meanwhile, in parts of the Sudan, this Mahdi is still remembered twice a day in the mosque prayer times.

It took the author two days on a train with no beds to get from the Northern border of Sudan into Khartoum. The route passes through some of the sites of the greatest battles between the British and the Mahdi's warriors. In Khartoum the Mahdi's tomb is still a major site for visitors to see despite being a very small building. In St Paul's Cathedral, London, Gordon's epitaph reveals a man of faith and courage, a hero victorious in faith and a Christian who laid down his life in service of others. 'Major General Charles George Gordon, C.B., who at all times and everywhere, gave his strength to the weak, his substance to the poor, his sympathy to the suffering, his heart to God. He saved an empire by his warlike genius, he ruled vast provinces with justice, wisdom, power, and lastly, obedient to his sovereign's command, he died in the heroic attempt to save men, women and children from imminent and deadly peril. "Greater love hath no man than this, that a man lay down his life for his friends." - St. John, xv. ch., v.13.'[10]

From Russia With Love: In 2001, Russian President Putin said, "One must agree with those who believe that without Christianity, without the Orthodox faith and the culture which sprang from it, Russia would have hardly existed as a state." Russian Christianity was very influential in shaping that nation, however in history, the failure of Russia to enter into liberty and the nation's eclipse into Communism could possibly be traced to the loss of almost all biblical Christianity within the nation. The Russian Orthodox Church became far removed from St Paul's writings about Christianity and was lost in ritual, superstition and tradition.

Lord Radstock (1833-1913) was a rich privileged English Lord, who became a great supporter of Christianity in Britain and became a living example of the priesthood of all believers. Without being ordained or asked to be a missionary, Radstock used his position to help rekindle biblical Christianity in Russia, throughout the highest levels of power in that nation. Much of his wealth was used in the service of Christ's Kingdom, but his personal adventures in Russia led to his witnessing for Jesus Christ in St Petersburg, the gathering place of all Russia's nobility and royalty, where even cabinet members became true believers. Princess Catherine Galitsin recalled, 'By heaven's power all doors were opened to him, halls, chapels and private houses: whole crowds pressed in to hear the glad tidings.'[11] Sharing and preaching, Radstock was the Lord's Apostle to Russia, for aristocracy would crowd in to hear the pure gospel message. Even Colonel Paschkoff, the wealthiest army officer in Russia was converted and later used his wealth to sponsor Bible distribution around Russia. Persecution soon followed the new converts and the nation suffered the horrors of Communism, but the small evangelical witness survived and grew, as Communism later diminished.

Cannibals Want Missionaries! China was a nation dead to the world and conflict with Western powers did little to help missionaries who wanted to open its doors to the gospel. Bursting into flames, mission houses were being destroyed and foreigners were fleeing. The city was in lockdown with guards posted to keep the 'foreign devils' out – for rumours had spread that the white man would kidnap people and eat them! Travelling through areas which no European had seen before, the team crossed rivers, navigated narrow ledges and escaped falling rocks on their way into the city. The British Consul could not believe they had found a way in and urged them to leave immediately. C.T. Studd (1860-1931) boldly declared that God had called them there and without doubt, they would stay and minister for Christ. As C.T. Studd attempted to sleep that ravenous night, we can only wonder if his mind went back to the memories of home. As a first-class cricketer he often stood before thousands of adoring fans, applauding every move which brought glory to his team. In 1883, the Cricketers Record stated: 'C.T. Studd, must, for the second year, be accorded the premier position as an all-round cricketer.' He had returned cricket's greatest trophy to England and became the hero of many. In his desire to follow the Master, Studd counted fame and fortune as nothing. All had changed in his life when he accepted Christ into his heart: 'At once, joy and peace came into my soul. I knew then what it was to be born again, and the Bible, which had been so dry to me before, became everything.'[12] The missionary endeavour made newspaper headlines; people could hardly believe that C.T. Studd and other Cambridge graduates were off to China. One of England's most famous sportsmen had forsaken all for the sake of His call!

During his time in China, Studd received a massive inheritance and as he prayed about what to do, the words of Jesus echoed in his heart, "Sell all that you have and give to the poor and come follow Me." Following the command of Jesus, C.T. Studd gave all his inheritance away to Christian organisations and looked to the Lord alone to provide. For many years Studd laboured in China, winning people to the Lord and teaching them the principles of Christian discipleship. Due to his wife's illness, he returned to England and later they completed missions in India.

'Cannibals Want Missionaries,' brought a large smile to C.T. Studd; it was this poster which caught his attention in England and during the meeting he heard of many unreached tribes in Africa. Now nearing the latter end of his life, with no money, poor health and a sick wife he picked up his cross again, and responded to the call. His plan was to go to the Sudan, but God began to burn into his heart, "This trip is not merely for the Sudan, it is for the whole unevangelised world!" It took him over half a year to enter the heart of Africa; a man who grew up in a wealthy home, laughed as he now lived in a mud hut – writing home his letters were always 'from Buckingham Palace.'

Life on the mission field was full of hazards and cruel at times, but C.T. always kept a light hearted view of things. Once a team member fired shots into the river, to scare away crocodiles as he baptised new believers and snakes found their way into his hut. Studd had left fame and fortune, to serve the Lord in China, India and Africa, and he founded the Worldwide Evangelistic Crusade (WEC). The author visited the WEC headquarters in England and found that the faith, vision and pioneering work of Studd still lives on vibrantly in the hearts and minds of those still willing to sacrifice all for Christ and His Great Commission.

Christianity and Mission: Faith, missions and adventure have always gone hand in hand and these Christian pioneers, like many others have often been the very first to go into the unknown to proclaim peace and in so doing planted Christianity into the heart of the world. President Theodore Roosevelt (1882-

1945) noted the contribution of missions in Africa by saying, "Even a poorly taught and imperfectly understood Christianity, with its underlying foundations of justice and mercy, represents an immeasurable advance."[13] In 1908, Winston Churchill expressed the contrast between the Christian areas of Africa and others, calling it 'another world' of 'clothed, cultivated, educated natives.'[14] In December 2008, Journalist and atheist Matthew Parris wrote: 'Missionaries, not aid money, are the solution to Africa's biggest problem...I've become convinced of the enormous contribution that Christian evangelism makes in Africa: sharply distinct from the work of secular NGOs, government projects and international aid efforts. These alone will not do. Education and training alone will not do. In Africa Christianity changes people's hearts. It brings a spiritual transformation. The rebirth is real. The change is good... Christians black and white, working in Africa, do heal the sick, do teach people to read and write.'[15]

The sociologist Professor Robert Woodberry spent fourteen years studying the long-term impact of missionaries. He found that 'areas where Protestant missionaries had a significant presence in the past are on average more economically developed today, with comparatively better health, lower infant mortality, lower corruption, greater literacy, higher educational attainment (especially for women), and more robust membership in nongovernmental associations.'[16]

During the nineteenth century the stories of Christian leaders inspired huge numbers of people, but Mark Greene wrote of this generation: 'Entertainment is the opiate of the masses, and we are distracted from reflective thought and radical action by the power, creativity and pervasiveness of our media.'[17] Teachers are also concerned about the way celebrity culture is misleading a generation of young people – in a recent survey 70% of teachers said that celebrity culture is 'perverting children's aspirations and expectations.'[18] Perhaps it's time for us to rediscover these Christians who mapped the unknown, ended human tragedy and changed the spiritual heritage of the world, and perhaps it's time for us to start writing another chapter in this story. The book *How to Plan, Prepare and Successfully Complete Your Short-term Mission* by Mathew Backholer was written to aid those who want to serve God on a STM.

Chapter Thirty-One

The Civil Rights Movement

"Therefore you shall not oppress one another, but you shall fear your God, for I am the Lord your God" (Leviticus 25:17).

The colour of one's skin determined everything in America for generations. For one nameless person, the reality of her situation only came home one terrible day. For years she had seen white people enter a beautiful restaurant and she only wanted to look inside. When she walked in, slowly opening the doors the restaurant went silent. People began to whisper about the sign outside which barred black people from entering and angry customers began to demand the management to do something. The words which were spoken to her that day were never forgotten, nor the sense of inferiority. She did not feel like a second class citizen, it was worse than that; a sense of shame took hold of her that day and a wish that she could deny who she really was. It was the Jim Crow Laws of 1881 which segregated black and white people that made this possible. These actions were a clear violation of the Civil Rights Act of 1875, but it seemed that even the Supreme Court had the power to degrade and devalue human life, for in 1883 it overturned it.

In 1942, James Leonard Farmer addressing the situation founded the Congress of Racial Equality (CORE), which was dedicated to peaceful, active promotion of black rights. In 1943, CORE members began a campaign of civil disobedience, and visited a Chicago restaurant that did not serve black people and staged a sit-in. In the land of the free, only white people knew freedom; even the buses were segregated for millions. It was an event on a bus which would change the entire course of history in the United States. It was December 1955, when Rosa Parks took a seat on a bus expecting an uneventful journey home. She had no idea that her actions would lead one day to *Time* magazine calling her one of the one hundred most influential people of the twentieth century. When a white man entered the bus, this little African American woman was expected to move, but she refused. It would have been easy and conventional to do what everyone else expected her to do, but she stood up for justice. "Since I have always been a strong believer in God," said Rosa later, "I knew that He was with me and only He could get me through that next step." She was apprehended by the police and her arrest was the catalyst which led to a year-long bus boycott in Montgomery, Alabama. Her defiance of the discriminatory rules led her to be called The Mother of the Civil Rights Movement. 'As a child,' she later wrote: 'I learned from the Bible to trust in God and not be afraid. I felt the Lord would give me the strength to endure whatever I had to face.'[1] This event accelerated the Civil Rights Movement which soon was led by Baptist minister Martin Luther King Jr. (1929-1968) who sought non-violent confrontation calling for justice and equality.

Leading the bus boycott to protest at segregation Luther said, "We must keep God in the forefront. Let us be Christian in all our actions." He encouraged his protesters not to hate white people saying, "Love is one of the pinnacle parts of the Christian faith." Years later, a quarter of a million people marched on Washington where one of Christianity's greatest orators gave a plea for equality and brotherhood between white and black people. "I have a dream that one day this nation will rise up and live out the true meaning of its creed: 'We hold these truths to be self-evident: that all men are created equal.' I have a dream that one day on the red hills of Georgia the sons of former slaves and the sons of former slave owners will be able to sit down together at a table of brotherhood...We will be able to speed up that day when all of God's children – black men and white men, Jews and Gentiles, Protestants and Catholics – will be able to join hands and sing in the words of the old Negro spiritual: 'Free at last! Free at last! Thank God Almighty, we are free at last!' "[2]

'The ideals for this organisation he took from Christianity,' explained Nobel Prize. 'King travelled over six million miles and spoke over twenty-five hundred times, appearing wherever there was injustice, protest, and action; and meanwhile he wrote five books as well as numerous articles. In these years he led a massive protest in Birmingham, Alabama, that caught the attention of the entire world, providing what he called a coalition of conscience.'[3] In 1962, American President Kennedy issued an Executive Order which forbade any racially motivated discrimination in government housing. In addition, James Meredith, an African American, was accepted by the University of Mississippi following a court order and 12,000 federal troops were assigned to the campus to maintain order during the rioting that followed.

Fannie Lou Hamer (1917-1977) was another civil rights leader whose sense of justice was rooted in the Bible. She became involved in the struggle after hearing a sermon speaking of biblical justice. She famously sang, "Let my people go," linking the story of Israelite slavery to the plight of African Americans and she was a source of inspiration for many. She became the Vice-Chair of the Mississippi Freedom Democratic Party and in 1964 attended the Democratic National Convention. Speaking of the violence which was endured she said, "All of this is on account we want to register, to become first-class citizens....Is this America, the land of the free and the home of the brave where we have to sleep with our telephones off the hooks because our lives be threatened daily because we want to live as decent human beings – in America?" President Johnson signed the 1964 Civil Rights Act into law which affected legislation for voting, schools, accommodation, federal aid, employment and treatment of civil rights cases.

Martin Luther King became the youngest man to be awarded the Nobel Peace Prize. He was tragically assassinated in 1968. The campaigns of Luther were not marred with the type of racism or hatred of white people for which similar campaigners who followed other religions were noted for. Luther had taken the high ground and it was the Christian faith that was always central. Millions of African Americans benefited from the campaigns of Martin Luther King Jr. and others like him. They helped form a legacy, not only for African Americans, but for every citizen of the world. For as America dealt with her problems at home, she was able to put pressure on other nations and helped set a precedent for equality.

The historian Simon Schama CBE, identified the source of the movement which changed America and the world. He said, "The Civil Rights movement wouldn't have happened at all without the black Church."[4] British Prime Minister David Cameron said, "The Bible has infused some of the greatest speeches from Martin Luther King's dream that Isaiah's prophecy would be fulfilled, and that one day 'every valley shall be exalted,'[5]" and it was.

Chapter Thirty-Two

Ending Apartheid

"God has shown me that I should not call any man common or unclean" (Acts 10:28).

My mother came home from work today, she is a cleaner in a white residence. Every day she visits a large elegant home full of modern equipment and prepares everything to be suitable for the owners. Then she comes back to a nine by twelve leaky shanty home and prepares dinner for all her children. A few months ago, her employer accused her of stealing something and told her that she would not get paid until it was returned. We did not eat for a week; finally they looked behind a cabinet and noticed that the item had fallen there; they never apologised and the money was never paid. Mother has been our wage earner for two years now. It happened in the middle of the night, when eight white police officers ransacked our home; they accused my father of sabotage and dragged him away. I never thought that would be the last day that I would see him.

After several months we were given access to the official papers which claimed he had died from natural causes. The pictures told another story – it was obvious he had been beaten to death; we never got to see his body and his death was never recorded as a crime. We used to live in another ghetto, but everything changed when government bulldozers rampaged their way through our homes. I can't tell you how soul-destroying it feels being poor, but to have everything taken in a minute is brutal. Two weeks ago, thousands of the black community came out to protest; we had no real weapons and were considered as nothing before their superior forces. They opened fire on us all and we ran for our lives; as I looked behind me, I saw bodies of children in the street, victims of a government who considers the greatest crime one can commit is the crime of being black.

Opposition: In Church Square, Cape Town, stands a statue of Andrew Murray in the grounds of his old church. Pushing the doors open reveals a titanic size house of God, with a pulpit rising almost to the ceiling and an organ which looks as if it belongs in the Royal Albert Hall, London. But more important than the grand feel, is the message that Andrew Murray (1828-

1917) preached from the pulpit. From the very beginning Murray was opposed to Afrikaner Nationalism, which eventually led to Apartheid and he was not the first. In 1828, missionary John Philip, who was working with William Wilberforce secured from Britain a declaration for South Africa that black Africans should have the same rights as the white settlers, and other missionaries raised the same concern. David Livingstone had also been confronted with Boer brutality towards the natives and his support for the indigenous tribes led to the Boers often treating him as an enemy, and they eventually destroyed his third mission station. The author visited the remains of this station just outside of Botswana's capital. All that is left are the foundation stones, which are marked out by a tiny link of chains and the unmarked grave of his infant daughter. However all the pressure did not bear results and over the years the racist attitude grew more extreme until from 1948 onwards Apartheid was enforced in South Africa.

Apartheid was a system of racial segregation in which citizens of European descent held the wealth and power of the nation; they used their power to create laws which dominated and discriminated against all other races. District Six, in Cape Town, is a chilling reminder of how ugly Apartheid became. 'In 1965, the Apartheid government, declared District Six 'white.' More than 60,000 people were forcibly uprooted and relocated onto the barren plains of the Cape Flats.'[1] The local church in this district became a focal point for opposition to Apartheid and because of this church's importance in the struggle, the authorities have turned it into a museum to tell the story of those years. In the late 1940s the resistance began with prayer meetings, later the church became a safe haven for freedom gatherings, until the police tried to shut them. The local papers tell the story of the church's victory in the courts and outside on the wall one can find the famous plaque of shame, which the church leadership unveiled to oppose Apartheid.

A former resident of District Six was the guide who showed the author around Robben Island, where Nelson Mandela was kept a prisoner for many years. Nelson received his first name when his teacher from the Christian school he attended crowned him 'Nelson.' His mother converted to Christianity when he was seven years old, and he outlines in his autobiography that he is a Christian, whose religious beliefs explain his convictions and actions later in life. Few could have imagined the struggle that took place in his lifetime or the suffering that many undertook for the cause. After our guide spoke of torture and virtual slave labour, one visitor asked in anger, "Why were these people not punished for these crimes?" The former prisoner and District Six resident said with a large smile, "Reconciliation...the miracle." Mandela is perhaps the first leader ever to take the Christian ideal of forgiveness and apply it to a whole nation. It appeared that without preaching, Mandela was asking the whole nation to embrace Jesus' Sermon on the Mount. At one point in history, the world believed South Africa would descend into a bloody civil war, but redemption was found through forgiveness.

When Mandela was in prison, the power vacuum was filled by Archbishop Desmond Tutu, who became the embodiment of the call for justice. During these days Tutu had the unique ability to raise a crowd to a frenzied apex of anger at injustice, but was still able to send them away with the message of forgiveness and reconciliation. Tutu said, "Many people think that Christians should be neutral or that the Church must be neutral. But...the Church in South Africa must be the prophetic Church which cries out, 'Thus saith the Lord,' speaking up against injustice and violence, against oppression and exploitation, against all that dehumanises God's children and makes them less than what God intended them to be....for my part, the day will never come when Apartheid will be acceptable. It is an evil system and it is at variance with the gospel of Jesus Christ. That is why I oppose it and can never compromise with it – not for political reasons, but because I am a Christian." In 1993 Tutu stood in front of a crowd of 120,000 people and led the people crying out, "We will be free! All of us! Black and white together!" His message was completed with his famous rainbow speech saying, "We are the rainbow people of God! We are unstoppable! Nobody can stop us on our march to victory! No one, no guns, nothing! Nothing will stop us, for we are moving to freedom!...For God is on our side!"[2]

In 1984, Tutu was awarded the Nobel Peace Prize for 'Desmond Tutu has formulated his objective as "a democratic and just society without racial divisions" and has set forward the following points as minimum demands: 1. Equal civil rights for all. 2. The abolition of South Africa's passport laws. 3. A common system of education and 4. The cessation of forced deportation from South Africa to the so-called "homelands." [3]

When international pressures caused the value of the rand to plunge, Tutu brought tens of thouands out onto the streets of Cape Town in peaceful protests. Tutu cried out, "Free our leader, free our leader." Mandela was soon released and the days of Apartheid were numbered. In 1994, South Africa had its first democratic elections and one of the most moving images of the next few years was that of Tutu breaking down and weeping at the Truth and Reconciliation Commission, which he chaired.

Professor Tony Campolo wrote: 'The collapse of Apartheid in South Africa offers another dramatic example of the churches bringing principalities and powers into submission to God's will. Archbishop Tutu, the leader of the Anglican Church in that country, was able to make the Church into a force for justice. There can be no question as to the crucial role the Church played in challenging the racism that had made black Africans into less than second-class citizens. Young people...found in Tutu a spokesperson and leader for their movement. American author (and my friend) Jim Wallis describes how, on one occasion, Tutu met with thousands of freedom-seeking young people in the cathedral of Cape Town. The atmosphere was electric with anticipation as Tutu took his place in the pulpit. He pointed to the policemen who had positioned themselves along the walls of the cathedral to intimidate the crowd. Then he lovingly spoke to the police: "Come join us! You know we will win, so why not be part of the victory?" Then he led the thousands of young people in singing freedom songs. The congregation rose to its feet, swayed to the music and started dancing in the aisles. There was no containing these young people, who were celebrating the coming end of Apartheid.'[4]

Chapter Thirty-Three

Prison Reform

"For I was hungry and you gave Me food...I was in prison and you came to Me" (Matthew 25:35-36).

In the eighteenth and early nineteenth centuries, prison conditions in Europe were appalling. Elizabeth Fry (1780-1845), a Bible-believing Christian, against protocol visited a local prison and was horrified by the cruelty she witnessed. There was mass overcrowding, a bucket in the corner was the communal toilet, and women and children slept on the floor together. In these tiny rooms they had to do their cooking and washing with little water, and they had to pay for everything. Elizabeth was shocked to discover that children were sent to prison for stealing food for survival, and punishments were harsh for the poor and lenient for the rich. She even discovered that some had been thrown into prison without a trial – violating the basic laws of England. There was little sympathy for the injustice which led the poor to crime, even if the person was caught stealing bread to survive. Some thought prisoners should be treated like animals and made to suffer, whilst Elizabeth believed people should be rehabilitated to play a role in society, or at least treated humanely. The conflict between the attitude of society and her Christian faith was revealed when she cried out, "Oh Lord, may I be directed what to do and what to leave undone."

Elizabeth Fry felt sympathy for the women and children incarcerated and organised a group to help female prisoners in a local prison. She made available schooling for children behind bars, and provided women with wool and sewing materials so they could make goods to sell. Her motivation was the words of Jesus, where prisoners are especially remembered by the Lord. 'Then the righteous will answer Him saying, "Lord, when did we see You hungry and feed You...when did we see You a stranger and take You in, or naked and clothe You? Or when did we see You sick, or in prison and come to You?" And the King will answer and say to them, "Assuredly, I say to you, inasmuch as you did it to one of the least of these My brethren, you did it to Me" ' (Matthew 25:37-40).

Eventually her sacrificial example earned her the right to speak to powerful people in parliament about the conditions of prisons.

Due to her labour and that of others, the 1823 Goad Act was passed which improved conditions. Also, prisoners shipped to Australia were no longer chained to the decks during the voyage, as they had been previously.

Her work is widely recognised, being only one of four women, including the Queen, who is featured on the Bank of England's legal tender (£5 note). Fry achieved much as an English prison reformer, social reformer and philanthropist. She helped force through legislation to make the treatment of prisoners more humane and challenged Europeans to treat prisoners as human beings. She aided the homeless by establishing night shelters, and created a nationwide society which visited and provided for the poor. She also opened a training school for nurses which assisted in inspiring Florence Nightingale. Through personal sacrifice and bravery she revealed the individual human face behind the label 'criminal,' and awoke the conscience of the nations of Europe to the ill-treatment, filth and inhumanity of the prison system.

Christian leaders have not only been concerned about improving conditions within prisons, but also preventing people from ending up there. Benjamin Rush (1745-1813) was an American Revolutionary leader and signatory of the Declaration of Independence. He believed that the way to prevent crime was to teach the Holy Scriptures. He said, "I lament that we waste so much time and money in punishing crimes and take so little pains to prevent them...we neglect the only means of establishing and perpetuating our republican forms of government; that is, the universal education of our youth in the principles of Christianity by means of the Bible."[1] Two hundred years later, many prisons are happy to open their doors to Christian chaplains because it has been proved time and again, that conversion to Christianity is a major help in stopping people re-offend and helping to establish them as responsible citizens.

Chapter Thirty-Four

Global Reform

'How beautiful are the feet of those who preach the gospel of peace, who bring glad tidings of good things' (Romans 10:15).

Britain's Dundee City Council wrote of missionaries: 'Like lambs to the slaughter, they came to a country with its river mists and overpowering heat, where diseases and infections were legion, and they succumbed in their hundreds to the very fevers from which the modern traveller is mercifully spared. Their average life expectancy was just a few years, and those who survived and returned home often endured recurring fevers and ill-health for the rest of their lives.'[1] Christian missionaries have always made huge personal, professional, financial and often physical sacrifices to obey the call, but despite their successful humanitarian works, they are often criticised. 'Political correctness now puts missionaries in the dock and charges them with being worldwide murderers of liberty, independence and culture. In the past this charge was laid by Communists, but more recently it has been taken up by other plainly anti-Christian historians, and retold by ill-informed teachers in many British schools and colleges,' wrote Dr Peter Masters.[2]

Heathenism To Holiness: Christianity spread like wildfire after the Lord's resurrection, and soon the gospel started to arrive in Europe and wherever the gospel went, it brought reform. In Julius Caesar's record of *The Gallic Wars* he describes Britain before Christianity. His record explains how Britons were governed by their religious teachers, who appeared to have been a separate caste with peculiar privileges. The people sacrificed in open-air temples, sometimes on immense stones. The author has travelled all over Britain, and visited many of these places of ancient worship and mysterious monuments, including the famous Stonehenge. 'On great occasions human victims were offered as vicarious propitiatory sacrifices. The elements of fire, earth and water, vegetation etc., were additional objects of their veneration.'[3] When the Anglo-Saxon's invaded Britain they brought their heathenism with them. In *Anglo-Saxon Britain* it states: 'The average heathen Anglo-Saxon religion was merely a vast mass of superstition, a dark and gloomy terrorism begotten of the vague dread of misfortune...where war and massacre are the highest business of every man's lifetime, and a violent death the ordinary way in which he meets his end.'[4] As time went on the new inhabitants of England accepted Christianity and their heathen ways were replaced with godly civilizing faith. Also the Christian religion helped bring peace to the land, as the wars between the peoples subsided, for now they had a common bond between them all. 'It was clear to everybody that this marvellous spread of Christianity brought great good to the Anglo-Saxon people, for instead of fighting against each other, they dwelt within their own borders and became a very prosperous race.'[5]

The Christian message ended the darkness of superstition in England and swept Europe into a Christian age. Having benefited greatly from the faith, Europeans themselves would later take the Christian gospel to the ends of the world, and call for the reform that Christianity had brought in their own lands. Speaking of the British faith based organisations that spread Christianity around the world in the nineteenth century, the historian Niall Ferguson considered that they were 'the century's most successful non-governmental organisations (NGOs).'[6]

Despite the humanitarian nature of Christian missionary work, they frequently found that non-religious people were the ones who hindered and criticised their work, just as they do today. Christians then, as today, are frequently at the fore of relieving suffering, providing medical care and education in the developing world, as well as spiritual encouragement and moral guidance. In the context of the fight to end slavery in Jamaica, the book *Missionary Triumph Over Slavery* by Dr Peter Master's states: 'Most of these missionaries were, at some time in their service banned, arrested, molested, slandered and impeded by those whose ongoing power and wealth depended on the continuance of ignorance and slavery. Proof of the social and religious sincerity of most missionaries is to be seen in the alarming short life-span that they faced, most dying from local fevers within three years of arrival.'[7]

A Missionary Fights For Women's Rights: The screams of the woman pierced the heart of the foreigner and they sent waves of fear down his spine. In a state of confusion his body was not sure if it should burn with rage, or vomit. A day after watching this cruelty, his hands were still shaking and he was still struggling to accept what he had witnessed was real. His own eyes had seen a healthy woman being forcibly burnt alive on the funeral fire of her dead husband and those who practiced it thought it was a noble religious practice. Suttee was a Hindu funeral custom in which a dead man's widow had to immolate herself on her husband's funeral pyre. In theory, this practice was supposed to take place on a voluntary basis, but the missionaries had discovered many cases of widows, and at times children being forced to burn to death with their dead relative. The process of banning this inhuman practice took over two decades, but by the eighteenth century many European nations had made it illegal in colonial territories.

Over time the British ruled much of the subcontinent of India, and it was the missionary William Carey who took up the challenge to bring a total ban to end this violence and murder of women. The East India Company was mostly concerned with keeping the peace and creating a climate where trading could continue unhindered, so William Carey's presence in India was at first considered undesirable. During Carey's lifetime he was first considered as a terrible nuisance by the authorities, but by the end of his ministry he had won the love and respect of all; now he was an essential partner for peace. On the mission field, Carey reported the horrific practice of Suttee and at home in Britain, William Wilberforce amongst many other evangelical believers began a campaign against it. 'Between 1813 and 1825 a total of 7,941 women died this way in Bengal alone,' wrote Niall Ferguson.[8] He then explained the case of a widow called Radhabyee in 1823, where eye-witnesses saw her escaping the flames of her husband's funeral fire, only to be dragged back by three men, who piled wood on top of her to keep her there. Managing to escape again, with almost her whole body burnt, she jumped into the river – the men followed and held her under until she drowned. This was real life and it was happening in the name of local religion, culture and tradition.

The pressure-cooker at home began to yield results as the East India Company started to consider banning the act and in 1813 the Bengal presidency started collecting figures on the practice. But for success Carey would need the support of local theologians and leaders. Ram Mohan Roy, a Bengali reformer began a campaign and taught that their religion did not require this act. At the end of 1829, Carey's faith was rewarded by the practice being banned in the Bengal presidency lands by Lord William Bentinck.

The author visited Carey's home and mission in India, and the neighbourhood still feels similar to the time of Carey. His work and ministry were excruciatingly sacrificial, with poverty, illness and the premature death of his two wives, and some children, all a part of his experience; yet the man who saw both his wives die in India, saved the women of India from having their lives taken from them. The battle to end Suttee took decades, but when the new law was issued, 'Carey was preparing to preach,' and, 'a courier from the governor-general arrived with an urgent dispatch, an order in council which Carey was requested immediately to translate into Bengali. It was nothing less than the famous edict abolishing Suttee throughout British dominions in India. Springing to his feet and throwing off his black coat he cried, "No church for today!" Without the loss of a moment he sent an urgent request to one of his colleagues to take service, summoned his pundit and then settled down to his momentous task. For twenty-five years he has been urging the necessity of this law and there should be no further loss of time and life – if he could prevent it. "If I delay an hour to translate and publish this, many a widow's life may be sacrificed," he said.'[9]

Language Resurgence: Christian missionaries have always been accused of destroying local culture, but the Father of Modern Missions was honoured in India for serving that nation, including helping the resurgence of the Bengali language. For Carey brought the first printing press to the nation, and worked hard to print works in local languages and translated much besides the Bible. Author Louise Creighton (1850-1936) wrote: 'Missionaries have not only done much for civilisation, they have also done much for science. All over the world they have been the first to reduce illiterate language to writing, to make grammars for them, to provide them with a translation of the Bible and other books. They have been foremost amongst discoverers and explorers of unknown lands, and their studies of the customs and primitive peoples have been a most important contribution to ethnology. Many of them have been distinguished as naturalists, geographers and scientific observers.'[10]

Jamaican Emancipation: William Knibb (1803-1845) was a missionary to Jamaica and an honest friend of its people. He was opposed and harassed by the land owners, and established clergy because of his non-conformist evangelical views. After his arrival in Jamaica he wrote home to England saying: 'The curse blast of slavery has, like a pestilence, withered almost every moral bloom. I know not how any person can feel a union with such a monster, such a child of hell. I feel a burning anger against it.'[11] When the local people revolted against slavery, much of the blame came to Knibb's door who was arrested for not being willing to fight to subdue the population. The uproar made the ears of every Englishman tingle and soon he was called to parliament to give an account. In England, Knibb spoke up for the Jamaicans, revealing the true horror of slave labour and managed to turn public opinion in favour of liberty. When emancipation was granted, Knibb was welcomed back as a hero and revival broke out! The story of this revival can be found in Mathew Backholer's book *Global Revival – Worldwide Outpourings*. In Jamaica, the authorities still considered Knibb as an enemy, but the locals saw him as their hero, who stood up for them in England where they had no voice.

'We are being told today that Christian missionaries of the past were tools of colonial oppression and destroyers of culture,' explained Dr Peter Masters, 'the story of William Knibb shows how wildly wrong this is. Persecuted by British rulers in Jamaica because he opposed settlers' abuses he was pivotal in swinging British public opinion behind legislation to end colonial slavery.'[12]

Ending Slavery Abroad: David Livingstone's (1813-1873) mission journeys inspired an entire generation. He worked endlessly to bring to naught the slave trade in Africa and after his witness, others followed in his footsteps. Creighton wrote: 'Livingstone had so impressed England with the needs of Central Africa that as a result of his exhortations the Universities Mission was founded. They had to begin by reducing Swahili to a written language...seven years later the slave market in Zanzibar was closed and a cathedral was built where it had been.'[13] The author has been inside the underground slave cells in Zanzibar, it was horrific; yet there was joy that Christianity closed (as the sign outside states), 'The last open slave market in the world.' The cathedral's high altar now stands on the exact spot where the old whipping post once was.

Changing Hearts, Changing Ways: In 1839 John Williams came ashore on the island of Eromanga, in the South Pacific and within a few minutes was martyred, cooked and eaten by the natives. John Geddie heard of this missionary and was inspired to go there to sacrifice himself in the work of the Lord. Dr Steel of Sydney wrote of these Canadian missionaries to the New Hebrides: 'The Geddie's had to pass through a hard and trying experience...their property was stolen, their house threatened with fire and their very lives imperilled. Meanwhile strangling widows on the death of their husbands continued. Intertribal fighting was chronic and people were afraid to go from one side of the island to the other, for fear of being killed, cooked or eaten.' When the people converted to Christianity, all the old sins and crimes against humanity had to be repented-of and forsaken. This missionary converted the soul to Christ and the mind to godly morality. In 1872, Geddie passed into glory.

Mathew Backholer researched these events and many others, telling them in *Global Revival – Worldwide Outpourings*, and in this book we discover that in recognition of this missionary's work, a wooden tablet was placed in a church he built and inscribed in the local language to the memory of John Geddie was: 'When he landed here in 1848 there were no Christians and when he left here in 1872 there were no heathen.'[14]

Defending Human Rights in Africa: Enraged, the two tribal warriors prepared for war and no man or chief dared stop them. As the crowd moved out of the way, one small woman stood between them and in Christ's name told them to stop. The warrior told her to get out of the way or die. "Shoot if you dare!" she called back. The stand-off of wills continued, until the mighty warriors had to concede defeat to the defenceless woman. Mary Slessor (1848-1915) was a missionary to Africa who served in an area known as the White Man's Grave. In her neighbourhood death stalked all missionaries and none were strangers to witch doctors, cannibals, swarms of insects, lions and deadly diseases. In Britain, she had worked twelve hours a day in a factory, waiting for a chance to serve God and by the age of twenty-nine she landed in West Africa. This young lady faced dangers beyond imagination and through courage, she not only ended much tribal warfare, but changed the spiritual landscape. A representative of Dundee City Council wrote: 'Witchcraft and superstition were prevalent in a country whose traditional society had been torn apart by the slave trade. Human sacrifice routinely followed the death of a village dignitary, and the ritual murder of twins was viewed by the new missionary with particular abhorrence. Her dedicated efforts to forestall this irrational superstition was to prove a resounding success.'[15]

"Oh Lord," she once prayed, "I thank Thee that I can bring these people Thy Word. But Lord, there are other villages back in the jungle where no man has gone. They need Jesus, too. Help me reach them!"[16] Mary trekked into unknown areas to preach the gospel, even though all people, including local chiefs warned her she would die. She was shocked by local customs which included killing the wives and slaves of important people upon their masters death, killing twins and worshipping the skulls of dead men. She preached the gospel, won the respect of all and brought crimes to an end. Mary also did much to improve the rights of women who were often considered inferior to animals.

Throughout her life, she suffered much through sickness and diseases, which would never have afflicted her at home. At her funeral stood many who loved her – former cannibals, chiefs, warriors and people whose lives were saved because the old practices had been abandoned. This woman, who had trekked through jungles in the darkness to help the lowest of all, was in death, given a state funeral and was later honoured by Queen Elizabeth II of Great Britain, who made a pilgrimage to her graveside. Her home nation recalls her achievements by depicting her on the £10 Clydesdale note and Dundee City Council concluded: 'Few have given so much of themselves to so many and under such appalling conditions.'[17]

Ending Human Sacrifice: Alexander Mackay gave his life to Africa and in 1878 he began his vision 'to connect Christianity with modern civilisation' and to train the young men in faith and science together. He wanted public works, railways and mines etc., but first, the local king had to be converted to Christianity by Henry Stanley. The previous ways of the king would shock Mackay; Creighton wrote that King Mtesa (of Uganda): 'Gave way to the wildest outbreaks of cruelty and vice. At such times he caused large numbers of men, women and children to be kidnapped and sacrificed as expiatory offerings to departed spirits. On one occasion as many as 2,000 innocent people were caught and killed in this way.'[18] Missionaries like Mackay, had to confront and bring an end to human sacrifice all over the world, from expiatory offerings in Africa, to cannibalism in the Pacific, and as the people turned to Christianity, the accepted crimes of another age were brought to the light and dealt with.

Confronting Abuse of Human Rights: Christianity also played an important role in bringing godly morality to local leaders, who then applied the Christian ethic to law in their lands. In the late 1800s, Khama, the chief of Bechuanaland was baptised and taught by a German missionary. When he became the chief, he desired to make progress for his people and Christianity would play an important role in redeeming the people's hearts and minds. In the book *Missions Their Rise and Development* the author explains: 'First he had to put down the hateful witch doctors, whose lies made the lives of the Bechuana a constant terror. Next he had to stop many heathen customs, the killing of weak children, the plan of allowing useless old people to starve, the right of a man to kill his wife and many horrible punishments...Khama said in after years, "I withstood my people at the risk of my life." ' The British government was impressed with Khama and they stated: 'His character entitles him to the respect and affection with which he is plainly regarded by his people and to the esteem entertained for him by all unprejudiced Europeans who have come in contact with him.'[19]

Confronting Business and Governments: Missionaries have always had confrontations with governments and business leaders because the Christian ethos was often in conflict with secular agendas. In India, William Carey was at first hindered because the East India Company was concerned that any missionary activity would hinder trading; in Africa, the same was true for missionaries who reported the state 'sanctioned' brothels for soldiers and closed them. Before the U.N. or investigative reporters dared to endanger their lives, it was often missionaries who reported on the abuse of locals. Creighton wrote: 'It was missionaries in the Congo that made known to Europe the atrocities perpetrated in the country which Leopold, King of the Belgians, had promised to develop for the good of the natives, but where he allowed them to be exploited and ruined with the most horrible cruelty for the good of his shareholders...and it is the missionaries who have done more to awaken the conscience of Europe to the havoc wrought by opium in China.'[20]

The British Empire was often kept accountable by Christian missionaries; in 1935 a mainstream history book was printed to educate the population, it stated: 'There was also another set of reformers, even more influential, who thought first of the treatment of native people in the regions under the British flag.' These missionaries and their supporters at home called for human treatment of all peoples and 'at the beginning of the nineteenth century they had very great influence with successive British governments because they had the opinion of religious people behind them.'[21] The Clapham Sect 'denounced the African slave trade' and the use of slaves in sugar plantations. They also expressed concern for indigenous peoples and fought to stop white people from taking land from the locals.[22] 'Not content with these efforts, the same party formed the Aborigines Protection Society to watch over the interests of the natives in those new colonies into which the new emigration was pouring its streams of settlers.' In today's New Zealand, a host of Westerners were settling and before the British were officially present, these areas were turning into 'a hotbed of crime and oppression. As a counteracting influence British missionaries made their appearance early in the nineteenth century and tried to introduce higher ideals.'[23] When British rule was beginning, the missionaries had a keen interest in making sure that the locals right to land was respected. Reviewing a new treaty the 'missionaries were pleased with it, since it seemed to safeguard the interests of the natives.'[24] These Christians angered the secular people who had no interest in protecting the rights of the locals and 'there was thus no love lost between them.'[25] When treaties were broken or pledges not kept, it was often the missionaries who were the first to write home, to inform the populist what their government was doing in their name and it was often Christian politicians who debated these subjects in parliament and helped bring change.

The Outcasts of the Outcasts: Mary Reed (1854-1943) was born in the U.S. and felt God calling her to aid the poor women and children of India. On a journey to the Himalayas to relax and recover from her exhausting work, she discovered five hundred miserable lepers, outcasts from society, poverty stricken and despairing of life. Neglected by all, these lepers were considered accursed and shunned; who could have imagined the tears that flowed from their eyes when an American woman said, ' "I have been called by God to come and help you." For the first time since they had been smitten by the terrible disease and so had become helpless outcasts, they heard kind words addressed to them.'[26]

Whilst many sceptics at home were criticising the works of Christian societies abroad, very few understood the personal hardships and sacrificial living that Mary Reed, and thousands of others like her endured on a daily basis because the love of Christ compelled them. As atheists attacked the work of missionaries, Mary Reed returned home to America because of poor health and discovered that she too had become a leper. It was this event which led her in 1891 to volunteer to work under the Mission to Lepers in London and for 52 years she brought relief, friendship, kindness and love to the lost lepers of India. Writing of her work she stated: 'Words are empty to tell of a love like His. He has enabled me to say, not with a sigh, but with a song, "Thy will be done." '[27]

The Konyak Tribe: When a member of the Konyak tribe died, they were not buried as is the custom in the West. In the book *Global Revival – Worldwide Outpourings* it states: 'They would place the corpse on a bamboo platform and after nine days or so they would separate the head from the dead body. They would then prepare a feast, place the head on the table and the family would talk to it as if it were a living person.'[28] Mathew Backholer explains in his book how revival changed everything. It was 1936 when the first church was planted amongst this tribe and by 1964 they had 52 churches with over 10,000 members, within three years the Church grew by 20%, and as the people became Christians, the old ways were put to the cross. Globally, there are unending stories of tribes converting to Christianity and deserting heathen ways. The BBC reported of the villagers in Fiji who apologised to the descendants of a missionary who was eaten 140 years ago; for 'cannibalism died out in Fiji in the mid-19th century with the acceptance of Christianity.'[29]

Saving Lives During World War II: A Japanese airplane flew overhead, signalling that their troops were near. It was World War II and the Empire of Japan showed no mercy in their treatment of Chinese people, as they massacred their way into China's provinces. In the midst of the turmoil was an English woman, who had been rejected as a missionary by the mission board – but by age thirty this former maid had saved enough money to make it to China on her own. She learnt the language, shared Jesus' message in the inn which she helped run, preached in the local villages and became a mother to the abandoned children of her area. The Japanese death machine was now coming close to her village and all would have to be abandoned. Gladys Aylward (1902-1970) had the choice now to save her own life, or to risk it all for her Chinese children; she chose to suffer with the people she was there to serve and decided to lead all her children to safety. The Japanese advance meant she was unable to take the regular routes of travel, so leading her children on foot they travelled for twenty-seven days, over one hundred miles, through rivers and over mountains, enduring the elements, hiding from the Japanese and daily being weakened through hardships. Anyone using simple logic would understand that it was impossible for this missionary to succeed in such a dangerous overland mission, with little supplies and a host of vulnerable children. The odds of a massive tragedy were high, yet against all hope she saved these children and took them to a safe place. She was always a strong leader, but the true cost to her was revealed on arrival, for when she knew everyone else was safe, she collapsed suffering from pneumonia, typhus, fever, malnutrition and extreme exhaustion. Her real life story of faith has inspired millions. The *Reader's Digest* was so inspired by her life that they covered it in their magazine and a Hollywood movie was made (which included a fictional romance). 'When *Newsweek* magazine reviewed the movie and summarised the plot, a reader, supposing the story to be fiction, wrote in to say, "In order for a movie to be good, the story should be believable!" '[30]

Time For Respect: Missionaries are perhaps the most undervalued and undermined humanitarians from the Western world. Together they helped end the slave trade and slavery. They kept governments and big business accountable and like investigative journalists they reported their findings to people at home. They opened schools and hospitals for those who would have lived and died without these benefits. They helped protect women's rights, and saved them and their children from death. They removed stone-age superstition and criminal activities, yet they also translated and preserved ancient languages from extinction. They comforted the lonely, the outcast, the leper and they saved the most vulnerable during times of great conflict. If we take away the name 'Christian' from them, the secular would probably hail them as some of the greatest heroes in the history of the world, but it was Christianity which was their motivation. There is an irony of course that those who most criticise these missionaries are in fact imposing their own values on others. Their views have become the 'absolute truth' which cannot be questioned and are 'centre ground,' yet despite having a stranglehold on the media and using the most of the opportunity to demand their values – our society has not in fact got better; instead there is a consensus that society is worse. Missionaries have changed the world for the better abroad, but first they improved our nations. It's a shame today that so much of their work has been undone, to the detriment of all.

We have only considered a few stories here, but there are tens of thousands of stories of missionaries who were the first to reach out into unknown areas, and still today there are hundreds of thousands who sacrifice much for His name's sake. On the author's visit to a remote Island in the Pacific, he discovered the story of one of many, who were martyred and eaten by the local tribe, yet despite it being a self-proclaimed death sentence more missionaries arrived. 'The missionaries who went forth in the nineteenth century to bring these great hymns to the Empire were, in most cases, extraordinarily brave and caring men and women,' explained journalist Mary Kenny. 'They built hospitals. They built schools. They extended faith and hope and music, which brought harmony and joy to the peoples they evangelised.'[31] The story of Western Protestant missionaries during the eighteenth and nineteenth centuries, is one of the greatest success stories of Church history. Not too long ago, Africa was non-Christian and Asia was without the light. Today Africa is the most Christian continent on earth and Christianity in Asia is exploding in many nations. South Korea is today the second largest mission sending nation in the world and on the author's visit to Malaysia and Singapore, he discovered huge numbers of Christians, including mega-churches. In India, the author found a vibrant growing Church and in China, even secular reports conclude that Christianity is the fastest growing religion in that nation. In Latin America, in the twenty-first century, millions are turning away from the traditions of the Church of Rome and discovering vibrant evangelical biblical Christianity. On an outreach in Latin America the author discovered that a massive percentage of the continent has now converted to become evangelicals.

During a fourteen year study of the impact of missionaries, Professor Robert Woodberry headed up a team of fifty research assistants and was shocked to find how missionaries had paved the way for democracy to flourish worldwide. "It was like an atomic bomb," he said, "the impact of missions on global democracy was huge." Published under the title, *The Missionary Roots of Liberal Democracy*, Woodberry's research was published in the respected *American Political Science Review* of 2012. Professor Daniel Philpott, who teaches political science at the University of Notre Dame, explained how the research showed, "Through devastatingly thorough analysis that conversionary Protestants are crucial to what makes the country democratic today – remarkable in many ways. Not only is it another factor, it turns out to be the most important factor. It can't be anything but startling for scholars of democracy."[32]

"Even the often-decried missionary activity of Christians in regions such as sub-Saharan Africa and Latin America has encouraged economic growth, and female literacy – a key sign of a successful society," said former American federal judge Ken Starr, now the president of Baylor University. "National University of Singapore political scientist Robert Woodberry argues that Protestant missionaries catalyzed the global spread of religious liberty, mass education, mass printing, newspapers, voluntary organizations and colonial reforms, thereby creating the conditions that made stable democracy more likely. In fact, Woodberry draws on historical evidence and sophisticated statistical methods to prove that the presence of Protestant missionaries explains about half the progress towards democracy in Africa, Asia, Latin America and Oceania."[33]

Chapter Thirty-Five

The Modern State of Israel

'Who has heard such a thing? Who has seen such things? Shall the earth be made to give birth in one day? Or shall a nation be born at once? For as soon as Zion was in labour, she gave birth to her children' (Isaiah 66:8).

The British Foreign Office, 2 November 1917. 'Dear Lord Rothschild, I have much pleasure in conveying to you, on behalf of His Majesty's government, the following declaration of sympathy with Jewish Zionist aspirations which has been approved by, the Cabinet: "His Majesty's Government view with favour the establishment in Palestine of a national home for the Jewish people, and will use their best endeavours to facilitate the achievement of this object, it being clearly understood that nothing shall be done which may prejudice the civil and religious rights of existing non-Jewish communities in Palestine, or the rights and political status enjoyed by Jews in any other country..." Yours sincerely, Arthur James Balfour.'[1]

'The people of Britain made a unique contribution to the establishment of the state of Israel,' explained Derek Prince, Bible teacher and former fellow of Cambridge University. 'For more than three centuries, Christians in Britain had nourished a vision, based on the Bible, that God desired to make of the Jewish people a sovereign nation once again in their own land. Politically, this vision found expression through such men as Lord Shaftesbury and Lord Balfour. In 1917 it was the Balfour Declaration made on behalf of the British government that set in motion the political processes that issued, thirty-one years later, in the establishment of the state of Israel. It was the British government too, that took the decisive step of placing before the United Nations the future of Palestine.'[2]

'The Church is rightly criticised for centuries of Christian anti-Semitism,' wrote Rabbi Jamie Cowen, 'but what is overlooked is the pivotal role British Christian Zionists played in the establishment of modern day Israel...the theology of British Puritans with regard to God's plan for the Jewish people so influenced British public opinion that governmental leaders in the nineteenth century began manoeuvring international events towards the re-establishment of a Jewish Israel.'[3]

It was the Christian statesman Oliver Cromwell who restored the English relationship with the Jews, by inviting them back to England during a time when persecution in Europe was fierce. As time went on, several books were published in England which spoke of the restoration of the Jews, most notably Thomas Witherby saw England as God's instrument, the 'new Cyrus' who would restore the land to the Jews. By 1838, the first diplomatic appointment in the Holy Land began with the British consulate, set up by Lord Shaftesbury. After the Crimean War, the British forced the Ottoman Turks, who ruled the Holy Land, to allow Jewish immigration; thus setting the scene for the mass influx of Jewish people. Derek Prince added, 'The names of nineteenth-century Christians who embraced the concept of a restored Jewish state read like a section of 'Who's Who'...the Earl of Shaftesbury, Lord Palmerstone...Robert Browning, George Elliot, John Adams and others.'[4] Benjamin Disraeli was also among them – he was Jewish by birth, but his parents converted to Anglicanism, and he rose to the heights of entering into the most powerful position in the world at that time, Prime Minister of Great Britain and her Empire. He did much to increase British influence in that area of the world and wrote about the Jews being restored to their historic homeland.

By 1902, the British were worried about the persecution of Jews, especially in Russia and decided to help. They offered land for a home to the Jews for self-rule in Sinai or Uganda; the British could not consider the Holy Land because at this point it was ruled by the Turks. But the leaders of the Zionist movement refused the British offer because they feared that if they accepted, it would never be 'next year in Jerusalem.' It was WWI, which gave Britain the opportunity to liberate the Holy Land, for the Turks sided with Germany and the British now had enemies in the Middle East, as well as in Europe.

In a small village in Dorset, England, the author visited the grave of an English officer which humbly resides with all the others; very few driving past this quiet village realise that the man buried in this cemetery changed the history of the Middle East and the world. T. E. Lawrence was a complex man, but he had the skills to unite the Arab tribes to throw-off the yoke of

Turkish rule. Lawrence of Arabia in *Seven Pillars of Wisdom* (from Proverbs 9:1), which inspired the film wrote: 'Arabs believe in persons, not in institutions. They saw in me a free agent of the British Government.'[5]

At the same time as the Arabs fought with Lawrence, the Christian General Allenby (1861-1936) wrought victory after victory against the Turks on their way to Jerusalem. Faith played an important role in the liberation of the Holy Land from Muslim rule. Major Vivian Gilbert wrote of a real life battle, where the Bible helped secure success: 'In the First World War a brigade major in Allenby's army in Palestine was on one occasion searching his Bible with the light of a candle, looking for a certain name. His brigade had received orders to take a village that stood on a rocky prominence on the other side of a deep valley. It was called Michmash and the name seemed familiar.'[6] After searching he found the story in 1 Samuel 14:1-16, where in the same location Jonathan had won a victory against the enemies of Israel. The British officer studied the plan, searched for the route which verse four revealed and planned an attack based on the Bible! Instead of sending a brigade, he sent one company who overpowered the Turks and the enemy fled. 'And so,' concludes Major Gilbert, 'after thousands of years British troops successfully copied the tactics of Saul and Jonathan.'[7]

General Allenby was a God fearing man who did not want to shed blood in the Holy City of His Lord. The Middle East expert Lance Lambert revealed that instead of forcing their way in, the British sent planes to drop leaflets over the city.[8] When the Turks received them they trembled in fear and fled because they feared God was against them, and so without a shot being fired, Allenby was able to liberate Jerusalem from Muslim rule.

'When British forces under General Allenby captured Jerusalem from the Turks in 1917, Ottoman rule ended and British mandatory rule began,' wrote Derek Prince. 'General Allenby, a Christian, dismounted from his horse and entered Jerusalem on foot saying, "No one but the Messiah should enter this city mounted." '[9] Broadcaster Michael Greenspan revealed that Jerusalem was freed by the British on 9 December 1917 in fulfilment of the prophecy of Daniel chapter 12, verse 12.[10] The Turks used a Muslim calendar in which the year was 1335.

A month before Jerusalem's liberation, Lord Balfour (1848-1930), had issued the Balfour Declaration which prepared the way for a Jewish state. For the first time since the first century a world power had recognised the right of Jewish people to live in their historic homeland. Derek Prince concluded: 'Lord Balfour was a Christian who believed in the restoration of Israel. His Declaration caused Christian Restorationists and Jewish Zionists to rejoice together.'[11] The Balfour Declaration set an international precedent, as the great powers of the world began to accept the concept of a restored Jewish state in the Holy Land. The original Balfour Declaration is now in residence at the British Museum and in another amazing twist of fate, the Cyrus Cylinder – which contains the description of the previous decree that led to the restoration of the Jewish state after the Babylonian exile is also there!

The Middle East and North Africa was the heartland of Christianity for hundreds of years, until the Islamic armies invaded. Then by 1517, the Ottoman Empire began its long rule of the Holy Land and it seemed impossible that a Jewish state could ever be re-born. But now everything had changed. With the overthrow of Ottoman rule, Britain became the ruling sovereign in the area. By 1920 the League of Nations, the forerunner to the U.N., gave a mandate to Britain to rule, setting a precedent in international law that British rule was only legitimate, if they carried out the expressed intent of the Balfour Declaration – to make a Jewish homeland.

When WWII broke out, almost all able Jewish men volunteered for the British army, but the limitation of immigration during that time caused great suffering for their people. After the war, the world learnt the true horrors of the Holocaust and the need for a Jewish state was recognised by many. In 1947, the future of the land was laid before the U.N. and the General Assembly approved a two state U.N. partition plan. David Ben-Gurion accepted the partition for the Jews, while the Arab League rejected it and violence grew into a state of undeclared war. The U.S. warned Jewish leaders not to declare a state because they feared the massive Arab armies would defeat them quickly.

For Jewish leaders, it was now or never, so on 14 May 1948, the state of Israel was proclaimed and the U.S. was the first to recognise the new nation. Soon after, Egypt, Transjordon, Iraq,

Syria and Lebanon invaded, with a plan to drive the Jews into the sea. The sons of David held-off Goliath and against impossible odds survived.

The year 1967 was another significant year for biblical prophecy, for in June Israel regained control of the Old City of Jerusalem for the first time since 70AD. The same enemies who attempted to destroy Israel at birth, were preparing for another push, with the support of other Arab nations, including Saudi Arabia, Kuwait and Algeria. The pre-emptive Six-Day War by Israel, humiliated her enemies and left the world in no doubt, that Israel was now the power in the Middle East. 'Those who war against you shall be as nothing..."Fear not, I will help you" ' (Isaiah 41:12-13).

What was once considered impossible, had now taken place. The Jews had their own state and Jerusalem was now in their hands and it was Christians, despite their governments' failure which helped shape the stage for the fulfilment of biblical prophecy. Today the political, economic and military support of the U.S. to Israel has been essential to Israel's survival, as over the years many Muslim nations have refused to even recognise the right of Israel to exist. The U.S. support is due in part to the Jewish community in America and the influence of Christians.

In the first century, Jesus' disciples believed that the Messiah would deliver a free, independent Jewish state, but Jesus was the suffering Messiah. After His resurrection, the disciples asked Him, "Lord will you at this time restore the kingdom to Israel?" Jesus replied, "It is not for you to know times or seasons..." (Acts 1:6-7). Nevertheless, nineteen centuries after Jesus Christ's resurrection, a free and independent Jewish state was created precisely because followers of Jesus had become powerful political figures and had moved world events with this intent. These men had nourished a biblical vision that dovetailed with the beliefs of Jews who were fighting for a homeland. Jesus was therefore a powerful inspiration for Christians to help create a free Jewish state. Israeli Prime Minister Benjamin Netanyahu told Christians in Jerusalem, "Christian Zionism preceded Jewish Zionism; in fact I believe it enabled it."[12]

Chapter Thirty-Six

Non-Conformists

The religious leaders 'called them and commanded them not to speak at all nor teach in the name of Jesus' (Acts 4:18). Then Peter, John and the Church ignored them and spread the gospel around the world!

After the English Act of Uniformity of 1662, 'non-conformist' became a term used for Christians who belonged to non-Anglican churches. These citizens were ready to struggle for their religious liberty and opposed state interference in their affairs. However, Christians have had a long history of being 'non-conformists' in one way or another. It was the non-conformist behaviour and dogma of Wycliffe, Luther, Knox, Tyndale, Wesley and Wilberforce etc., that shaped the history of our nations. Their failure to 'conform' to what was expected was a shaft of light which helped produce a Western paradigm shift, setting the stage for a new world to emerge.

The non-conformist beliefs of the early Puritans transformed parliament in Great Britain and led to the slow demise of the power of the Monarch in the English speaking world. The non-conformist attitudes of the settlers in North America, led not only to religious liberty, but to political liberty and the conception of a new nation. St Paul, Peter, John and the early disciples were non-conformists in their day; the religious establishment and political powers often feared and harassed them. Why have Christians always been considered a threat to rogue states and an asset to free states? Across the globe today, the authorities in oppressive states fear and persecute their own Christian citizens. Why is that? Is it because they realise that Christianity teaches the fundamental equality of all and that wherever biblical Christianity has had a satisfactory period to express itself, it leads to liberty? If you check your news today, whilst reporting on battles for liberty around the world, you will often find a Christian leader speaking out for the poor or vigorously supporting the need for democratic reform.

Non-conformist Christianity was essential in helping to forge modern democracy, liberty and freedom of speech and over time this non-conformity became embedded into educated thought. If we can imagine that the story of the Western world is like a long river that flows through 2,000 years of history, then at every twist of that river, there were Christian non-conformists emptying buckets of ideas into the flow. As the years went on, the fundamental consistency of the river changed as one idea was blended into another. Each new generation drew from this source and added their own; but more recently this river was split into two, one was called secular and the other Christian. People went to draw from the two outlets, but because people tend to only recall recent history, they have no idea that the source of both flows was once one. Finally the Christian and the secular were considered totally separate sources and much was made to diminish the Christian tributary; later it appeared that only one of the sources had led to liberty, but those who looked back realised that the river had a much longer history than just the recent twist or turn. History is His story.

Jesus Christ was the greatest non-conformist ever, yet He never lived for self, but strived for a better world. Britain's Queen Elizabeth II said, "We can surely be grateful that, two thousand years after the birth of Jesus, so many of us are able to draw inspiration from His life and message, and to find in Him a source of strength and courage."[1]

The essential substructure of modern democracy, human rights, liberty of speech, thought and assembly, all found their genesis in non-conformity, and non-conformity found its most faithful lifelong partner in Christian believers, whose battle for religious and political liberty became one and the same. Faith based non-conformist attitudes are still widespread in the Church today; before making poverty history was fashionable Christian displays and leaders highlighted unfair trade rules, and before mainstream shops stocked fair-trade products, the Church promoted these goods. It is the Church who still often checks the moral tone of a nation, questioning promiscuity, abortion, scientific ethics and calling for family values. Non-conformity is still alive and well, and is still forcing change and challenging the accepted.

'And do not be conformed to this world, but be transformed by the renewing of your mind' (Romans 12:2).

Chapter Thirty-Seven

Treasuring Our Heritage

'A posterity shall serve Him. It will be recounted of the Lord to the next generation, they will come and declare His righteousness to a people who will be born, that He has done this' (Psalm 22:30-31).

As the world follows the example set by the Protestant nations and more countries benefit from freedom, democracy and compassionate capitalism, there is a danger that the clear link between Christianity, and the development of our rights and freedom will be lost; in much European public opinion this may have already happened. To avoid this continuing, we must keep the link alive and disperse its knowledge until it becomes common, yet our heritage is under assault.

One British journalist wrote of the 'official intolerance towards Christian traditions' explaining that 'each attack on a Christian tradition puts the precious freedoms enjoyed by all Britons in jeopardy...this nation is an old one and draws immense strength from its ancient roots. Christianity lies at their heart. Unless it is defended by believer and non-believer alike, the whole basis of our tolerant civilisation will be imperilled.'[1] Historian Dan Snow, explained that after the Romans left Britain in 410AD, civilisation collapsed; but the nation was saved from the dark vacuum 'by reintroducing Christianity and its civilising components to a Britain that had fallen into barbarism.'[2] Christianity rescued the country and started the process which led it to become a pioneer nation.

In the U.S., Congressman James Randy Forbes asked, "If America was birthed upon Judeo-Christian principles; at what point in time did our nation cease to be Judeo-Christian?" He explained: "The first act of America's first Congress in 1774 was to ask a minister to open with prayer and to lead Congress in the reading of four chapters of the Bible. In 1776, in approving the Declaration of Independence, our founders acknowledged that all men "are endowed by their Creator with certain unalienable rights..." and noted that they were relying "on the protection of Divine Providence" in the founding of this country. John Quincy Adams said, "The Declaration of Independence laid the cornerstone of human government upon the first precepts of

Christianity..." In 1800, Congress approved the use of the Capitol building as a church. Both chambers approved the measure, with president of the Senate Thomas Jefferson, giving the approval in that chamber. Throughout his terms as both vice president and president, Jefferson attended church at the Capitol, including January 3, 1802, just two days after writing his infamous letter in which he penned the phrase "the wall of separation between church and state." Nearly 100 years later, in 1892, in *Church of the Holy Trinity v. United States,* the United States Supreme Court held that America is a "Christian nation." Presidents Washington, Adams, Jefferson, Jackson, McKinley, Teddy Roosevelt, Wilson, Hoover, FDR, Truman, Eisenhower, Kennedy, Reagan all referenced the importance of Judeo-Christian principles in the birth and growth of our country."[3]

In Canada, one journalist wrote: 'The evangelical movement is experiencing double-digit growth, with 10 to 15 percent of Canadians calling themselves evangelical Christians.' TV anchor Kevin Newman said, "With our current prime minister among those who believe in this new version of church, we need to examine the evangelical movement for what it is, not what secular Canada assumes it is."[4]

In the West we should be honouring our heritage, yet we often show it great discourtesy. For our history is not the story of strangers, but it is the story of our grandparents and their forefathers and their forefathers, and so forth. Our institutions often show great disrespect for the achievements of our forefathers, for at the same time as we profit from their labour and Christian heritage, we often openly mock their beliefs, belittle their success, focus on their failings and feel ashamed to talk about our common history. Our schools often attempt to disenfranchise our religious history, our governments tend to emphasize the contribution of all other civilisations, and the Christian contribution is often ignored or the story is told, but with little reference to the Christian faith that was the inspiration.

The Rt. Rev. Michael Nazir-Ali, the Pakistan-born Bishop of Rochester in England said, "Every society, for its wellbeing, needs the social capital of common values and the recognition of certain virtues which contribute to personal and social flourishing. Our ideas about the sacredness of the human person at every stage of life, of equality and natural rights and, therefore, of freedom, have demonstrably arisen from the tradition rooted in the Bible. Different faiths and traditions will not necessarily produce the values and virtues which have been so prominent in the history of this country...One of the surprising aspects of what you could call our values vacuum is the historical amnesia which is so prevalent today – or, rather, a selective sort of amnesia. The perfectly virtuous pages of history, such as Magna Carta, the campaign to abolish the slave trade and later, slavery itself, the easing of conditions of labour for men, women and children and the introduction of universal education, which all took place under the inspiration of the Christian faith, are forgotten or ignored."[5]

General Sir Francis Richard Dannatt, whilst the head of the British Army and a devout Christian said British society, "Has always been embedded in Christian values...it is said that we live in a post Christian society. I think that is a great shame. The broader Judeo-Christian tradition has underpinned British society. It underpins the British Army."[6] In a poll launched for the BBC Faith Diary, people responded overwhelmingly that they did not want a 'secularist wipe-out of religion in Britain.' Almost two-thirds of those questioned said the law 'should respect and be influenced by U.K. religious values' and a similar proportion agreed that 'religion has an important role to play in public life.'[7] In another recent poll, Jesus Christ came number one, as the person most people would like to meet. A spokesman for the poll said, "These results show that Jesus Christ will always be the British public's superstar."[8] Jesus is highly regarded, because His message was great. The Archbishop of Canterbury said recently, "Christianity takes it for granted that whether you succeed or fail, you're valuable. God's view of you doesn't depend on how you do – it's always the same love, always giving you a second chance....you still have your dignity before God, so you still have a future."[9] If the positive Christian influence in Western civilisation is so evident, why is there so much hostility towards Christianity by a small influential group? Yet at the same time, the Church too needs to honour her heritage, for it is easy to criticise another, but what sacrifices are we personally making to build upon the achievements of other Christian generations? Will they look at us knowing that we had more money, people and democratic influence, yet less impact? We have only considered a small part of our Christian history, yet we have discovered many men and women who were willing to sacrifice much for a greater cause than self. Generations of believers were propelled into action by their faith to challenge and change the status quo and often it began with just one motivated individual. One study showed 'nearly three-quarters of all charity organisations in the late nineteenth century were run by evangelical Christians.'[10] In twenty-first century Britain, the Church still plays a major role. Mark Greene wrote: 'No one contributes more to this society voluntarily than local churches and the pastors who lead them. And it is a contribution increasingly recognised by both central and local government.'[11] The same is true in the U.S. and other English speaking nations.

This final chapter could be devoted to what Christianity is achieving today, in global education, medication and in all forms of philanthropy. We could recall that the Church in Britain and the U.S. are often the number one suppliers of youth work and at the centre of community – where the needs of people from toddler groups to the retired are met. We could recall the numerous people involved on a voluntary basis in caring for the homeless, sick, elderly and the downcast. We could recall churches which provide drop-in sessions for isolated mums, after-school meetings and holiday clubs for children. We could consider the statistics of all the finances which are poured into others, from mandatory education, food banks to counselling, and the rehabilitation of troubled people. We could retrieve the statistics of missionaries abroad, the unknown thousands who give freely to heal the sick, help the poor, educate the young and share the message of the gospel. We could combine the global contribution of Christian charities, which battle injustice, fight for change and publicise the cause of the hurting, abused, hungry and harassed. But instead of thinking about what is being done, maybe we should consider what could be done if only we all played a part. Perhaps the best way to value our heritage is to build upon the sacrificial foundations others laid.

Today people in the West are experiencing many liberties, rights and prosperity all unqualified in our history. There is still much work to be done at home, yet there are millions of people who know nothing of their basic rights or freedoms which could be found by the gospel message bearing fruit in their lands. Should the West of today rejoice in our liberty in Christ without sharing it with the world? Should we benefit from victories which others won, but avoid our own battles?

Sphere of Influence: In Matthew 25:14-30 Jesus tells a parable which concerns the gifts and talents which He has given to His people. The parable reveals that God expects us to use our talents, abilities and power for the King and His cause. Every Christian has a sphere of influence which he or she can use to help spread the gospel and create a world of greater justice. Every individual in the West has a democratic voice, a customer's point of view and a financial influence. Christians can use their power to spread the good news or they can support institutions, companies, artists, musicians, entertainment industries and politicians whose views are fundamentally opposed to their Christian values.

The Consumers Who Forgot The Great Commission: The credit crunch and financial crisis beginning in 2008 was for many a wake-up call. For Christians it revealed how wasteful the West had become and exposed to believers how much of our diminishing expendable income had been squandered on 'anything but the gospel.' Before this a non-Christian may have received the impression that Jesus' last words to His Church was, "Go into all the world and consume!" Research revealed that in Britain only 31% of Christians tithed[12] and in the U.S. the figure was 23%.[13] Practically this meant the financial influence of 69% of British Christians and 77% of American Christians was lost from Christianity. In 1920 the Church gave 10% of the total offering to missions, but this is not the case now.[14] In the U.S. research shows that it takes on average 7.6 churches to send out one missionary, in Britain it's 5.6, in South Korea it's 4.2, in Australia it's 3.3, in Finland it's 1.5![15] Why is our missionary vision small, when Jesus Christ's last command was to take His message to the world?

The Baton: Every generation of Christians receive the 'baton' from another. They have passed onto us their successes, achievements and progress. Just think about it – somebody took the gospel from the Holy Land or wider Middle East, or later from Europe to your nation; and someone gave of his or her own money so the gospel could get to your town! More recently many worked hard to build the church in which we were taught God's word and other people paid for the meetings in which we were saved. In the same way, someone fought to change the law so that we could be free – another fought to end the tragedy of human suffering abroad, others opened hospitals, schools and orphanages to make the world a better place. This book should not be the story of others who made the world a better place, but of us and the opportunities we have to leave a godly legacy to the world. Should we benefit from the price others have paid and refuse ourselves to make the smallest of sacrifices? If someone sacrificed and gave so much so that we could get saved, should we take this blessing and never do our part to pass it on to others? Could we imagine our lives without God's gift of salvation, the Bible or without the Holy Spirit's presence? Billions live without these blessings and we have the power to help. Rick Warren in *The Purpose Driven Life* wrote: 'Make your goal to be a Kingdom builder rather than just a wealth builder.'[16]

'Do not withhold good from those to whom it is due, when it is in the power of your hand to do so' (Proverbs 3:27).

The Youth: Another way the Church helps complete the Great Commission is to give the gospel to the next generation; yet when we study youth work we often find that many churches have a bigger budget for church flowers, than for youth work! Do we really think our flowers are more important than imparting the gospel to our children? The world is spending billions on reaching our youth with their products and secular values; why then do we starve their work of the means to get the job done? How can we complain that our nations are going down hill, if we are not raising up the next generation in the ways of the Lord? Studies show that over ninety percent of Christians are converted before the age of twenty-two, yet the Church is still spending over ninety-five percent of its evangelistic resources on reaching those who don't respond and keeping its resources from those that do! We are like a weapons factory which spends all their money on trying to persuade pacifists to buy, whilst ignoring the military that are already waiting in our store looking for a reason to purchase.

The Question: The question all believers must ask themselves is, 'Am I using my influence for Christ?' What if every Christian today put their influence into action for the Kingdom of God, instead of indirectly supporting another kingdom by inaction?

This is not only a challenge to us all, but an opportunity. This is a chance for us to leave a legacy outside of our immediate home, a chance for us to make our lives count, and to know that our existence has meaning and purpose. Today is our opportunity to act and leave a legacy! God's Kingdom requires missionaries, but that does not necessarily mean being in 'full-time' Christian employment or going abroad. God wants to raise up missionaries in the media, in politics, in art, music and film. He is calling for reformers at home and abroad, as well as business people with a passion for Him. He calls forth doctors, engineers, teachers, lawyers...all to take His Kingdom into their world. From cleaners to computer experts and from farmers to footballers, all can be used by Him to be salt and light, but will we be ready? Will we take up our cross and follow Him, or take up our blessing and expect Him to follow us? The Wilberforce of today is already among us, but will he or she stand up? Perhaps it's someone you know, perhaps it's you!

God not only calls for preachers, but as this book shows, He calls believers to be active every day for Him. Just consider what the BBC said of our great Christian politician: 'Although Wilberforce is most famous for his battle against the slave trade, he was also active in many other social and religious areas. Most of England had become unchurched by the 18th century and Wilberforce was determined to draw people back into the Christian faith. But he didn't just want people to return to a Christianity limited to church on Sundays; he wanted them to embrace a Christianity that would change the whole fabric of British society. He worked with the poor, he worked to establish educational reform, prison reform, healthcare reform and to limit the number of hours children were required to work in factories. To deal with many of these problems they established organisations that would work to improve or rectify the particular social injustice that they were dealing with.'[17]

The world in which we now live owes much to Christianity. In the English speaking world we owe our liberty, our rights and our democracies to those who took the Christian faith seriously. Many gave all that they had in Christ's name and by doing so they changed the world for the better. Today we are Christ's servants, and we all have a contribution to make to shape the world and leave a godly legacy. We have been called to stand in the gap on behalf of the land, but His purposes cannot be accomplished unless we all do our part and surrender everything to His will, so His will shall be done here on earth as it is in heaven. Christianity did make the modern world; it is not responsible for everything, but it was the greatest driving force behind many of the values which we all now hold dear, because our rights were often fought for and won by non-conformist Bible-believing Christians.

We have a great Christian legacy and the best way of honouring that legacy will be to add to it. When every Christian realises they can make a valuable contribution where they live and work, and by joining hands with others worldwide, they can be directly involved with fulfilling the Great Commission – perhaps the Church's aspirations will be turned into direct action. When every believer realises they have a voice and decide to find out how to use it, perhaps the change that we all grumble about at home, will actually take place! When every Christian moves from being a consumer, to a believer consumed with His commission, then the world will be rocked. Some sit at home and complain about the darkness, others go out into the world as salt and light to start a fire. Which one are you?

Jesus said to them, "Go into all the world and preach the gospel to every creature" (Mark 16:15).

Books by the Author

- *Celtic Christianity*
- *Britain, a Christian Country*
- *Jesus Today, Daily Devotional. 100 Days with Jesus Christ.* Two minutes a day of Christian Bible inspiration
- *Holy Spirit Power: Knowing the Voice, Guidance and Person of the Holy Spirit*
- *Heaven: A Journey to Paradise and the Heavenly City*
- *The End Times: A Journey Through the Last Days*
- *The Exodus Evidence In Pictures – The Bible's Exodus:* 100+ colour photos
- *The Ark of the Covenant – Investigating the Ten Leading Claims:* 80+ colour photos
- *Samuel Rees Howells: A Life of Intercession* by Richard Maton, with Paul and Mathew Backholer

Sources and Notes

Preface
1. *The Legacy of Rome* by Cyril Bailey, Clarendon Press, 1928, p.9.
2. Much of the writings of Apollonius are lost, many are of disputed authorship. *On Sacrifices* is often considered as authentic.
3. *Description of Greece* contains his personal observations in ten books.
4. *De Civitate Dei Contra Paganos* by Augustine of Hippo, book II, 5th century.
5. *The History of Western Philosophy* by Bertrand Russel, Touchstone, 1964, p.194.
6. *Rome and the West* by William Stearns Davis, Allyn and Bacon, 1912, p.285.
7. *The History of Christianity, Tenth Century* by Harry Rosenberg, A Lion Handbook, 1977, 1990, p.244.
8. What would Wilberforce do? ChristianityToday.com, March 2007.
9. WWII casualty numbers vary between sources. Includes civilians.
10. *History of the World* edited by W.N. Weech, Odhams Books, 1905, p.407.
11. *Haley's Bible Handbook* by Henry H. Haley, Zondervan, 1965, pp.18-19.
12. Ibid. pp.18-19.
13. English Literature, King James Bible, *Encyclopaedia Britannica, Student Edition,* CD-Rom, Published by Encyclopaedia Britannica (UK) Ltd, 2003.
14. The Prime Minister's King James Bible Speech by David Cameron, www.number10.gov.uk/news/king-james-bible, 16 December 2011.

Chapter One - Christianity and Liberty
1. German Minister of Propaganda during 1933-1945.
2. Speech by Prime Minister Gordon Brown concerning Hope 08, 10 Downing Street, December 2008.
3. Don't cringe at your own culture, be proud by Simon Heffer, *Daily Mail*, 26 April 2004.
4. Back to God, *Time* magazine, 7 March 1955.
5. How Britain is turning Christianity into a crime by Melanie Phillips, *Daily Mail*, 7 September 2006.
6. Biblical Worldview University. The Bible: The Foundation of Liberty by Paul Strand, CBN News, 24 April 2007.
7. One Solitary Life. A Sermon by Dr James Allan Francis (1864-1928).
8. Empires and superpowers of Portugal, Spain, Netherlands, France, Britain, Germany, U.S. etc. 83% of the world surface was run by Europeans and North Americans.
9. U.S., Britain, Canada, Australia & N.Z. The British Empire was dominant between the 19th and early 20th century and the U.S. thereon.
10. The British Empire ruled around 1/3 of the world's surface in its entire history - not at one time. It peaked between 1919-39 at 1/4 of the planet; adding all former colonies to this creates almost 1/3 of the world.
11. Most recent Islamic expansion can be explained by biological growth. Muslims tend to have large families and it is often illegal and always culturally unacceptable to change or doubt one's Islamic faith.
12. *Operation World* by Patrick Johnstone & Jason Mandryk, CLC, 1993, 2001, p.2.
13. Due to persecution 'underground' Christians do not show up on official statistics; official figures will always come short. Therefore consider Christianity is China's new social revolution by Richard Spenser, *Telegraph*, 30 July 2005. Also, Christianity in China, sons of heaven, *The Economist*, 2 October 2008. In addition, see the last two pages of the chapter Empires and Superpowers.

Chapter Two - The Christian Legacy
1. One Solitary Life, a sermon by Dr James Allan Francis (1864-1928).
2. Time Traveller's Guide to Victorian Britain, U.K. Channel 4 online.
3. The Prime Minister at Faithworks in London. Tony Blair Lecture, 22 March 2005.
4. Warren squares off with atheist, *The Christian Post*, April 2007.
5. *Time* magazine by Jim Wallis, 16 February 2007.
6. Sir John Mortimer, *The Daily Telegraph*, 28 April 1999.
7. Can't my children be taught their own religion? by J.Parkin, *Daily Mail*, 26 July 2006.
8. Ashamed to be Christian by Simon Heffer, *Daily Mail*, 10 June 2005.
9. *Celebrating Our Heritage, A Journey Through Christian England* by Joanna Bogle, Marshall Pickering, 1988, p.3.
10. The Queen's Christmas Message, 25 December 2000. 11. Ibid. 2002.
12. The British presided over a 100 year peace and America is now responsible for relative global peace. Smaller localised wars are the exception, Sudan 1898 or Iraq 2003 etc.

Chapter Three - Great Reformers
1. *A Book of Golden Deeds* by Charlotte Yonge, Macmillan, 1865.

2. Saving the slums by Donald Lewis, christianitytodaylibrary.com, January 1997.
3. *The Christian Travelers Guide to Great Britain* by Irvin Hexham, Zondervan Publishing House, p.28.
4. Speech to Social Service Congress, Liverpool, 1859.
5. Conservative Party's Leader at Faithworks in London, Michael Howard Lecture, 23 February 2005.
6. Stephen Timms, MP for East Ham, Faithworks Conference, 2 November 2007.
7. Chasing Australia's Christian vote, Treasurer Peter Costello by Phil Mercer, BBC.co.uk, 20 September 2004.
8. A Point of View: Two cheers for human rights by John N. Gray, BBC.co.uk, 27 December 2013.

Chapter Four - The End of The Slave Trade
1. Empire, How Britain Made The Modern World by Niall Ferguson, Penguin, 2003, 2004, p.116.
2. Ibid. p.118.
3. *Celebrating Our Heritage, A Journey Through Christian England* by Joanna Bogle, Marshall Pickering, 1988, p.72.
4. U.N. definition of Western & Northern Europe does not include Italy or Greece etc.

Chapter Five - The End of Slavery
1. *In Empire's Cause* by Ernest Protheroe, Epworth Press, 1927, p.370.
2. William Wilberforce House of Commons Speech, 19 July 1811.
3. U.S. Census, 1830 Statistics. 4. Ibid.
5. The U.S. National Archives, Charters of Freedom.
6. The faith factor by Nancy Gibbs, *Time* magazine, 21 June 2004.

Chapter Six - The Birth of Modern Campaigning
1. *Thomas Clarkson, The Friend of Slaves* by E.L. Griggs, G Allen & Unwin, 1936.
2. The birth of modern campaigning by Brian Wheeler, BBC.co.uk, March 2007.
3. Rt Rev. Stephen Sykes, Clarkson Memorial Dedication, Westm. Abbey, 1996.
4. The birth of modern campaigning by Brian Wheeler, BBC.co.uk, March 2007.

Chapter Seven – Workers' Rights
1. *What Are Churches For?* by Frank Ballard, Elliot Stock, 1891, p.83.
2. Charlotte Elizabeth Tonna, Enotes.com, March 2007.
3. Tolpuddle Martyrs Museum, Dorset, England, March 2007.

Chapter Eight - Children's Rights
1. Julian Marsh, The George Müller foundation, April 2007.
2. Julian Marsh, The George Müller foundation, April 2007.
3. The U.K. National Archives, Child Labour, April 2007.
4. *Yarns On Christian Pioneers* by Ernest H. Hayes, The Religious Education Press, 1928, 1942, p.95.
5. Who are we? The history of Barnardos, May 2007.
6. BBC Songs of Praise, 2 July 2007.
7. Testimony of Mary Ellen, 10 April 1874.
8. The story of Mary Ellen, American Humane Association, May 2007.
9. The story of Mary Ellen, American Humane Association, May 2007.
10. National Society for the Prevention of Cruelty to Children, History, June 2007.
11. The Faithworks Awards, hosted by Steve Chalke, England, 8 June 2009.
12. Christianity is part of our national heritage, message by Indian Prime Minister to the World Council of Churches, 20 October 2008.
13. Empire: Doing Good by Jeremy Paxman, BBC, March 2012.

Chapter Nine - Women's Rights
1. The ultimate leading man by Clive James, BBC.co.uk, 26 December 2008.
2. Divine Women by Bettany Hughes, BBC, May 2012. 3. Ibid.
4. Fearless women of Iran by Edwina Currie, *Daily Express*, 16 June 2009.
5. Victorianweb.org, Hannah More, June 2009.
6. The Christian contribution to medicine by Rosie Beal-Preston, Christian Medical Fellowship.
7. *Elsie Inglis, The Woman With The Torch* by Eva Shaw, McLaren, 1920, ch. 1.
8. Mary Slessor, mother of all the peoples. Dundee City Council, Scotland, May 2007.
9. Man who hates his own Church by Mary Kenny, *Daily Mail*, 3 November 2005.

Chapter Ten - Education: Schools and Universities
1. Oxford University, About, May 2007.
2. *Illustrated Notes on English Church History* by Rev. C.A. Lane, Society For Promoting Christian

Knowledge,1898, pp.230-231.
3. William Elphinstone, Abdn.ac.uk, May 2007.
4. *The Ten Greatest Revivals Ever* by Elmer Towns, Douglas Porter, Servant Publications, 2000, p.94.
5. Ivy league faith by Wendy Griffith, CBN, 10 April 2007.
6. *Men of Science Men of God* by Henry M. Morris, Master Books, p.39.
7. To The Citizens of Philadelphia - A Plan for Free Schools. A letter by Benjamin Rush, 28 March 1787.
8. Education in England online, author unknown, May 2007.
9. *AD*, Anno Domini, FIEC, Day One Publications, p.6.
10. Why does Labour hate faith schools? Cristina Odone, Telegraph, 11 January 2010.
11. Queen Elizabeth II, address to the 9th General Synod of the Church of England, 23 November 2010.
12. Lecture of Theology by Lord Blair, Theos, 16 November 2010.
13. *The Ten Greatest Revivals Ever* by Elmer Towns, Douglas Porter, Servant Publications, 2000, p.45.
14. *The Personal Life of David Livingstone* by William G. Blaikie, London, John Murray, 1881, p.510.

Chapter Eleven - The Right to Healthcare
1. Herophilos works were lost but were much quoted by Galen in the 2nd century and preserved by Sextus Empiricus.
2. The Christian contribution to medicine by Rosie Beal-Preston, Christian Medical Fellowship.
3. *Yarns on the Human Quest* by Ernest H. Hayes, The Religious Education Press, 1933, 1948, p.6.
4. *AD*, Anno Domini, FIEC, Day One Publications, pp.8-9.
5. History of Hospitals online, author unknown, May 2007.
6. Inauguration Sermon: The Archbishop of York, 1 December 2005.

Chapter Twelve - The Impoverished Masses
1. *The History of Christianity* by A. Skevington Wood, 1977, 1990, p.452.
2. *What Are Churches For?* by Frank Ballard, Elliot Stock, 1891, p.84.
3. The Salvation Army, about Booth, July 2007.
4. The Salvation Army's International Heritage Centre, July 2007. 5. Ibid.
6. *Yarns on Christian Torchbearers* by Lilian E. Cox & Ernest H. Hayes, The Religious Education Press, 1941, 1958, p.36.
7. Inauguration Sermon: The Archbishop of York, 1 December 2005.
8. The Prime Minister's King James Bible Speech by David Cameron, www.number10.gov.uk/news/king-james-bible, 16 December 2011.

Chapter Thirteen - The Preservation of Nature
1. *Time* magazine, April 2004.
2. Environmentalism - Big Ideas That Changed The World, UK Channel 5, 2007.
3. *Our Nation's Heritage* by J.B. Priestly, The Temple Press, 1939, 1940, p.119.
4. Visitcumbria.com, Canon Rawnsley, July 2007.
5. Time Traveller's Guide To Victorian Britain, U.K. Channel 4 online.
6. The National Trust, History 1884-1912, July 2007.
7. The National Trust, History of the Charity, July 2007.
8. *God's Wilds: John Muir's Vision of Nature Environmental History* by Dennis C. Williams, A&M University Press, 2002.
9. *A Thousand Mile Walk to the Gulf* by John Muir, Sierra Club, chapter 6.
10. Inside The Sierra Club, Sierraclub.org, August 2007.
11. John Muir, The Yosemite, Sierra Club History, 1912.
12. Bioenergy: Fuelling the food crisis? by Steph. Holmes, BBC.co.uk, 4 June 2008.
13. The cooling world by Peter Gwynne, *Newsweek*, 28 April 1975.

Chapter Fourteen - Animal Welfare
1. *Kindness To Animals: The Sin of Cruelty Exposed and Rebuked* by Charlotte Elizabeth Tonna, J.M. Dent & Sons, 1845, p.14.
2. RSPCA.org.uk, August 2007.

Chapter Fifteen - Time
1. We are not considering the scientific question, what is time? Consider particle physicist professor Brian Cox in What Time Is It? Horizon, BBC, 20 December 2008.
2. Article VII, of the U.S. Constitution.
3. Calculations made in 525AD by Dionysius Exiguus, a Scythian monk. Many believe the birth of Jesus should more correctly be placed about 4BC.

4. Greenwich 2000, wwp.greenwich2000.com.
5. Famous Derbyshire People: www.derbyshireuk.net/flamstead.html, March 2006. 6. Ibid.

Chapter Sixteen - Music
1. Larry Norman, the growth of Christian music, Crossrhythms.co.uk, 11 October 2006.
2. President Bush honours Black Music Month, the White House, 17 June 2008.
3. Elvis's childhood church to be added to the Elvis Presley Birthplace and Park, Elvis.com, 22 January 2008.
4. Pride, In the Name of Love, U2's 1984 album The Unforgettable Fire.
5. Rebecca St James double celebration, BMI news, 8 July 2003.
6. Tomlin picks up platinum and gold records. Hip hymns are in by Belinda Luscombe, *Time* magazine, 19 November 2006.
7. Delirious? Rock the Cathedral, BBC.co.uk, 2 February 2004.
8. The Gospel Music Association 2002-2007 - CDs, cassettes, digital albums and digital tracks. Average total yearly sales of over 41 million units.
9. Composer James MacMillan warns of liberal elite's 'ignorance-fuelled hostility to religion' by Martin Beckford, *Daily Telegraph*, 1 October 2008.
10. Rev. Michael Nazir-Ali: Britons suffer 'cultural amnesia' about Christian art by Martin Beckford, *Telegraph*, 13 September 2008.
11. The Prime Minister's King James Bible Speech by David Cameron, www.number10. gov.uk/news/king-james-bible, 16 December 2011.

Chapter Seventeen - Art and Architecture
1. The Campbell Morgan Memorial Bible Lectures, number two, Westminster Chapel, London, 1950.
2. About Michelangelo, National Gallery, London, England, January 2009.
3. God is behind some of our greatest art - Richard Dawkins' secular army must be stopped or future generations will be denied a source of inspiration by Mark Ravenhill, The Guardian, 14 April 2008.
4. The Campbell Morgan Memorial Bible Lectures, number two, Westminster Chapel, London, 1950.
5. *Christian Art: A Very Short Introduction* by Beth Williamson, Oxford University Press, 2004, p.110.
6. The Campbell Morgan Memorial Bible Lectures, number two, Westminster Chapel, London, 1950.
7. A cure for national Amnesia by Michael Nazir-Ali, *Standpoint* magazine, November 2010.

Chapter Eighteen - Language
1. *Illustrated Notes on English Church History* by Rev. C.A. Lane, Society For Promoting Christian Knowledge, 1898, p.235.
2. The Bible Revolution presented by Rod Liddle, U.K. Channel 4, April 2007.
3. The ultimate leading man by Clive James, BBC.co.uk, 26 December 2008.
4. *The History of Christianity*, Paul D. Steeves, Lion Handbook, 1977, 1990, p.316.
5. Except 1 & 2 Kings because they were a warring people.
6. *History Of The Church*, ii.5 by Philostorgius, (368-433).
7. The Prime Minister's King James Bible Speech by David Cameron, www.number10. gov.uk/news/king-james-bible, 16 December 2011.
8. International Bible Society, August 2008.
9. *Missions Their Rise and Development* by Louise Creighton, Williams & Norgate, 1912, p.193.
10. First Day Cover and Stamp, Department of Posts, India, 9 January 1993.
11. *William Carey* by Pearce, Hodder & Stoughton, 1923.
12. The Rosetta Stone contains a passage in two Egyptian language scripts and in classical Greek. Its home since 1802 has been the British Museum.
13. Egypt, Discovering A Lost World, BBC, 2006.

Chapter Nineteen - Law and Order
1. *Christianity and Law: An Enquiry into the Influence of Christianity on the Development of English Common Law* by Stephen C Perks, Avant Books, 1993, 2003.
2. *Illustrated Notes on English Church History* by Rev. C.A. Lane, Society For Promoting Christian Knowledge, 1898, p.43.
3. AD, Anno Domini, FIEC, Day One Publications, p.4.
4. The Bible: A History by Ann Widdecombe, Channel 4, 7 February 2010. 5. Ibid.
5a. A cure for national Amnesia by Bishop Nazir-Ali, *Standpoint* magazine, November 2010.
6. Christianity & Law, Creation Ministries International.
7. *The Trumpet Sounds For Britain*, Volume Two by David E Gardner, Jesus Is Alive Ministries, 1980s, 2003, p.29.
8. *The Bible Lessons of John Quincy Adams for His Son, edited by* Doug Phillips, The Vision Forum Inc., 2001, p.61.
9. *Commentaries on the Constitution of the United States* by Joseph Story, Hilliard Gray and Co, 1833, p.593.

9a. Lord Denning, The Daily Telegraph, 6 March 1999.
10. George Polson, QC, Speech on The Christian Content of the Rule of Law and its Contribution to Human Rights, 19 February 1969.
11. Christianity and Law: An Enquiry into the Influence of Christianity on the Development of English Common Law by Stephen C Perks, Avant Books, 1993, 2003.
12. The Trumpet Sounds For Britain, Volume Two by David E. Gardner, Jesus Is Alive Ministries, 1980s, 2003, p.29.
13. Christianity, A History, episode 2, presented by Michael Portillo, U.K. Channel 4, January 2009.
14. Britons 'back Christian society,' BBC.co.uk, 14 November 2005.
15. Archbishop's speech on the Criminal Justice and Immigration Bill, 5 March 2008.
15a. The Prime Minister's King James Bible Speech by David Cameron, www.number 10.gov.uk/ news/king-james-bible, 16 December 2011.
16. Harry Truman Presidential Term 1945-1953.
17. MSNBC Poll, Should the motto 'In God We Trust' be removed from U.S. currency? Internet polls are not scientific, but nine million responses show weight of feeling. Msnbc.msn.com/id/10103521.
18. Can't my children be taught their own religion? by Jill Parkin, Daily Mail, 26 July 2006.
19. Speech on the UDHR by Said Rajaie-Khorassani, Iranian representative to the United Nations, 1981.
20. The Cairo Declaration of Human Rights in Islam (CDHRI) is severely criticised for not upholding the fundamental right of equality for all. The Center for Inquiry wrote to the United Nations that CDHRI: 'Undermines equality of persons and freedom of expression and religion by imposing restrictions on nearly every human right based on Islamic Sharia law.' See, Center for Inquiry defends freedom of expression at the U.N. Human Rights Council, 17 September 2008.
21. CIA world fact book, 2006.
22. The European Court of Human Rights, judgement in the case of Refah Partisi and others verses Turkey, 13 February 2003. See also the Solemn Hearing of the European Court of Human Rights - opening of the judicial year, 22 January 2004.

Chapter Twenty - Family and Community

1. U.N. African Recovery Briefing Paper, 11 April 1998.
2. Land Of The Walking Marriage - Mosuo people of China by Lu Yuan & Sam Mitchell, State University of New York Press, 2000.
3. Marriage online, author unknown, May 2006.
4. Marriage is best for bringing up children, says Tory study by Graeme Wilson, Telegraph, 7 September 2006.
5. Centre for Social Justice by Iain Duncan Smith, 19 January 2010.
6. If the head of our Church can't uphold the standards that shaped us, what hope is there? by Lord Tebbit, Daily Mail, 8 August 2008.
7. Marriage benefits, The Telegraph, 23 August 2008.
8. From cancer to heart disease, the amazing life-saving benefits of marriage by Roger Dobson, Daily Mail, 26 August 2008.
9. Religion and Ethics - Judaism, BBC.co.uk, August 2008.
10. Her Majesty Queen Elizabeth, The Queen Mother, January 1997.
11. The Bible's Buried Secrets by Nova, narrated by Liev Schreiber, PBS, 2008.
12. Inauguration Sermon: The Archbishop of York, 1 December 2005.
13. The Queen's Christmas Message, 25 December 2001.
13a. The Prime Minister's King James Bible Speech by David Cameron, www.number 10gov.uk /news/king-james-bible, 16 December 2011.
14. Government favours Islam says C.O.E. Report, Daily Mail, 9 June 2008.
15. Duncan Smith praises churches for transforming communities, Christiantoday.com, 4 April 2008.
16. Government underestimates Church contribution to welfare, Christiantoday.com, 9 June 2008.
17. Barack Obama visiting Ohio's East Community Youth, Zanesville, 1 July 2008.
18. A unlikely ally in France's Sarkozy, Times of Malta, 11 September 2008.
19. The path of Europe and the public role of the theologies by Dr Wolfgang Schäuble, Berlin, 8 March 2007.
20. Truth or Weak Faith: Dialogue on Christianity and Relativism by René Girard and Gianni Vattimo, published by Pier Vittorio and Associates, 2008.
21. Anthropologist foresees a Christian Renaissance, Zenit.org, 17 December 2007.
22. Christmas still seen as religious, The Scotsman, 7 December 2008.
23. The Queen's Christmas Message, 25 December 2008.
24. Haley's Bible Handbook by Henry H. Haley, Zondervan, 1965, pp.18-19.
25. The Queen's Christmas Message, 25 December 2011.

Chapter Twenty-One - Spiritual Revival and Social Cohesion

1. Time Traveller's Guide To Victorian Britain, U.K. Channel 4 online.

2. W.E. Gladstone speaking in The House of Commons, 5 March 1880.
3. *The Mission of Christianity* by Frank Ballard, Elliot Stock, 1891. p.95.
4. Unknown author's letter to Diognetus.
5. *Idea* magazine by Mark Greene, U.K. Evangelical Alliance, LICC. March/April 2003, p.11.
5a. Legal expert H. Potter said, "Since the late 1970s, governments seem to have become increasingly addicted to enacting new laws... what was once a light dusting of new legislation first of all became a snowstorm and then an avalanche threatening to overwhelm the entire legal system." The Strange Case of the Law by H. Potter, BBC, June 2012.
6. National Statistics Online, U.K. Gov. 2005.
7. The British Crime Survey, Years 05/06. Crimestatistics.org.uk.
8. Department For Work And Pensions, January 2007.
9. Help the Aged, 2007.
10. Key child protection statistics, NSPCC, March 2006.
11. Child sex offender plan condemned, BBC.co.uk, NSPCC, 1 June 2007. 12. Ibid.
13. The Home Office, domestic violence. 14. Ibid.
15. Child sex offender plan condemned, BBC.co.uk, NSPCC, 1 June 2007.
16. Yob attacks total 35 million a year, Metro.co.uk, 4 February 2009.
17. Advert, International Aids Charity, August 2006.
18. The Independent by Jeremy Laurance, 16 April 2007.
19. Tories seek tougher rape laws, BBC News / Home Office, 12 November 2007.
20. Teen pregnancy rates increase, 2002 statistics, BBC.co.uk, 5 March 2004.
21. Child poverty, Sky News, 11 June 2007.
22. The British Crime Survey, Years 05/06, Crimestatistics.org.uk.
23. Child Support Agency, April 2006.
24. Avon Longitudinal Study Of Parents and Children, 12 April 2007.
25. Paternity Tests, August 2007.
26. U.S. sex offenders younger, more violent, CNN, 10 June 2007.
27. Assaults on police 'hit 60 a day,' BBC.co.uk, 24 March 2006.
28. Teacher Support Network, 2005. 29. Ibid.
30. One-a-day violence against teachers, BBC.co.uk, 20 March 2007.
31. Attacks on nurses 'cost £100m a year' by Stephanie Condron, *The Daily Telegraph*, 27 February 2007.
32. Figure for 2004, BBC News, 18 May 2007.
33. Attacks on nurses 'on the rise,' BBC.co.uk, 28 February 2006.
34. Britain becomes a Prozac nation by David Rose, *The Times*, 14 May 2007.
35. English 'booze culture' targeted, BBC.co.uk, 5 June 2007. 36. Ibid.
37. Home Affairs Committee third report - "The Government's drug policy: Is It working?" 2002.
38. Disordered-eating.co.uk, May 2007.
39. Management of Deliberate Self-Poisoning In Adults In Four Teaching Hospitals: Descriptive Study by A Creed, Fetal Kapur, N, House, 1998.
40. Cannabis hospital admissions rise - study over ten year period, BBC.co.uk, June 2007.
41. *Idea* magazine by Mark Greene, U.K. Evangelical Alliance, LICC. March / April 2003, p.16.
42. Faithworks.info, April 2010.
42a. The Prime Minister's King James Bible Speech, by David Cameron, www.number 10.gov.uk/news/king-james-bible, 16 December 2011.
43. *Revival Fires And Awakenings - Thirty Moves of the Holy Spirit* by Mathew Backholer, ByFaith Media, 2006, pp.70-71.
44. *150 Years of Revival* by Mathew Backholer, ByFaith Media, 2007, p.104.
45. Congregation and Community: Identity in the South West woollen industry, 1760-1850, a lecture by Dr Claire Strachan, University of Leicester, 10 February 2010.
46. Christianity remains the foundation for Britain, *Daily Express*, 5 December 2007.
47. *A Pastor from Egypt*, Life and Ministry of Dr Rev. Menes Abdul Noor by Naiim Atef, back cover summary, Call of Hope Publications, 2002.
48. Declining values and gang violence, BBC.co.uk, 5 September 2008.
49. God is behind some of our greatest art by Mark Ravenhill, *Guardian*, 14 April 2008.

Chapter Twenty-Two - Empires & Superpowers
1. *The City of God* by Augustine of Hippo, 5th century, book IV, chapter 33.
2. *Antiquities of the Jews* by Josephus, book XI, chapter I, section two.
3. *Expansion of England* by J.R. Seeley, 1883.
4. *The River War* by Winston Churchill, Longmans, Green and Co., 1899, p.2.
5. Oxfam Report: Africa's wars cost billions, CNN, 11 October 2007.
6. The battle took place on the 22 January 1879.
7. *Empire, How Britain Made The Modern World* by Niall Ferguson, Penguin, 2003, 2004, p.4.
8. Ibid. p.5.

9. *Haley's Bible Handbook* by Henry H. Haley, Zondervan, 1965, pp.18-19.
10. Adam Brown's speech in Gore Park, Hamilton, Canada, 26 January 1901.
11. *Livingstone* by Thomas Hughes, Macmillan and Co. Ltd, March 1889, p.94.
12. Botswana National Museum, Gaborone, 'Protest in England 1895.'
13. *Africa On A Shoestring, Botswana* by Becca Blond, Lonely Planet, March 2004, p.865.
14. *Empire, How Britain Made The Modern World* by Niall Ferguson, Penguin, 2003, 2004, p.366.
15. *Malawi the Warm Heart of Africa*, The Ministry of Tourism, Wildlife and Culture, Central Africana Limited, p.28.
16. Ibid. p.20.
17. Adopted in 1968, words by Andrease Enoke Fanyana Simelane, music by David Kenneth Rycroft.
18. Speech at the Constitutional Convention, 28 June 1787.
19. Instructions for the Virginia Colony, granted by King James I, on 10 April 1606.
20. Speech by John Quincy Adams, Committee for Celebration of Independence, Washington, 4 July 1821.
21. Some question the authenticity of various quotes concerning American history. Therefore those quotes in question are used when they appear to be consistent with other quotes in such settings from those to whom it concerns. All four quotes. *Haley's Bible Handbook* by Henry H. Haley, Zondervan, 1965, pp.18-19.
22. Address to General Assembly of the state of Virginia by James Madison, 1778.
23. A letter by Charles Carroll to James McHenry, 4 November 1800.
24. A sermon by Jedidiah Morse, delivered at The Day of National Fast, Charlestown, 25 April 1799.
25. State of the First Amendment 2007, The First Amendment Centre, 11 September 2007.
26. Pledge of Allegiance Poll, Fox News, 30 November 2005.
27. Obama and McCain's test of faith by Amy Sullivan, *Time* magazine, 15 August 2008.
28. The Arsenal of Democracy radio broadcast by President Franklin D. Roosevelt, on the 29 December 1940.
29. President Bush, second term inaugural address, 20 January 2005.
30. Saddleback Church Presidential Forum, Barack Obama & John McCain, moderated by Rick Warren, 16 August 2008.
31. Linked by a Bible by Ronald C. White Jr, *Los Angeles Times*, 17 January 2009.
32. President Barack Obama's Inauguration Speech, 20 January 2009.
33. *The Chinese* by David Bonavia, Pengiun books, 1980, p.55.
34. China's churches facing leader shortages by G. Thomas, CBN, 27 August 2008.
35. Appeal of the Chinese House Church, Henan Province, 22 August 1998.
36. *Jesus in Beijing* by David Aikman, Monarch Books, 2003, p.291.
37. Ibid. p.285.
38. Chinaaid.org, April 2008.
39. Christianity in China, sons of heaven, Beijing and Shanghai, *The Economist*, 2 October 2008.
40. *Jesus in Beijing* by David Aikman, Monarch Books, 2003, pp.9-10.
41. BacktoJerusalem.com, April 2008.
42. *Global Trends 2025, A Transformed World*, Chaired by C. Thomas Fingar, National Intelligence Council, November 2008.
43. No tolerance without Christianity by Judge Ken Starr, USA Today, 16 December 2013.

Chapter Twenty-Three - Capitalism: Creating Wealthy Productive Nations

1. *Time* magazine, 26 April 2004.
2. *Empire, How Britain Made The Modern World* by Niall Ferguson, Penguin, 2003, 2004, p.217.
3. Ibid. p.288.
4. Ibid. p.165.
5. Ibid. p.377.
6. Countries and outlying territories by total area, Wikipedia.com.
7. *Empire, How Britain Made The Modern World* by Niall Ferguson, Penguin, 2003, 2004, p.378.
8. The Bible: The foundation of liberty by Paul Strand, CBN News, 24 April 2007.
9. Is capitalism morally bankrupt? by Dr Michael Schluter volume 18, number 3, Jubilee Centre, September 2009.
10. The Protestant Revolution, episode 4 by Tristram Hunt, BBC, 3 October 2007.
11. *The Bottom Billion* by Paul Collier, Oxford University Press, 2007.
12. *Working For The Few*, Oxfam, January 2014.
13. *Tale of Two Britains*, Oxfam, March 2014.
14. *Asia and the West* by Maurice Zinkin, International Secretariat, 1953, p.208.
15. *The British Empire And Commonwealth* by J.A. Williamson, Macmillan, 1935, p.368.
16. Jesus in *Beijing* by David Aikman, Monarch Books, 2003, p.5.
17. International Business Times by Jijo Jacob, 21 November 2013.
18. China getting rich less quick by Quentin Sommerville, BBC.co.uk, 26 October 2008.
19. China on the brink by Wei Jingsheng, *Daily Express*, 16 January 2009.

Chapter Twenty-Four - The Industrial Revolution and Compassionate Capitalism
1. The Industrial Revolution online, author unknown, April 2008.
2. *Memoirs of Samuel Slater* by George S. White, Phildelphia, 1836, p. 265.
3. His holy calling by Heather Sells, CBN, 15 April 2007.
4. *Yarns on Social Pioneers* by Ernest H. Hayes, The Religious Education Press, 1924, 1943, p.72.
5. *Life of George Cadbury* by A.G. Gardiner, Cassel, 1923.
6. *What Are Churches For?* by Frank Ballard, Elliot Stock, 1891, p.40.
7. Joseph Rowntree Charitable Trust - Our Founder, June 2008.
8. The Last Will and Testament of Henry J. Heinz, 1919.
9. The Higher Life and Social Enterprise, Wisdomonwealth.org, June 2008.
10. *Working For The Few*, Oxfam, January 2014.

Chapter Twenty-Five - A Fair Deal - Justice Not Charity
1. *Letters To A Young Evangelical, Why the Church Is Important* by Tony Campolo, Basic Books.
2. The Prime Minister at Faithworks in London, Tony Blair Lecture, 22 March 2005.
3. Makepovertyhistory.org, June 2008.
4. Stephen Timms, MP for East Ham, Faithworks Conference, 2 November 2007.
5. Fern Britton meets Tony Blair, BBC, 13 December 2009.
6. There's a God-shaped hole by Rachel Sylvester, *The Times*, 21 October 2008.
7. Gordon Brown, Premier Radio, 4 January 2010.
8. Archbishop Desmond Tutu on the pledges to Africa, DATA report One, 11 June 2009. 80% of the failure of pledges due to Italy and France.
9. MicahChallenge.org, June 2008.
10. PM endorses new Micah Challenge book on Church responsibility to poor, Christiantoday.com, 16 April 2008.
11. Gordon Brown, Number10.gov.uk/page23068, 2 April 2010.
12. U.N. Secretary-General Ban Ki-Moon, addressing the National Association of Evangelicals, Sheraton Crystal City Hotel, Arlington, Va., 11 October 2007.

Chapter Twenty-Six - The Foundations of Modern Democracy
1. *The British Empire And Commonwealth* by J.A. Williamson, Macmillan, 1935, p.233.
2. *The American Presidency* by William H. Riker. Democracy, Grolier Multimedia Encyclopaedia.
3. *Multi New Testament Commentary*, C.H. Spurgeon, John Hunt, p.195.
3a. The Prime Minister's King James Bible Speech by David Cameron, www.number10. gov.uk/news/ king-james-bible, 16 December 2011.
3b. *Religion and Rationality: Essays on Reason, God and Modernity*, ed. Eduardo Mendieta, MIT Press, 2002, p.149. And Habermas, Jurgen, *Time of Transitions*, Polity Press, 2006, pp. 150-151.
4. *Illustrated Notes on English Church History* by Rev. C.A. Lane, Society For Promoting Christian Knowledge,1898, p.208.
5. The Magna Carta, Article 1.
6. The U.K. National Archives, Citizenship, Magna Carta, April 2008.
7. *Haley's Bible Handbook* by Henry H. Haley, Zondervan, 1965, pp.18-19.
8. Genesis 1:26.
9. *Illustrated Notes on English Church History* by Rev. C.A. Lane, Society For Promoting Christian Knowledge, 1898, p.208.
10. Ibid. p.244.
11. *Calvin Studies Colloquium*, Kelly in Leith and Raynal, Eds. p.67.
12. *The Emergence of Liberty in the Modern World* by Douglas F. Kelly, P&R Publishing, 1942, 1992, p.140.
13. *History of the Westminster Assembly* by R Hetherington and J. Gemmell, 1878, p.68.
13a. Two cheers for human rights by John N. Gray, BBC.co.uk, 27 December 2013.
14. *Virtual History* by John Adamson & Niall Ferguson, Basic Books, 2002, p.92.
15. Alaska Governor Sarah Palin, http://gov.state.ak.us, 31 August 2007.
16. *History of the English Speaking Peoples*, Habeas Corpus by Winston Churchill, Orion Publishing Co, 1956, 2002.
17. Citizenship, Bill of Rights, 1689, The U.K. National Archives.
18. England's Glorious Revolution by Professor Wilkes, Uni./Georgia School of Law.
19. *More What If?* by Theodore K Rabb & Robert Cowley, Pan Macmillan, 2002, p.125.
20. *More What If?* by Theodore K Rabb & Robert Cowley, Pan Macmillan, 2002, p.126.
21. *Thomas Paine: Social and Political Thought* by Gregory Claeys, Routledge 1989, p.20.
22. A History of Britain, Forces of Nature, presented by Simon Schama BBC, 2002.
23. Christianity & Democracy, *Time* magazine, 25 June 1951.
24. *Chartism in Scotland* by Richard Brown, June 2008.
25. *The Chartist Movement in Scotland* by Alexander Wilson, Manchester U.P.

26. The Northern Echo by W.T. Stead, 14 October 1870.
27. Lecture on Democracy by Ernest Jones, York 1868.
28. Gordon Brown on liberty & the role of the state, Chatham House, 13 December 2005.
29. Time Traveller's Guide To Victorian Britain, U.K. Channel 4 online, June 2008.
30. David Pollock, 23 May 2003.
31. UK 'must celebrate Christianity,' BBC.co.uk, 5 December 2007.
32. *In Empire's Cause* by Ernest Protheroe, Epworth Press, 1927, p.375.
33. Obama calls for strong UK links, BBC.co.uk, 26 July 2008.
34. Ancient Greece, BBC.co.uk, July 2008.
35. Athens: The Dawn of Democracy by Bettany Hughes, channel 4, July 2007. 36. Ibid. 37. Ibid.
38. Ibid.
39. Are Christians being persecuted? BBC, 7 April 2010.
40. How I made peace with God by Peter Hitchens, Daily Mail, 13 March 2010.

Chapter Twenty-Seven - American Democracy

1. *The British Empire And Commonwealth* by J.A. Williamson, Macmillan, 1935, p.249.
2. Ibid. p.52.
3 U.S. National Archives, Charters of Freedom, June 2007.
4. *Woodrow Wilson: A Life of World Peace* by J.W. Schulte Nordholt, University of California Press, 1991, p.47.
5. Jamestown, America's Birthplace, A Time Team Special, U.K. Channel 4, 1 May 2007.
6. Cape Henry: Spiritual roots of a nation by Craig von Buseck, CBN, April 2007.
7. President George W. Bush Welcomes Her Majesty Queen Elizabeth II to the White House, 7 May 2007.
8. The Mayflower, Historyplace.com, June 2008.
9. *The Mayflower Pilgrims* by Edmund J. Carpenter, Christian Liberty Press, 2007, p.37.
10. Ibid. preface by Michael J. McHugh, p.V.
11. *The Rights of Colonies Examined* by Stephen Hopkins, William Goddard, 1765, pp.23-24.
12. VisitBritian.com, January 2009.
13. *The British Empire and Commonwealth* by J.A.Williamson, Macmillan, 1935, p.100.
14. Ibid. p.102.
15. *The History of Christianity*, A. Skevington Wood, Lion, 1977, 1990, p.438.
16. Charters Of Freedom, Part 1, U.S. National Archives.
17. *A History of American Christianity* by Leonard Woolsey Bacon, Scribner's Sons, 1898, p.181.
18. Declaration of Independence, The 56 Signatures, U.S. National Archives.
19. Letter to Thomas Jefferson by John Adams, 28 June 1813.
20. A nation of Christians is not a Christian nation by Jon Meacham, *New York Times*, 7 October 2007.
21. John Adams in a letter written to Abigail on the day the Declaration was approved by Congress.
22. *An Essay Concerning Human Understanding* by John Locke, by Alexander Campbell Fraser from 1690 original, 1959, Dover Publications inc, New York, p.xlix.
23. To The Citizens of Philadelphia: A Plan for Free Schools, A letter by Benjamin Rush, 28 March 1787.
24. George Mason's Last Will and Testament, 1792.
25. *The Federalist on the New Constitution*, Benjamin Warner, 1818, p.53.
26. Speech by John Quincy Adams, the Jubilee of the Constitution, the New York Historical Society, 30 April 1839.
27. Speech by John Quincy Adams, to the town of Newburyport, 4 July 1837.
28. *A Defence of the use of the Bible as a School Book*, Benjamin Rush, Thomas & Samuel Bradford, 1798, p.112.
29. *History of the United States*, by Noah Webster, Durrie & Peck, 1832, p.6.
30. *Democracy in America* by Alexis de Tocqueville, Barnes & Co., 1851, pp.336-7.
31. *Haley's Bible Handbook* by Henry H. Haley, Zondervan, 1965, pp.18-19.
32. Herbert Hoover, U.S. President 1929-1933.
33. The Bible: The foundation of liberty by Paul Strand, CBN News, 24 April 2007.
34. Graham's crusade saved America by Mark D. Tooley, CBS News, 10 June 2007.
35. Saddleback Presidential Forum, Obama & McCain - Rick Warren, 16 August 2008.
35a. The Prime Minister's King James Bible Speech by David Cameron, www.number 10gov.uk/news/king-james-bible, 16 December 2011.
36. Obama and McCain's test of faith by Amy Sullivan, *Time* magazine, 15 August 2008.
37. Christianity and Law, Creation Ministries International.
38. British Prime Minister Gordon Brown, speech on liberty, 25 October 2007.
39. Terror, Robespierre and the French Revolution, BBC 11 July, 2009.
40. Napoleon, Mastering Luck, PBS, November 2000.
41. Napoleon, Summit of Greatness, PBS, November 2000.

42. Napoleon's genocide on par with Hitler by Colin Randall, Telegraph, 26 November 2005.
43. Napoleon, the End, PBS, November 2000.
44. Ibid.
45. When Britain/France nearly married by Mike Thomson, BBC.co.uk, 15 January 2007.
46. British Prime Minister Margaret Thatcher, G7 summit, France, July 1989.
47. Canadian Prime Minister Stephen Harper, 2006.
48. Strong Christian support by Lauren Wilson, Coredata.com.au, 16 August 2007.
49. The American Future: A History, 3 of 4 by Simon Schama, BBC, 24 October 2008.

Chapter Twenty-Eight - The Founding Fathers of Modern Science

1. Science, a creation of God by Gailon Totheroh, CBN News, 25 April 2007.
2. The Christian Travelers Guide to Great Britain by Irvin Hexham, Zondervan Publishing House, 2001, p.184.
3. Ivy League Faith by Wendy Griffith, CBN News, 10 April 2007.
4. Men of Science Men of God by Henry M. Morris, Master Books, 1982, 2003, pp.1-2.
5. Ibid. p.23.
6. Empire, How Britain Made The Modern World by Niall Ferguson, Penguin, 2003, 2004, p.168.
7. Men of Purpose, Dawn of Electricity by Peter Masters, Stephens & George, p.9.
8. Science, a creation of God by Gailon Totheroh, CBN, 25 April 2007.
9. Men of Purpose, Dawn of Electricity by Peter Masters, Stephens & George, 1973, 2003, p.19.
10. Christian Social Reformers Of The Nineteenth Century by Hugh Martin, Student Christian Movement Press, 1927.
11. Men of Purpose, Pioneer of Power by Peter Masters, Stephens & George, p.125.
12. John Logie Baiird was the first to demonstrate a working TV in 1926. The first image he transmitted privately was a cross. The second was a boy.
13. Is Richard Dawkins still evolving? by Melanie Philips, Spectator.co.uk, 23 October 2008.
14. The Protestant Revolution, episode 3 by Tristram Hunt, BBC, 26 Sept. 2007.
15. Does Science Need Religion? by Roger Trigg, Faraday Papers, No. 2, 2007. See also Science and Religion: Some Historical Perspectives by John Hedley Brooke, New York, N.Y. Cambridge University Press, 1991.
16. Men of Science Men of God by Henry M. Morris, Master Books, 1982, 2003, pp.1-2.
16a. The King James Bible, the book that changed the world by Lord Melvyn Bragg, BBC, March 2011.
17. Ibid. pp.99-101.
18. Did Darwin Kill God, presented by Conor Cunningham, BBC, 31 March 2009.
19. Celebrating a landmark experiment, BBC.co.uk, 21 May 2009.
20. The Apollo 8 Christmas Eve Broadcast NASA, 24 December 1968.
21. The bizarre life of Buzz by Peter Sheridan, Daily Express, 12 June 2009.
22. He landed on the moon by Dan Wooding, Assist News Service, 15 July 2009.
23. A chemist and God by S. Joshua Swamidass and Shoba Spencer, World magazine, 18 October 2008.
24. The Narnia Code, BBC, 16 April 2009. 25. Ibid.
26. Subtle is the Lord - The Science and the Life of Albert Einstein by Abraham Pais, Clarendon Press, Oxford, 1982.
27. About NHGRI, Former Director, Genome.gov, October 2008.
28. White House Awards Ceremony, 14 March 2000.
29. U.S., Britain urges free access to human genome data by Eileen O'Connor / Reuters, CNN, 14 March 2000.
30. Speaking at the C.S. Lewis Foundation's International Summer Institute, Oxbridge, Cambridge, August 2008.
31. God vs. Science by David Van Biema, Time magazine, 5 November 2006.
32. Genome announcement brings new possibilities, CNN, 30 June 2000.
33. Professor John Lennox speaking at the U.K. National Prayer Breakfast, 2013.

Chapter Twenty-Nine - Great Authors and Freedom Fighters

1. Bedesworld.co.uk, The Age of Bede, March 2006.
2. Yarns on Christian Torchbearers by Lilian E. Cox & Ernest H. Hayes, The Religious Education Press, 1941, 1958, p.22.
3. Yarns on Social Pioneers by Ernest H. Hayes, The Religious Education Press, 1924, 1943, p.13.
4. Illustrated Notes on English Church History by Rev. C.A. Lane, Society For Promoting Christian Knowledge, 1898, p.258.
5. John Knox's Tomb, St Giles' Cathedral, Edinburgh, Scotland.
6. Daniel Defoe, Answers.com, October 2008.
7. William Hogarth, The Book Of Days, 15 December 2008.
8. Pride And Prejudice by Jane Austen, Penguin Classics, 1813, 2003.

9. The Missionary by Charlotte Brontë.
10. Faith and Despondency, by Emily Brontë.
11. *Haley's Bible Handbook* by Henry H. Haley, Zondervan, 1965, pp.18-19. 12. Ibid. 13. Ibid.
14. Ibid.
15. Oxford's C.S. Lewis. His Heresy: Christianity, *Time* magazine, 8 September 1947.
16. Christianity Today by Chris Armstrong, 1 August 2003.
17. Linked by a Bible by Ronald C. White Jr, *Los Angeles Times*, 17 January 2009.
17a. Ibid.
18. The Prime Minister's King James Bible Speech, by David Cameron, www.number10.gov.uk/news/king-james-bible, 16 December 2011.

Chapter Thirty - Great Explorers and Adventurers
1. Historic Figures, David Livingstone, BBC.co.uk, May 2006.
2. *On the Indian Trail* by Egerton Young, The Religious Tract Society, 1897.
3. *General Gordon Saint And Soldier* by J. Wardle, (21 September 1867), Henry B. Saxton, 1904, p.57.
4. *Empire, How Britain Made The Modern World* by Niall Ferguson, Penguin, 2003, 2004, p.165.
5. *The English In Egypt, Life of General Gordon*, James Sangsler & co. 1886, p.118.
6. *General Gordon Saint And Soldier* by J Wardle, Henry B. Saxton, 1904, p.55. 7. Ibid., p.17.
8. *Empire, How Britain Made The Modern World* by Niall Ferguson, Penguin, 2003, 2004, p.375.
9. Clash of Worlds, episode 2, BBC, 4 November 2007.
10. General Charles Gordon's Epitaph, St Paul's London, England.
11. *Men of Purpose*, The Lord Apostol by Peter Masters, Stephens & George, 1973, 2003, p.54.
12. *Yarns on Christian Torchbearers* by Lilian E. Cox & Ernest H. Hayes, The Religious Education Press, 1941, 1958, p.66.
13. *Scribner's* magazine, August 1910.
14. *Evangelical Awakenings in Africa* by J. Edwin Orr, Bethany Fellowship Inc, 1912, 1970, p.153.
15. As an atheist, I truly believe Africa needs God by Matthew Parris, *The Times*, 27 December 2008.
16. The surprising discovery about those colonialist proselytizing missionaries by Andrea Palpant Dilley, Christianitytoday.com, February 2014.
17. *Idea* magazine by Mark Greene, U.K. Evangelical Alliance, LICC, March/April 2003, p.11.
18. Action plan to tackle cult of celebrity, ChristianToday.com, 27 April 2008.
19. Woodrow Wilson, 28th president of US (1856-1924).

Chapter Thirty-One - The Civil Rights Movement
1. *Quiet Strength* by Rosa Parks, Zondervan, 1995.
2. I Have A Dream Speech by Martin Luther King Jr., Lincoln Memorial, Washington, D.C., 1963.
3. Nobel Peace Prize, Martin Luther King Jr., 1964.
4. The American Future: A History, 3 of 4 by Simon Schama, BBC, 24 Oct. 2008.
5. The Prime Minister's King James Bible Speech, by David Cameron, www.number10.gov.uk/news/king-james-bible, 16 December 2011.

Chapter Thirty-Two - Ending Apartheid
1. District Six Museum, About Us, Cape Town, South Africa, July 2008.
2. Tutu's Speech at the funeral of Chris Hani, April 1993.
3. Desmond Tutu, The Nobel Peace Prize, 1984. NobelPrize.org.
4. *Letters To A Young Evangelical, Why the Church Is Important* by Tony Campolo, Basic Books.

Chapter Thirty-Three - Prison Reform
1. To The Citizens of Philadelphia: A Plan for Free Schools, A letter by Benjamin Rush, 28 March 1787.

Chapter Thirty-Four - Global Reform
1. Mary Slessor 1848-1915, Dundee City Council, Scotland, October 2006.
2. *Missionary Triumph over Slavery* by Peter Masters, Stephens & George, 2006, p.7.
3. *Illustrated Notes on English Church History* by Rev. C.A. Lane, Society For Promoting Christian Knowledge,1898, pp.2-3.
4. *Anglo-Saxon Britain* by Grant Allen, The Society For Promoting Christian Knowledge, 1881.
5. *Illustrated Notes on English Church History* by Rev. C.A. Lane, Society For Promoting Christian Knowledge,1898, p.71.
6. *Empire, How Britain Made The Modern World* by Niall Ferguson, Penguin, 2003, 2004, pp.119-120.
7. *Missionary Triumph over Slavery* by Peter Masters, Stephens & George, 2006, p.8.
8. *Empire, How Britain Made The Modern World* by Niall Ferguson, Penguin, 2003, 2004, pp.141-142.

9. *William Carey, Missionary, Pioneer and Statesman* by Walker R. Deaville, Moody Press, 1951, pp.252-253.
10. *Missions Their Rise and Development* by Louise Creighton, Williams & Norgate, 1912, p.193.
11. *Missionary Triumph over Slavery* by Peter Masters, Stephens & George, 2006 p.11.
12. Ibid. Back cover summary.
13. *Missions Their Rise and Development* by Louise Creighton, Williams & Norgate, 1912, p.173.
14. *Revival and the Great Commission* by Mathew Backholer, ByFaith Media, 2007, pp.66-69.
15. Mary Slessor, mother of all the peoples, Dundee City Council, Scotland, May 2008.
16. *Mary Slessor: Mission Africa* by George R. Collins, Faith For The Family, 1977.
17. Mary Slessor, mother of all the peoples, Dundee City Council, Scotland, May 2008.
18. *Missions Their Rise and Development* by Louise Creighton, Williams & Norgate, 1912, pp.175-176. 19. Ibid. pp.185-187. 20. Ibid. pp.191-192.
21. *The British Empire And Commonwealth* by J.A. Williamson, Macmillan, 1935, p.197. 22. Ibid. p.186. 23. Ibid. p.268. 24. Ibid. p.268. 25. Ibid. p.198.
26. *More Yarns On Christian Pioneers* by Ernest H. Hayes, The Religious Education Press, 1933, 1955, p.71.
27. *Mary Reed of Chandag* by E Mackerchar, The Mission of Lepers, 1938.
28. *Revival and the Great Commission* by Mathew Backholer, ByFaith Media, 2007, p.106.
29. Eaten missionary's family gets an apology, BBC.co.uk, 13 November 2003.
30. Gladys Aylward, Missionary to China, Anglican Resources, June 2008.
31. Man who hates his own Church by Mary Kenny, *Daily Mail*, 3 November 2005.
32. The surprising discovery about those colonialist proselytizing missionaries by Andrea Palpant Dilley, Christianitytoday.com, February 2014.
33. No tolerance without Christianity by Judge Ken Starr, USA Today, 16 December 2013.

Chapter Thirty-Five - The Modern State of Israel
1. The Balfour Declaration, 2 November 1917.
2. *The Last Word On The Middle East* by Derek Prince, Chosen Books, 1982, pp.47-48.
3. The untold story: The role of Christian Zionists in the establishment of modern day Israel by Rabbi Jamie Cowen, Leadership University, 13 July 2002.
4. *The Last Word On The Middle East* by Derek Prince, Chosen Books, 1982, p.34.
5. *Seven Pillars of Wisdom* by E. Lawrence, Oxford, 1922, Introduction.
6. *Romance of the Last Crusade* by Major Vivian Gilbert, Appleton, 1927. 7. Ibid.
8. Jerusalem, The Covenant City, presented by Lance Lambert, Hatikvah Film Foundation, Distributed by Evangelical Films.
9. *The Last Word On The Middle East* by Derek Prince, Chosen Books, 1982, p.37.
10. Against All Odds: In Search Of A Miracle, Michael Greenspan, American Trademark Pictures.
11. *The Last Word on the Middle East* by Derek Prince, Chosen Books, 1982, p.37.
12. A night to honour Israel, Jerusalem, Israel, 9 March 2010.

Chapter Thirty-Six - Non-Conformists
1. The Queen's Christmas Message, 25 December 2008.

Chapter Thirty-Seven - Treasuring Our Heritage
1. Christianity remains the foundation for Britain, *Daily Express*, 5 December 2007.
2. How the Celts saved Britain by Dan Snow, BBC, 25 May 2009.
3. Congressman James Randy Forbes, the House Floor, Congress, May 2009.
4. For a growing number of Canadians, it's hip to be holy by L. Liepins, Canada.com, 21 May 2009.
5. Rt. Rev. Michael Nazir-Ali, Bishop of Rochester, resignation speech, 5 April 2009.
6. Government stunned by Army chief's Iraq blast, *Daily Mail*, 13 October 2006.
7. Faith Diary by Robert Pigott, BBC.co.uk, 24 February 2009.
8. Heaven's Above! by Gareth Bebb, *Daily Express*, 8 June 2009.
9. Archbishop of Canterbury's Easter Message, April 2009.
10. AD, Anno Domini, FIEC, Day One Publications, p.21.
11. *Idea* magazine by Mark Greene, U.K. Evangelical Alliance, LICC, March 2003, p.16.
12. How Christians use their money, published by Christian Research.
13. The Barna Group, Barna.org, May 2005.
14. *World* magazine by Gene Edward Veith, 22 October 2005.
15. *Operation World* by Patrick Johnstone & Jason Mandryk, CLC, 1993, 2001, U.S. p.751, U.K. p.750, S. Korea p.749, Australia p.752, Finland, p.750.
16. *The Purpose Driven Life* by Rick Warren, Zondervan, 2002, p.243.
17. Religion, Wilberforce, BBC.co.uk, May 2008.

ByFaith Media Books

Holy Spirit Power: Knowing the Voice, Guidance and Person of the Holy Spirit by Paul Backholer.

Revival Fires and Awakenings – Thirty-Six Visitations of the Holy Spirit by Mathew Backholer.

Reformation to Revival, 500 Years of God's Glory: Sixty Revivals by Mathew Backholer

How to Plan, Prepare and Successfully Complete Your Short-Term Mission by Mathew Backholer.

Revival Fire – 150 Years of Revivals by Mathew Backholer.

Discipleship for Everyday Living by Mathew Backholer.

Global Revival, Worldwide Outpourings, Forty-Three Visitations of the Holy Spirit by Mathew Backholer.

Understanding Revival and Addressing the Issues it Provokes by Mathew Backholer.

Extreme Faith – On Fire Christianity by Mathew Backholer. Powerful foundations for faith in Christ!

Revival Answers: True and False Revivals by Mathew Backholer. What is genuine and false revival?

Short-Term Missions, A Christian Guide to STMs, For Leaders, Pastors, Students… by Mathew Backholer.

Budget Travel, A Guide to Travelling on a Shoestring Explore the World by Mathew Backholer

Prophecy Now, Prophetic Words and Divine Revelations, For You, the Church and the Nations by Michael Backholer.

Samuel Rees Howells: A Life of Intercession by Richard Maton. Learn how intercession and prayer changed history.

Samuel, Son and Successor of Rees Howells by Richard Maton. Discover the full biography of Samuel Rees Howells.

The Holy Spirit in a Man by R.B. Watchman. Autobiography.

Tares and Weeds in your Church: Trouble & Deception in God's House by R.B. Watchman.

Heaven: A Journey to Paradise by Paul Backholer.

The Exodus Evidence In Pictures – The Bible's Exodus by Paul Backholer. 100+ colour photos.

The Ark of the Covenant – Investigating the Ten Leading Claims by Paul Backholer. 80+ colour photos.

Jesus Today, Daily Devotional by Paul Backholer.

Britain, A Christian Country by Paul Backholer.

Lost Treasures of the Bible by Paul Backholer.

ByFaith Media DVDs

Great Christian Revivals on 1 DVD is an uplifting account of the stories of the Welsh Revival (1904-1905), the Hebridean Revival (1949-1952) and the Evangelical Revival (1739-1791).

ByFaith – Quest for the Ark of the Covenant on 1 DVD. Four episodes. Search for the lost Ark of the Covenant.

ByFaith – World Mission on 1 DVD. A global short-term missions adventure through 14 nations.

Israel in Egypt – The Exodus Mystery on 1 DVD. Find the evidence for the Bible's exodus.

www.ByFaithBooks.co.uk – www.ByFaithDVDs.co.uk

CPSIA information can be obtained
at www.ICGtesting.com
Printed in the USA
BVOW03s2102081117
499754BV00029B/57/P